BK 277.4 G274G
GREAT AWAKENING IN NEW ENGLA
C1957 .00 F

3000 185118 30015
St. Louis Community College

277.4 G274g 1957
FV
GAUSTAD
GREAT AWAKENING IN NEW
ENGLAND
2.25

JUNIOR COLLEGE DISTRICT
of St. Louis - St. Louis County
LIBRARY
7508 Forsyth Blvd.
St. Louis, Missouri 63105

The Great Awakening in New England

Edwin Scott Gaustad was born in Rowley, Iowa, and studied at Baylor University and Brown University. He is the author of *Historical Atlas of Religion in America* and *A Religious History of America*. He is at present Professor of History and chairman of the department at the University of California, Riverside.

The
Great Awakening
IN NEW ENGLAND

By
EDWIN SCOTT GAUSTAD

QUADRANGLE PAPERBACKS
Quadrangle Books / Chicago

Q

THE GREAT AWAKENING IN NEW ENG-
LAND. ©1957 by Edwin Scott Gaustad. This book
was originally published in 1957 by Harper &
Brothers, New York, and is here reprinted by
arrangement.

First QUADRANGLE PAPERBACK edition
published 1968 by Quadrangle Books, Inc., 12 East
Delaware Place, Chicago 60611. Manufactured in
the United States of America.

To Virginia

ACKNOWLEDGMENTS

It is pleasant to recall the kindness of many who made this work possible and endurable.

It was at the suggestion of Edmund S. Morgan of Yale that this study was begun and through his generous counsel that many pitfalls were avoided. William J. Robbins, formerly of Brown, granted me the benefit of a painstaking criticism of the manuscript. Leonard J. Trinterud of McCormick Theological Seminary courteously corrected some statements and suggested clarification of others, while H. Shelton Smith of Duke has offered not only enlarged perspective but also invaluable encouragement.

I wish to express my appreciation further to the library staffs at Harvard, Yale, Brown, and Dartmouth; to the Massachusetts Historical Society, Boston Athanaeum, Andover-Harvard Library, Boston Public Library, and John Carter Brown Library. From all I have received considerate and liberal aid, but particularly from the John Carter Brown Library whose staff I have most often troubled. This Library has also granted permission for the inclusion of the three pages of illustrations copied from the originals in its possession.

Finally, grateful acknowledgment is made to The Mississippi Valley Historical Review *and to the Institute of Early American History and Culture, publishers of the* William and Mary Quarterly, *for permission to reprint material first appearing in those publications.*   E. S. G.

CONTENTS

The Great Awakening in New England

. . . after longe beating at sea they fell with that land which is called Cape Cod; the which being made & certainly knowne to be it, they were not a little joyfull. After some deliberation had amongst them selves & with the master of the ship, they tacked aboute and resolved to stande for the southward (the wind & weather being faire) to finde some place aboute Hudsons river for their habitation. But after they had sailed the course aboute halfe the day, they fell amongst deangerous shoulds and roring breakers, and they were so farr intangled ther with as they conceived them selves in great danger; & the wind shrinking upon them withall, they resolved to bear up againe for the Cape, and thought them selves hapy to gett out of those dangers before night overtooke them, as by Gods providence they did. And the next day they gott into the Cape-harbor wher they ridd in saftie . . . Being thus arrived in a good harbor and brought safe to land, they fell upon their knees & blessed the God of heaven, who had brought them over the vast & furious ocean, and delivered them from all the periles & miseries therof, againe to set their feete on the firme and stable earth, their proper elements.—Bradford's History "Of Plimoth Plantation."

PIETY and the PURITAN

"BUT JESUS SAID TO HIM, 'DO NOT FORBID HIM; FOR HE that is not against you is for you.'"[1] So early in Christian history is there both the witness to, and the sanction of, theological diversity. Although the sanction has not often been invoked or even acknowledged, the witness has been all too evident in Judea, Samaria, and the uttermost parts of the earth. The doctrinal development of the Christian religion is a chiaroscuro whose unity is most readily seen at considerable remove. To become absorbed in a small portion of the painting, and at close range, is to imagine that only one shade "belongs" or is "right." To forsake the closer scrutiny, however, is to remain ignorant of the delicate relationships and rich diversity. It may be well, therefore, to survey this ecclesiastical mural whole, then to step nearer, curiously and appreciatively.

"What is Christianity?" Adolf Harnack asked (and replied). Is it the possession of a single sect, a single century, a single school? The foregone answer but points to the contrasts and shadings which delineate the dominant faith of the Western world. The first four centuries of this faith's history reveal Jewish Christian in contrast with Gentile Christian, legalism with charismatic spontaneity, dogmatism with eclecticism, asceticism with indulgence, monasticism with formalism, philosophy with history, perfectionism with realism, and to cover a multitude of sins—on both sides—orthodoxy with heresy. Succeeding centuries, following the alliance of church and state—a blessing palpably mixed—display the increasingly irresistible divergence of East and West. Language, theology, worship, organization, and only incidentally creed point up this opposition.

The medieval church of the West, no monolith, is characterized by a tolerance, a latitudinarianism if you will, not easily imagined or readily admitted. Nominalism *versus* realism and Abelard's *Sic et Non* indicate only one aspect of this variegation. Reason and faith, of which there shall be occasion to speak at length later, reveal from Anselm to

Ockham striking mobility. But also there was Teuton now overshadowing Latin, the primitive adjoining the cultured. Mysticism was juxtaposed with sensualism, literary and artistic renaissance with moral debacle. Sacrificial and earnest mendicants took communion in the company of illiterate and sybaritic priests. Neoplatonists rebutted Aristotelians, while the countless crusaders combined zealous devotion with amoral opportunism. And Giovanni Boccaccio and Thomas à Kempis were near contemporaries.

So obvious are the contrasts of the Reformation era together with the pitiless wars waged in its aftermath that one may simplify too quickly. There are nuances here also, not to be observed if one sees only the misleading blacks and whites of medievalism against modernity, authority against freedom, superstition against rationalism, nobility against peasantry, true against false. The seventeenth century was dedicated in part to making certain that Catholic and Protestant were unmistakably distinguished. But it was also most crucially a time when intellectual leadership in the West passed, for the first time in over a millennium, out from the influence of the Church. While biblical revelation no longer supplied the context of, and limitations to, philosophy, Science was capitalized and religion grew irrelevant.

Now the tableau must be approached more closely, for the eighteenth century is at hand. Here, where the tense drama of the Great Awakening is played, are the forces that require our close attention. True, some of the issues might well be found elsewhere, the premises be held by those of centuries gone by or yet to come, the animosities and alliances be far from unique. On the other hand, this century reduplicates no other and the tinges of shading found here are, in that special combination, found here alone.

New England in the eighteenth century manifests, with all the peculiarities of its own locale, the vying factions abroad. Household names like Voltaire and Paine suggest one aspect of that century, while John Wesley and Jonathan Edwards call to mind another. The Enlightenment, as this first aspect has come to be called, was a movement and mood which in several ways and to varying degrees lauded the capacity of men's minds to reason and to know. Pietism, as the other aspect is often designated, was a movement and mood which in several ways and to varying degrees affirmed the capacity of men's hearts to feel and to believe. Broadly—and therefore to a degree inaccurately—speaking, the former recalled Greece and the renaissance, the latter, Judea and the reformation. Whereas the Enlightenment was anthropocentric, pietism was theocentric; the first embraced common sense and what was "natural" in religion and morality, while the second spoke of a sense of the heart and asserted revealed religion and supernaturally sanctioned morality. One was utilitarian, prudential; the other absolutist and committed. The Enlightenment assumed man's nobility and prowess, pietism built upon God's goodness and power.

The premises and tempers of both movements were readily passed across political and linguistic barriers. Sometimes a single individual carried the germinal ideas of one or the other, planting them wherever he journeyed. Wesley stayed with Count Zinzendorf's pietist brethren in Saxony, returned to England to associate with George Whitefield, and the latter, as we shall see, powerfully moved the American colonies. But far more often, the nameless wanderers, the immigrants, the merchants, students and soldiers together with the tracts and books made for a community of ideas that almost belied the heightened nationalism.

Thus Methodism in England, the Moravian Brethren on the Continent, and the Great Awakening in New England are part of a single broad, bold stroke of the brush. In each case, the role of the laity was emphasized, with efforts renewed to arrive at a priesthood that approached the universal. Conversely, the established ministry was regarded at least with indifference and not infrequently with hostility. Theology was simplified and, despite Wesley's "Free Grace," erected on common Calvinist assumptions. A strong ethical interest pervaded pietist circles where personal consecration and holiness were the expected norm. Finally, the work of God was something pre-eminently internal, something to be keenly felt and gratefully responded to; and from such direct contact with the divine, new insight and new truth would come.

It would, however, be folly to assume that perfect analogies can be drawn among the several manifestations of this eighteenth-century evangelical piety. Methodism, for example, had overtones of a social revolution which other circles of piety lacked. German pietism revolted against a formal scholasticism in a distinctive manner, while the movement in New England stands alone for having stimulated a significant theological school. And because this present account is chiefly concerned with piety and Puritanism in New England, it is necessary to examine these intently in that specific setting. We shall note, first, Puritanism's planting; second, piety's waning.

The earnest British colonists who migrated to New England in 1620, and in far greater numbers in the 1630's, looked upon the Church of

England as temporizing and adulterated. Puritanism, a word with many meanings,[2] points to the desire of these churchmen to purify the national church of those elements which impeded a vigorous Protestantism. Not only were reforms in doctrine and liturgy to be instituted, but also the membership of the local church was to be kept pure. That is, members should give every evidence of being saved to God and separated from the world. Most New England settlers stopped short of formal schism from the mother church, for the true church, Augustine had noted, is not schismatic. That mother church was, to be sure, steeped in error and gave no indication of altering its course; on the contrary, it oppressed and threatened those who were disposed in any way to modify or ignore the prescribed polity and liturgy. It was therefore impossible for these Puritans to set up their pure church even as it was indefensible to withdraw from what was nonetheless the body of Christ. Such a position was fundamentally untenable. A propitious escape between the horns of this dilemma was provided by the colonization opportunities. In New England, away from the greater part of the pressures on conscience, a true Church of England, not schismatic, not anarchical, could be legally and freely established.

The Puritans who settled New England were motivated by religious considerations not only of an institutional, semipolitical sort. There were reasons of the heart. The immediate sense of God's presence and rule, the full-bodied experience of receiving his grace, the demanding response of total stewardship, the sustaining faith in things not seen— these were no less a part of the colonists' spiritual adventure. Furthermore, these very factors connote in the eighteenth century the essence of pietism. In England, Puritanism and piety were friendly toward each other; in New England, every effort was made to establish between them a permanent and happy union.

Within the first generation of the new settlement, a peculiar *modus vivendi*, a "New England way," had been established. In 1644, John Cotton, distinguished Massachusetts divine, wrote of the "Church of a particular Congregation," noting that "in the Old Testament the Church set up by him [Christ] was Nationall, in the New, Congregationall. . . ."[3] The "Doctrines and Practices of our way" (i.e., of these Congregational churches), he later wrote, are distinctive in the following respects: (1) episcopacy and conformity are burdens too onerous to bear, (2) the use of the Book of Common Prayer is a violation of the second commandment, (3) "the visible Church of a Congregation . . . [is] the first of the power of the Keyes," (4) church members are to be visible saints, and (5) the church is to be organized around a mutual covenant of the believers.[4] Even while acknowledging their divergence from the National Church, the colonists still deemed it crucial "to put a great difference between Separation and Nonconformity."[5]

New England church polity followed a course somewhere between literal congregationalism and the synod control for which the Presbyterian branch of the Puritan party stood. Though in theory all authority was given to the congregation, in fact this democracy was mitigated by granting to the church officers much power. John Cotton affirmed that "the Brethren of the church are the first subject of church-liberty, and the Elders thereof of church-authority; and both of them together are the first subject of all church-power needful to be exercised within themselves. . . ." The power of rule is not seated in the congregation and by them delegated to an elder; rather, "they invest him with rule, partly by chusing him to the office which God hath invested with rule, partly by professing their own subjection to him in the Lord. . . ." In its position of leadership as the dominant church in New England, Congregationalism soon became aware of the necessity of control and uniformity. As a "state church"[6] it could not afford the luxury of radical innovation and absolute democratization.

Autonomy of the "Church of a particular Congregation" did not in New England imply the isolation of that body from all other churches. From 1629 when the Plymouth church extended the "right hand of fellowship" to the Salem church, throughout the subsequent history of Congregationalism, there existed among the several churches associations of varying degrees of formality and power. "Synods orderly assembled," set up by the Cambridge Platform,[7] did not have the power to enforce their decisions but since their decisions were an authoritative interpretation of the Word of God, no power was necessary. New England's Congregationalism thus had a greater cohesion than did the Independent churches of old England.

A group of persons (visible saints) could form a church when by voluntary agreement and consent they, living in the same society, would covenant to observe the ordinances of Christ. The officers elected by such a group were pastor, teacher, elder, and deacon. The pastor was to take care of the pragmatic or ethical part of Christian instruction, while the teacher was responsible for the theological or doctrinal aspects. The office of deacon was limited to "the care of the temporall good things of the church," including keeping the church treasury and preparing the elements for the "Lord's Table." When the churches came to be supported largely through public taxation, the duties and significance of deacons were greatly reduced. Because the New Testament summarily names "widows" or "deaconesses," the Cambridge Platform does also, but with even greater brevity. They were to help care for the sick and "others in like necessities." There is no evidence that the office was of any moment, nor indeed that it was often filled. At first, all church officers were ordained; later, only pastors and teachers received the ceremonial imposition of hands from the elders of their own and neighboring churches.

Worship was studiedly nonliturgical. The long prayer which opened the Sunday morning service, though sometimes a quarter of an hour in length, followed no conscious form. The next element of the service, reading a passage of Scripture, included a verse-by-verse exposition of the biblical excerpt, for to read it through without comment ("dumb reading") smacked of prelacy if not popery. Because the place of music was highly suspect in Puritanism, the colonists compromised by contributing to their service an element that could only with reservations be regarded as music. Psalms were "lined out" for the congregation who, without books or with books without notes, endeavored to repeat the tune which had been set for them. The tunes were rarely kept pure, and because no instrumental accompaniment was permitted, congregational singing was not the greatest asset of Puritan churches. Mather Byles, Boston's ministerial poetic wit, characterized a deacon's setting of a psalm in church as follows:

> The Deacon full resolved upon't,
>   To make a doleful sound,
> Twang'd thro' his Nose a murder'd grunt,
>   And all the People Groan'd.[8]

The psalm was followed by the sermon, the major portion of the colonial service. Generally about an hour in length it was delivered either from memory or from brief notes, although the eighteenth century witnessed a trend toward the reading of sermons. After the sermon the blessings of God on the preached Word were invoked in a short prayer. Occasionally there was then another psalm, but more often the service was at that point concluded with a benediction.

The Puritans of the seventeenth century were conscious of no considerable doctrinal difference from the English Protestants. In matters of discipline and polity they were aware that changes which they felt essential had been made. The inclusion of the Westminster Confession into the Cambridge Platform was not a subterfuge; it was an expression of the feeling of unity with English Presbyterians who in turn were regarded as differing little from Anglicans in belief. John Cotton writes (*The Way of Congregational Churches Cleared*) that the churches of New England cannot justly be described as a sect, "for we professe the Orthodox Doctrine of Faith, the same with all Protestant Churches; we celebrate the same Sacraments; and submit to the spirituall government of the same lawfull Guides, so farre as Christ and our choyce hath set them over us." (Part I, chap. 3.) The Calvinistic character of the Thirty-Nine Articles should be kept in mind, and the latter may be compared with the Westminster Confession of the following century. Because of this unanimity, doctrinal disputation was at a minimum and theological singularity was not self-conscious. The large portions of doctrine which every sermon contained represented to the colonist, not a theology, but theology *per se*; it was the Word of God, particularly the New Testament, interpreted, systematized, and clarified.

Yet with the wisdom which hindsight provides, it is possible to discern a theological ancestry, a kinship which might be described as Calvinism twice removed. In the sixteenth century the pattern and influence of Geneva were impressed on English soil chiefly by way of the Marian exiles. In Geneva itself as in other continental centers of Calvinism were to be found congregations of exiled English Protestants—Protestants who agitated for an extension of Reformation principles and practices. In the transmission and assimiliation of Calvinism, however, there was a shift of emphasis: the dealings of God with man were now described in terms of a covenant relationship.

The covenant idea was not original either with German Reformed or English Puritan theologians. It has ample biblical basis (e.g., Is. 42:6; Hos. 6:7; Heb. 9:15-17; Rom. 8:3; Lu. 22:20) and is prominent in the writings of Irenaeus. On the other hand, covenant theology, i.e., an entire theological system woven about the concept of the divine covenants, is a phenomenon first appearing in the sixteenth century, becoming soon thereafter a recognized branch of Calvinistic or Reformed theology. This federal school (L. *foedus*, covenant) began in Germany in the sixteenth century, producing in the seventeenth century its best-known representative, John Koch (1603-1669). In the second half of the previous century, covenant theology appeared in English in the writings of John Preston (1587-1628) and William Ames (1576-1633) whose student Koch was. Popular authors of the following century, Baxter, Ussher, and Owen, adopted and dispersed this characteristic thought. From the English writers New England divines in the seventeenth century received their inspiration and pattern. When this federal school had invaded Puritanism in sufficient strength to be incorporated as an article in the Westminister Confession (chap. VII), its prominence in American theology—both Congregational and Presbyterian, and to a lesser extent also Baptist—was assured.[9]

The relationships between an immutable, inscrutable God and contingent, finite man could by means of the covenant idea be more clearly expounded and more readily accepted. There were three types of covenants, each satisfying a theological, ecclesiastical, or social need.[10] The basic covenant, on which all communion between God and man rested, was the covenant of grace. Displacing the covenant of works made between God and Adam, this covenant, first made with Abraham (sometimes Noah or Moses), is the way in which God recognizes the salvation imparted to those foreordained to receive divine, saving grace. It is individual, between God and each of his created elect; it is sure, for God no less than man is bound by the terms of the covenant; it is essential, for in no other way does God convey his salvation or draw men unto himself.

A church came into being as those bound to God by the covenant of grace, and living in proximity to one another, did voluntarily covenant together to worship and to serve God. This second type of covenant, corporate not individual, bound together the Father and the body of visible saints. When the visibility of one's sainthood is poor, when it appears that one has fallen short of his "solemne and publick promise before the Lord," then that person is cut off, separated from the body of the church. The covenant of the Salem church, gathered in 1629, is a useful example of this type: "We covenant with the Lord and one with an other; and doe bynd our selves in the presence of God, to walke together in all his waies, according as he is pleased to reveale himself unto us in his Blessed word of truth."[11]

Finally, the covenant became social and political as it was extended to bind a total society, saints and sinners, to the active dominion of God. If the Puritan commonwealth may properly be described as theocratic, it is in the most literal sense of God ruling via the covenant. In the Old Testament from which the covenant of grace is mined, God rules the people as a whole. The people repent, the nation is punished, the tribe is forgiven. The individual sin of Achan jeopardized the entire camp, while the righteousness of only ten men could have saved the cities of Sodom and Gommorah. So in New England the civil covenant was logically deduced from the individual covenant of grace. The social covenant then, a contract between God and the whole people, was needed to insure external conformity to the divine laws which the magistrate under God vowed to reveal and to enforce.

A society, however, could be persuaded to follow the pillar of cloud only so long as a large number possessed that prior, private understanding with God. On the one hand, if all members of society were visible saints, the church could be the state and a social covenant would be superfluous. If, on the other hand, the elect were outnumbered by the mixed multitude, fulfillment of the state's covenant would be impossible. If the Babylonians invaded in strength, Jerusalem would fall. Still more alarming, if the piety of the saints became less visible and less a reality, the walls of the Puritan city of God might be breached from within. On so precarious a balance the fate of the grand experiment rested.

One innovation, the Half-Way Covenant, seemed to augur this feared decline in piety. New England's first divines, as we have seen, agreed that "Visible Saints are the only true and meet matter, whereof a visible Church should be gathered. . . ."[12] Visible saints included not only those persons whose profession and practice implied conversion, but also their children. While declaring a mature faith to be the invariable concomitant of salvation, these Congregationalists baptized only those infants whose parents were church members. Because they could not themselves acknowledge the church covenant, the baptized children were not fully church members; Hooker calls them *non confederate*. Yet in some sense they did share in the covenant of their parents. Moreover in receiving baptism they received one of the signs or seals of the covenant of grace. Baptism was not the means of their sharing in the covenant of grace, only the sign that they already had, by being born of Christian parents, acquired a share in that covenant. One could therefore come within the church either by birth or by experience, but only those who joined by the latter method were to enjoy the full privileges of membership. If upon reaching maturity they accepted the obligations of church membership, agreed to abide by the discipline of the church, and acquainted themselves with the truths of the gospel, then they continued to enjoy this special type of church affiliation. Finally, when they experienced the reception of divine grace, when they were "savingly converted" and therefore truly Christian (and it was assumed that this would normally ensue), at that time they became full church members, full participants in the covenant of grace, being now permitted the other seal: the Lord's Supper.

A perplexing problem arose when these quasi-church members did not complete their membership by having the anticipated conversion experience. Not scandalous in life they were nevertheless not to be classified as visible saints, for they made no profession to sainthood. The difficulty became most acute when one of these unregenerate would present his children for baptism. In the Old Testament there was precedent for children being included in the covenant of their fathers, but what of succeeding generations? Could a person who enjoyed this membership by birth transfer to his children that same minimum degree of church membership? To the last question Hooker gave a negative answer:

> It belongs not to any Predecessors, either neerer or further off removed from the next Parents . . . to give right of this privilege [Baptism] to their children.[13]

In 1645, about the time that Hooker was rendering this opinion, the Reverend Richard Mather of Dorchester answered the question affirmatively:

> . . . the Children of such Parents ought to be baptized: the Reason is, the Parents as they were born in the Covenant, so they continue therein, being neither cast out, nor deserving so to be, and if so, why should not their Children be baptized, for if the Parents be in Covenant, are not the Children so likewise?[14]

When the Cambridge Platform was drawn up in 1648, Mather's position was not adopted, probably because of the strong opposition of the Reverend Charles Chauncy.[15]

The difficulty was not resolved by postponing its solution. The churches were in danger of losing control over much of society if some provision were not made whereby those of upright life could be encompassed within them. At the instigation of the Connecticut General Court an association of seventeen ministers from Massachusetts and Connecticut colonies met in 1657 to consider requirements regarding baptism and church membership. Their conclusions, endorsed by the Connecticut General Court, were echoed in the Synod of 1662 called by the Massachusetts Court. At this representative meeting, the question "Who are the subjects of baptisme?" was considered with much care and debate. Finally, and not without opposition, the position championed earlier by Richard Mather was adopted. The Fifth Proposition of that synod, rephrased, rebutted, and thrice submitted to the whole assembly, read in its final form as follows:

Church-members who were admitted in minority, understanding the Doctrine of Faith, and publickly professing their assent thereto; not scandalous in life, and solemnly owning the Covenant before the Church, wherein they give up themselves and their Children to the Lord, and subject themselves to the Government of Christ in the Church, their Children are to be Baptized.[16]

This position is caricatured by the name Half-Way Covenant. Only visible saints, the regenerate under the covenant of grace, were fully within the church covenant. Members of this other group constituted an inferior class of church membership; they could neither partake of the Lord's Supper[17] nor vote in church affairs.[18] This significant compromise changed the character of the "only true and meet matter, whereof a visible Church should be gathered" from visible saints to those "not scandalous in life." Superficially similar, the two concepts are greatly disparate. Instead of a church whose membership is comprised of the elect only, the position of earlier Congregationalism, there was to be a church where membership was of varying degrees and was based on moral or even social acceptability. With the adoption and rapid spread of the Half-Way Covenant, New England churches wandered from the path of personal piety and were recalled to it only after the Great Awakening.

The extent of Half-Way Covenant practice cannot be determined with complete accuracy. Though very popular it was never universal. Its adoption both in Connecticut and Massachusetts was largely a matter for each church to determine for itself. While some churches did not go as far as authorized by the Synod, others went beyond the provisions of the Half-Way Covenant by admitting to baptism the children of parents that were of good character whether themselves members by birth or not. The relation of the covenant of grace to the church covenant was thus completely obscured.

Once the church door was opened enough to allow the worldly to enter, and that legally, it proved difficult if not impossible to maintain nice distinctions between "full" and "half-way" members. Half-way covenanters had received one of the signs of the covenant of grace: viz., baptism. But like the children of visible saints before the days of the Half-Way Covenant, they were denied the other seal, the Lord's Supper. The inevitable question was soon asked: If these persons are permitted one of the sacraments, then why not grant them the other? To the appeal for consistency was added the attractive contention that participation in the Lord's Supper might be a means of converting the unregenerate, even as preaching the Word was assuredly a means predestined by God for the salvation of the elect. Instead therefore of barring those who had no experience of personal conversion to relate, they—if of blameless life and thirsting after righteousness—should be urged to participate in the service of communion. This modification, Stoddardeanism,[19] became firmly entrenched in the Connecticut valley but was never as widely practiced as the Half-Way Covenant. Insofar as it was adopted, it represents a further departure from Browne, Barrowe, Ames, Preston, Cotton, Hooker *et al.*, who conceived the church to be distinct from the world, not of the world, composed of true believers only and purified regularly in order to maintain that distinction.

Opening wider the churches' doors seemed a hopeful way of halting piety's decline. But it was not. By the end of the seventeenth century, the decline had in no way abated. Perhaps the blame lay elsewhere for this "great and visible decay of the power of Godliness amongst many Professors in these Churches."[20] In searching about, many clergymen alighted upon laxity of church discipline and diversity in church practice as the real source of the trouble. And the remedy for this double weakness was clear: firm control of ecclesiastical affairs. A "Reforming Synod," held in Boston in 1679, addressed itself to this problem and passed some resolutions which, in the manner typical of resolutions, were ignored. Continued agitation for stringent control over the churches led to the Proposals of 1705, put forward by a committee of Massachusetts ministers. It was therein suggested that regional associations of ministers be formed to hear questions and cases of importance, to advise associated pastors with respect to action "likely to produce any imbroilments," and to examine accusations levied against any ministerial members. The proposals further urged that a single congregation no longer be allowed to ordain any person it chose as its pastor, but that it employ only those "Recommended by a Testimonial under the Hands of some Association." The second section of the Proposals directed that

these Associated Pastors, with a proper Number of Delegates from their several Churches, be formed into a standing or stated Council, which shall Consult, Advise and Determine all Affairs that shall be proper matter for the Consideration of an Ecclesiastical Council within their respective Limits. . . .

These "Consociated Churches" are to act "in all holy Watchfulness and Helpfulness towards each other" and may withdraw communion from a church that refuses to be healed of "such gross Disorders as plainly hurt the common Interest."[21] The steps suggested here, steps clearly leading in the direction of Presbyterianism, were only partly taken in Massachusetts where the ministerial associations, already existing, continued to grow. But the stated councils called for in the second part of the Proposals never materialized in the Bay colony. There an influential liberal faction centering around Harvard successfully resisted this *coup d'église*. The Massachusetts government, under its new charter and under its episcopal-minded governor, Joseph Dudley, was in no position or mood to pass legislation designed to protect the religious integrity of the haughty colonists. Finally a skillful satirist and able thinker, the Reverend John Wise, dealt the presbyterianizing tendency a heavy blow in his *The Churches Quarrel Espoused* (1710), and again in *Vindication of the Government of New England Churches* (1717).[22]

It was otherwise in Connecticut. There the leading ministers who had co-operated in the founding of Yale in 1701 witnessed the efforts of Massachusetts in 1705 to achieve stricter church control. With this effort they sympathized and from it they took their cue. In 1707, the governor of Connecticut, Gurdon Saltonstall, was not only friendly to Congregationalism, but was himself a leading Congregational minister. That colony's liberal charter of 1662 was moreover still in force, Edmund Andros notwithstanding, making English oversight less of a factor in Connecticut than it was at this time in Massachusetts. In May, 1708, the General Court passed a bill summoning ministers and messengers from all the colony's churches to meet at Saybrook the following September in order to "draw a form of ecclesiastical discipline." The resulting Saybrook Platform incorporated some of the Proposals of 1705 verbatim, and followed their spirit where it did not follow their words. The General Court approved this platform in October, opening the way for severe encroachments upon the autonomy of the local congregations. Although this act was accepted on varying terms from county to county, the principles which it advocated were in general operation within a year's time. These steps toward rigidity and formalism are unmistakable steps away from a spontaneous, institutionally careless pietism.

Prior to the Great Awakening, however, the many ministerial lamentations concerning the "decline of piety" did not refer primarily to doctrinal dilution, episcopal or synodical encroachments, nor even to Rhode Island's antinomianism, but to a laxity in personal morality and religion. As religion became more institutional and less personal, more a product of instruction than of experience, and more an affair of the intellect than of the emotions, piety waned. Brattle Street Church, founded in Boston in 1699, eliminated the testimony of personal religious experience not merely as a concession to the modesty of potential members: it was more a recognition that there was little such experience to relate. Religion was losing its dramatic, experiential quality. Sermons were preached with little feeling, and were heard with an emotional response proportional to the stimulus. Leslie Stephen's remark that a critical vocabulary of dull, duller, and dullest was sufficient to describe the English homilies of this period may be a bit severe for the sermons in New England where religion had not been wholly identified with morality. Yet a measure of Whitefield's sudden success lay in the conspicuous absence of dullness in his preaching style. The neglect of public worship and other lapses in external religious behavior, moreover, were usually regarded as tokens of this decay. The Reforming Synod of 1679 had pointed with a trembling finger to the apostasy, pride, neglect of "Church Fellowship, and other divine Institutions," profaning the name of God by oaths and irreverent behavior in church, sabbath-breaking, decline in family worship, "inordinate passions," intemperance, lying, worldliness, refusal to reform, self-seeking, and unbelief.[23] Jerusalem was no longer pure.

Another popularly accepted witness to defilement of the ancestral faith was the alleged growth of a rationalism that rivaled if it did not ridicule revelation. The strident alarms concerning "deistical principles" in the early seventeenth century seem almost ludicrous in view of the late seventeenth century; but of course none then knew what evils lay ahead. Those rays of the Enlightenment that did manage to filter into New England before the Awakening were largely focused on Arminianism which in turn was largely concentrated in the Church of England. Even this, however, proved unsettling. Well-publicized cases of conversion from the "New England way" to the Anglican way together with a rapidly increasing sense of insecurity made the warnings of the orthodox shrill and incessant. It is true that isolated cases of this limited sort of liberalism did appear within Congregationalism and college students, as always, did not limit their reading to the approved lists. Notwithstanding, the Enlightenment was not yet a brilliant beacon leading wayward wanderers out of a Calvinist gloom.

Finally, from the Olympus which passing time provides the historian, it is possible to view this lamented decline in religion as one aspect of a broad, irresistible cultural transformation. The Puritan commonwealth was entering the modern world. Pietism, for good or ill, rests most comfortably upon those who are least comfortable. When peace is made with the world, there is—as every Puritan well knew—a resulting enmity with God. And peace was being made. A thriving West Indian trade augmented the native fishing and shipbuilding industries, bringing a measure of prosperity to the New England colonies. This luxury, even moderate luxury, had its sinful concomitants. Economic oppression was the temptation of both the scarce laborer and of the possessor of even scarcer capital. Pride expressed itself in contention and fashionable clothes, in idleness and tavern-frequenting. In the election and fast-day sermons, the clergy's acute consciousness of the declension of New England from the purity of its fathers is abundantly evident. These woeful exhortations—Perry Miller aptly styles them jeremiads—testify fully to the growing sinfulness aggravated by indifference; the voices cry for repentance, but there is no repentance.[24] Ministers "berated the consequences of progress, but never progress itself. They deplored the effects of trade upon man's religion but they did not ask men to cease from trading."[25] As economic independence was ill-suited to cosmic insignificance, so also was serving mammon to serving God. It indeed seemed true that powerful cultural forces "often lead men to discard ideas which they may not have properly disproved."[26]

By the time the eighteenth century was under way, New England had become a "mixed multitude" religiously.[27] The dominant religious group, Congregationalism, was losing its monopoly and its integrity as was the dominant theology, Calvinism. As sainthood became more synonymous with respectability, Congregationalism became more like the world in which it lived, less like a pure fellowship of saints called out from society. Unable to rule over others, the established churches united to rule over themselves. With the altered economy and the threat of rationalism, God became less respected as man became more respectable. It cannot both be that God and man are masters of all destiny. The decline of this Puritan piety was marked by the rise of "many and great Impieties,"[28] a fall in "the power of godliness,"[29] and a "time of extraordinary dullness in religion."[30] New England, nodding sleepily, was soon to be awakened with a start.

CHAPTER 2

RIPPLES of REVIVAL

IN THE FIRST HALF OF THE EIGHTEENTH CENTURY revivalism was a phenomenon as wondrous as it was inexplicable, to be classed with meteorites and rattlesnakes. There was no revival technique. The extraordinary "outpourings of the spirit of God" were regarded as being truly from God, while the minister or church was only a channel through which that spirit was poured. How or why the revivals began or stopped, here and not there, were divine secrets. The wind blew where it listed, but none could tell whence it came or whither it went. Edwards' account of the revival at Northampton is of "surprising conversions"; the element of surprise in this and other early revivals is real.

Always a feature of revival times was the presence of a "remarkable religious concern." If this concern were the sole criterion of revivals, then it could be said of the early New England colonies that they were in a state of perennial revivalism. Such would of course be an abuse of the term, for Puritan life was not undulatory. Characterized by a sober religious preoccupation that prompted the dissenters to scrutinize their neighbor's piety carefully and to question their own continuously, first-generation Puritans gave indifference toward religion few ports of entry. Yet it was this remarkable concern that the pious of succeeding generations sought to recapture; and because revivals invariably aroused this concern they were regarded as wondrous blessings of God. Many of the third and fourth generations, haunted by a sense of apostasy and by a feeling of religious inferiority, looked back with envy and guilt to the older, sterner forebears.

Sensitive to their spiritual decline, the Puritans often regarded severe disasters or afflictions as divine reminders of their collective backsliding. On Sunday night, October 29, 1727, New England's earth quaked and trembled; so did many of its citizens, who gathered around the churches early the next day. There was "a greater resort to ministers and to the house of God than before, and greater numbers were added to the churches, yet in too many instances, it appeared to be rather the consequences of fear, than of genuine conviction, and a thorough change of heart."[1] Earlier, in 1721, Windham, Connecticut, had seen a "remarkable concern . . . among the people" which resulted in eighty persons being admitted to full church membership within a period of six months. "The town was full of love, joy, thanksgiving and praise. . . . But while this place was so remarkably wet with the dew of heaven, the ground was dry all round it."[2] Of these events no great notice was taken, nor was much significance attached to them. They were, as Trumbull suggests, oases of spiritual concern in a desert of growing indifference.

In Northampton, far to the northwest of Windham, revivalism was more than an isolated phenomenon. There periods of "wetness" tended to constitute a stream, a stream which suddenly broadened in 1734 sending its ripples into much of New England. In a powerful ministry of nearly sixty years at Northampton, Solomon Stoddard (1643-1729) had exercised a profound influence not only over his own frontier congregation but throughout Massachusetts and Connecticut colonies. During his long ministry, there were five periods in which a large number of persons were "converted," i.e., felt themselves to be now of the "elect," recipients of a divine and saving grace. In these five seasons of religious concern (called "harvests" by Stoddard) which began as early as around 1680 and continued through 1719, "the greater part of the young people in the town, seemed to be mainly concerned for their eternal salvation."[3] Described by Perry Miller as the first great "revivalist" in New England, Stoddard opened wide the doors of his church and urged all who would to enter.[4] Though a believer in, and extender of, covenant theology, Stoddard looked upon the covenant as in no way mitigating the arbitrariness with which God acts. He proclaimed, as did the preachers of the Great Awakening, an absolute and sovereign God and a miserable eternity for those whom God did not please to save. Some of Stoddard's writings expressing his tolerant evangelism were republished during the later and more intense revival interest in New England.[5]

Jonathan Edwards, Stoddard's tall and comely grandson, left his post as a tutor at Yale to come to Northampton in 1727.[6] For two years Edwards had the opportunity of laboring with Stoddard, "but there was nothing of any general awakening." When in 1729 Solomon Stoddard died, it seemed to Edwards that the local citizenry was "very insensible of the things of religion."

. . . licentiousness for some years greatly prevailed among the youth of the town; they were many of them very much addicted to night walking, and frequenting the tavern, and lewd practices, wherein some by their example exceedingly corrupted others. It was their manner very frequently to get together in conventions of both sexes, for mirth and jollity, which they called frolicks; and they would often spend the greater part of the night in them, without any regard to order in the families they belonged to: and indeed family goverment did too much fail in the town. It was become very customary with many of our young people to be indecent in their carriage at meeting. . . .[7]

As early as 1733, however, the young people in particular were more disposed to hear and to heed pastoral advice and "grew observably more decent in their attendance on public worship." By 1734 the whole town showed an increased anxiety about irreligion, harboring the "fear that God was about to withdraw from the land." As the people were diligently seeking a way more acceptable to God, "there was then some things said publicly . . . concerning justification by faith alone . . . it proved a word spoken in season here; and was most evidently attended with a very remarkable blessing of heaven to the souls of the people in this town."[8] Following the conversion of a young woman of questionable morality, the tempo of religious activity and interest thereabouts rapidly increased. ". . . religion was with all sorts the great concern, and the world was a thing only by the by."

This work of God, as it was carried on, and the number of true saints multiplied, soon made a glorious alteration in the town; so that in the spring and summer following, anno 1735, the town seemed to be full of the presence of God: it never was so full of love, nor so full of joy; and yet so full of distress as it was then. There were remarkable tokens of God's presence in almost every house. It was a time of joy in families on the account of salvation's being brought unto them; parents rejoicing over their children as new born, and husbands over their wives, and wives over their husbands. . . . Our public assemblies were then beautiful; the congregation was alive in God's service, every one earnestly intent on the public worship, every hearer eager to drink in the words of the minister as they came from his mouth; the assembly in general were, from time to time, in tears while the word was preached; some weeping with sorrow and distress, others with joy and love, others with pity and concern for the souls of their neighbors.[9]

News of what was happening in Northampton spread to nearby towns, mostly by means of eyewitness reports. When the court met or public lectures were held, visitors came from the environs. In the town they at least heard of what was transpiring; often, they "had their consciences smitten, and awakened, and went home with wounded hearts." Even the roving tradesmen noted the "showers of divine blessing that God rained down here, and went home rejoicing; till at length the same work began evidently to appear and prevail in several other towns in the county." In March, 1735, there were unmistakable signs of revival in South Hadley and in Suffield. The characteristics of concern—a profound and disturbing consciousness of sin with a subsequent feeling of relief and joy—then appeared in Sunderland "and soon overspread the town."

✓ . . . About the same time it began to appear in a part of Deerfield, called Green River, and afterwards filled the town, and there has been a glorious work there: it began also to be manifest in the south part of Hatfield, in a place called the Hill, and after that the whole town, in the second week in April, seemed to be seized, as it were at once, with concern about the things of religion: and the word of God has been great there. There has been also a very general awakening at West Springfield, and Long Meadow; and in Enfield; there was, for a time, a pretty general concern amongst some that before had been very loose persons. About the same time that this appeared at Enfield, the Rev. Mr. Bull of Westfield informed me, that there had been a great alteration there, and that more had been done in one week there than in seven years before.— Something of this work likewise appeared in the first precinct in Springfield, principally in the north and south extremes of the parish. And in Hadley old town, there gradually appeared so much of a work of God on souls, as at another time would have been thought worthy of much notice. For a short time there was also a very great and general concern, of the like nature, but in every place God brought saving blessings with him, and his word attended with his Spirit (as we all have reason to think) returned not void.[10]

✓ The news of so much zeal and fervor acted and reacted as a stimulant to others. Edwards reports that when Northampton heard what was happening elsewhere, the intelligence "did doubtless, for a time, serve to uphold the work amongst us." As indicated above, the revival was not limited to Massachusetts, "but many places in Connecticut have partook in this same mercy." In Windsor, also in East Windsor where Edwards' father was minister, there were stirrings of concern. In the latter parish, there had been "four or five seasons of the pouring out of the Spirit" since 1694. On Coventry, Lebanon (under Eleazar Wheelock), Durham, Ripton in Stratford (under Jedediah Mills), Mansfield (under Eleazar Williams), Tolland, Hebron, Bolton, and elsewhere in Connecticut this divine blessing had been showered. Two Connecticut ministers, Benjamin Lord of Preston and John Owen of Groton, traveled to Northampton for the single purpose of observing the events occurring there. Lord later told Edwards that upon returning home and relating what he had seen and heard, the same phenomenon appeared in Preston, prevailing "till there was a general awakening."

The importance of this word-of-mouth transmission is emphasized by the location of the communities experiencing revivals in this period. Revivals appeared along the banks of the Connecticut River and spread toward the east as that river approached the ocean.[11] From Northfield to Saybrook Point, the religious stirrings of Northampton were known many months before Edwards sat down to write his *Narrative*. With reference to some of the places mentioned, however, Edwards notes that "we had no knowledge of each other's circumstances." Was there any other factor contributing to the generality of renewed religious interest? Since the tendency of revivals to follow divine chastisement has been noted, contemporary calamities or public distresses may be interpreted as a possible provocation of the religious solicitude.

A phenomenon of disastrous proportions—sufficient to have caused a religious reaction or a popular revolt—was the epidemic of 1735 to 1740 known as the "throat distemper." Causing more deaths in the New England colonies than any war before the Revolution, the diphtheria plague was most severe in the New Hampshire and Maine areas.[12] In Kingston, New Hampshire, the epidemic of little more than a year's duration brought death to more than one-third of that town's children. In a nearby town of twelve hundred inhabitants, there were in one year, 1736, two hundred and ten deaths. In view of such incidence the distemper might easily provoke abnormal behavior. Since religious upheavals were both contemporary with and subsequent to it, is there not some causal relation between the two? That question cannot be answered affirmatively for the following reasons: the epidemic appeared in New Jersey in 1735, long after the revival movement had been under way there; in Connecticut and Massachusetts, the severity of the epidemic in any given area bears no observable relation to the intensity of the revival in that area, either before or after Whitefield; in New Hampshire the epidemic was all over by 1736, making difficult an explanation of the five-year lapse between its terminus and the beginning of the Great Awakening in the Kingston-Hampton Falls area; and finally, while the epidemic was from four to five times as severe in New Hampshire and Maine as in Connecticut and Massachusetts, it was in the latter areas that the revival was most pervasive.

In the preface to Edward's report of the revivals Drs. Watts and Guyse of London wrote:

'Tis worthy of our Observation, that this great and surprizing Work does not seem to have taken its Rise from any sudden and distressing Calamity or publick Terror that might universally impress the Minds of a People: Here was no Storm, no Earthquake, no Inundation of Water, no Desolation by Fire, no Pestilence or any other sweeping Distemper, nor any cruel Invasion by their Indian Neighbours, that might force the Inhabitants into a serious Thoughtfulness, and a religious Temper by the Fears of approaching Death and Judgment.

If it be thought that a contemporary witness on the other side of the Atlantic is of little value, it should be remembered that there existed an Anglo-American community that often made London more familiar than Charleston, South Carolina, with what might be happening in and around Massachusetts Bay. To grant that the "throat distemper" was the cause of every revival in New England would in no way minimize or detract from those revivals, according to the prevailing thought. There would certainly be no attempt to conceal a causal relation if there was one, for the epidemic too was of God. Thomas Prince calls attention to the smallpox epidemic of 1721 which caused many young people to be "greatly awakened." Then, with reference to another siege of smallpox in 1729, Prince remarks with obvious disappointment that it left them "unawakened, ungrateful, unreformed."[13]

Edwards' formal account of these events, in and around Northampton, had considerable effect in acquainting many with New England revivals. In the *Narrative,* which is in fact a protracted letter to Benjamin Colman and was published first in London, then the following year, 1738, in Boston, Edwards acts as a reporter of the inexplicable and unexpected occurrences.[14] He neither defends nor discriminates as he describes the religious experiences of young and old, male and female, moral and profligate, joyous and melancholy. Because of many inquiries concerning this "work of God," Edwards endeavored to give as full a report as possible, including detailed, almost morbid, recitation of case histories. The feeling that "there is no one thing I know of that God has made such a means of promoting his work amongst us, as the news of others' conversion" moved Edwards—as it did later prorevivalists—to be as full as possible. By the time that his *Narrative* was published, however, zeal and concern in Northampton had declined. After perusing Edwards' letter, Colman wrote of the great pleasure it gave many to know how the Spirit of God had worked in that frontier area. Edwards in a letter of reply thanked Colman for his kind regard, adding "but yet at the same time it is a great damp to that Joy to consider how we decline, and what decays that lively Spirit in religion suffers amongst us, while others are rejoicing and praising God for us. . . ."[15] It appeared also that the Spirit was withdrawing elsewhere as people became more concerned with this world; religion nevertheless persisted as "the main subject of conversation for several months after this."[16] The revival halted with an abruptness not unlike that with which it had begun, while through it all man could only behold and wonder. "God is pleased to let us see how entirely & immediately the great work lately wrought was his, by withdrawing, & letting us see how little we can do, and how little effect great things have without him . . ."[17]

Like a true Calvinist, Edwards continued, however, to do the little that he could, confident that a "true and righteous Judge" would bless and make use of whatever glorified His name. In 1738 he published *Discourses on Various Important Subjects, Nearly concerning the great Affair of the Soul's Eternal Salvation*, a collection of sermons which he had preached during the peak of the religious excitement three to four years previously. Included here is Edwards' significant series on justification by faith, which doctrine, he now believes, was vindicated in and by the revival—"a remarkable Testimony of God's Approbation of the Doctrine."[18] Published because they were found to be particularly effective and plainly relevant, these discourses are notable for their lack of stirring emotional appeals. Filled with much theology and overflowing with ratiocination, they bowed the intellect before they swayed the heart. Edwards regarded a doctrinal confusion rather than a lethargic disposition as the chief sore to be healed. The fourth discourse, "The Justification of God in the Damnation of Sinners," as well as the doctrine that "we are justified only by faith in Christ, and not by any manner or virtue or goodness of our own," were thrusts of a Calvinism pure and uncompromised.

The American edition of the *Narrative*, published in Boston the same year as the *Discourses*, included an attestation of six "ministers of Hampshire" confirming the accuracy of Edwards' reporting. The first of the six names affixed is that of William Williams of Hatfield, an uncle of Jonathan Edwards and a hearty supporter of the revival in his own parish. By May of 1736, Williams had preached and prepared for publication a group of sermons entitled *The Duty and Interest of a People among whom Religion has been planted, To Continue Stedfast and Sincere in the Profession and Practice of it. From Generation to Generation.* While not greatly stressing the necessity for an experience of regeneration, Williams here urged his flock to display or revive that fidelity and zeal characteristic of their progenitors; the children had sinned against the God of their fathers. Published with this series were *Directions for such as are Concerned to obtain a true Repentance and Conversion to God,* more clearly showing Williams' proximity to his nephew in an intelligent support of the religious freshening. Cautioning his hearers against a false sense of conversion, Williams gave specific and detailed advice for those who in "the present Season of Grace" continue to search for the divine grace necessary for salvation, urging them "especially if it be a Day of Conviction and Awakening with you, [to] carefully improve and attend to such a Season."

From these two points along the west bank of the Connecticut River, Northampton and Hatfield, the revival had moved upstream and down, migrating overland only in a southeasterly direction. Affecting about twoscore towns or parishes, this awakening attracted the attention of many of the colonies as well as of England and Scotland—chiefly by means of Edwards' *Narrative.* Yet the revival was far from general in New England, being limited to the River valley in Massachusetts and extending less than thirty miles to the east of that valley in Connecticut. Where the movement did appear, it was most often only a ripple leaving little trace of its presence. No churches were split, no legislative or ecclesiastical measures were called forth, no elaborate apologetic or sustained attack apropos of revivalism was advanced at this time.

This "frontier revival" is usually regarded as a phase or precursor of the violent religious upsurge of the 1740's. Especially since Edwards was prominent in both, the former readily appears to many as something more than simply the temporal antecedent of the latter. It "seemed to prepare the way in diverse places for that more extensive revival of religion which in five years after followed."[19] Though a consideration of the causes of the later revival must be reserved for the next chapter, it may here be noted that Edwards regarded the two movements as distinct. In the *Memoirs of David Brainerd,* he remarks that "this awakening [i.e., of January, 1741] was at the beginning of that extraordinary religious commotion, through the land. . . . It was for a time very great and general at New-Haven; and the college had no small share in it."[20] By 1737, the frontier revival was "very much at a Stop." When the Great Awakening broke forth under Whitefield, the scene was by some three to four years and, in its initial phases, by many miles removed from the earlier one.

There was, however, one element of continuity between the two: the spirit of revivalism among the Presbyterians of New York and New Jersey. In the Middle Colonies revivals had been a factor since about 1720 when the Dutch Reformed under Theodore J. Frelinghuysen's pietistic, evangelical, impassioned preaching were rudely shaken. In the *Narrative* Edwards refers to a revival "under the ministry of a very pious young gentleman, a Dutch minister, whose name as I remember, was Freelinghousen."[21] Both the Jonathan Dickinson group of the New York Presbytery and the Tennent group of the New Brunswick Presbytery (organized in 1738) accepted the unusual religious devotion and interest attending revivals as of divine origin, and therefore to be encouraged and promoted. Though there is before 1740 little direct influence of this Middle Colony group on New England,[22] many ministers with Presbyterian affiliation labored on behalf of the Great Awakening.[23] There were Presbyterian pastors within New England itself: notably, Jonathan Parsons, who had studied under Edwards in the early 1730's, and then presided over a church at Lyme, Connecticut, and later at Newburyport, Massachusetts; John Moorhead, who since 1730 had pastored a Presbyterian flock in Boston; and David Mac-Gregore, who had guided the West Society of Londonderry, New Hampshire, since its inception in 1739. In the years between 1737 and 1740, when revivals in New England were negligible, interest in such occurrences was kept high by the Presbyterian activities outside of that area.[24] And in June and July of 1740 Ebenezer Pemberton, pastor of the Presbyterian church in the city of New York, preached a series of very evangelistic sermons in Boston,[25] speaking at the important Thursday lecture as well as in the leading meetinghouses on Sundays. For six provocative years, New England's emotions and interest had been aroused by these religious pulsations. Eager with anticipation and overready for the climax, New England on September 14, 1740, received George Whitefield.

CHAPTER 3

THE GRAND ITINERANTS

AT TEN O'CLOCK IN THE MORNING, SEPTEMBER 15, 1740, George Whitefield preached his first sermon in New England. Having sailed from Charleston he arrived at Newport, Rhode Island, on Sunday, September 14, and immediately wrung from the local Anglican minister a reluctant invitation to speak from his pulpit the following day. So on Monday at ten o'clock and again at three, the eloquent and irrepressible young English cleric prayed and preached in the "very commodious" parish church.

It was more than filled in the afternoon.—Persons of all Denominations attended—God assisted me much. I observed Numbers affected, and had great Reason to believe the Word of the Lord had been sharper than a two-edged Sword in some of the Hearers Souls.[1]

These words from Whitefield's Journal open the record of the greatest single evangelistic tour in New England's history. Into an atmosphere electrified with expectancy and emotion Whitefield came, bristling, crackling, and thundering.

It is easy, deceptively so, to regard the Great Awakening in New England as the exclusive work of two of three dramatic, explosive figures. So prodigious were their labors, so striking the results, that such a simplification has much validity. We look initially, then, upon the persons of George Whitefield, Gilbert Tennent, and James Davenport, in whom the tumultuous sweep of the revival is first and most clearly seen. Of these three, Whitefield was first in time and in eminence; he was "the Grand Itinerant" *par excellence*. Born in Gloucester in 1714, Whitefield had while at Oxford become intimate with John and Charles Wesley. His popularity as a preacher grew with extraordinary rapidity and in 1738 he found himself briefly in Georgia on a mission of mercy to the homeless and poor. Shortly after his ordination to the Anglican priesthood in 1739, Whitefield, meeting resistance in England to his "methodism," adopted the procedure of

itinerant, open-air preaching. When he arrived in the colonies toward
the end of that year, he employed the same technique as he bustled
from Savannah to New York and back, raising funds for an orphanage
which he was building in Bethesda, Georgia.

Preparation for Whitefield's coming to New England took the form
not only of the earlier revivals, but more specifically of ample publication of writings pertinent to the excitement of the times. Following
the example of Philadelphia and New York, Boston in 1739 published
seven separate items written by Gilbert Tennent. In that same year,
Whitefield's writings began to appear in the American colonies, half
of the total number published being printed in Boston. While one of
Boston's leading ministers, Benjamin Colman, was busy carrying on
a correspondence with Whitefield,[2] Boston newspapers carried extensive advertisements of books or tracts by or about Whitefield, even
noting books of which the young English evangelist approved.[3] News of
Whitefield's successes elsewhere, testimonies to his piety, eulogies of
his character, his own ill-concealed egoism—these constituents augured
if they did not conjure up an "extraordinary outpouring of the spirit of
God" on New England.

Newport heard Whitefield twice on that Monday in 1740 and again
on Tuesday when he preached, he informs us, "with much Flame,
Clearness and Power to still greater Auditories than Yesterday. It
being Assembly Time, the Gentlemen adjourned in order to attend
the Service, and several Invitations were given me to come to other
adjacent Places. The People were exceedingly attentive. Tears trickled
down their Cheeks. . . ." Wednesday morning the preacher of flame
ferried to Bristol, departing thence for Boston the next morning. Of his
Boston visit the *News-Letter* writes:

Last Thursday Evening the Rev'd Mr. Whitefield arrived from Rhode-
Island, being met on the Road and conducted to Town by several Gentle-
men. The next Day in the Forenoon he attended Prayers in the King's
Chappel, and in the Afternoon he preach'd to a vast Congregation in the
Rev'd Dr. Colman's Meeting-House. The next Day he preach'd in the
Forenoon at the South Church to a Crowded Audience, and in the Afternoon to about 5000 People on the Common: and Lord's-Day in the
afternoon having preach'd to a great Number of People at the Old Brick
Church, the House not being large enough to hold those that crowded to
hear him, when the Exercise was over, He went and preached in the Field,
to at least 8000 Persons. . . .[4]

On Monday Whitefield, having addressed about six thousand persons at Webb's meetinghouse that morning, proceeded to Checkley's church in Summer Street in the afternoon. So great and unruly was the crowd awaiting him that by the time Whitefield arrived, what should have been a prayerful congregation was in fact a turbulent mob. When the zealous orator was informed that five persons had killed themselves in ill-advised leaps from the gallery he decided that the Commons might be safer, if less sacred, ground and there led his hearers. Tuesday at Second Church with Joshua Gee; Wednesday at Harvard College; Thursday delivering the weekly lecture in First Church at the invitation of Thomas Foxcroft. Concluding his first incredible week in Boston Whitefield dined with the governor, Jonathan Belcher, then crossed by ferry to Charleston. In a hastily written letter, the evangelist noted, "So many persons come to me under convictions, and for advice, that I have scarce time to eat bread. Wonderful things are doing here. The word runs like lightening. Dagon daily falls before the ark. . . ."[5]

From Boston, Whitefield went to Roxbury, Marblehead, Ipswich, Newbury, Hampton, Portsmouth, and on Wednesday, October 1, he arrived at York, Maine, his northernmost point.[6] The next day he began retracing his steps toward Boston, this time pausing to preach in Salem as well as in the aforementioned parishes. After preaching at Prince's and Sewall's Old South Church on Thursday, October 9, young George Whitefield noted in his journal:

For I am verily persuaded, the Generality of Preachers talk of an unknown, unfelt Christ. And the Reason why Congregations have been so dead, is because dead Men preach to them. O that the Lord may quicken and revive them for his own Names Sake. For how can dead Men beget living Children? 'Tis true, God may convert people by the Devil, if he pleases, and so he may by unconverted Ministers; but I believe he seldom or never makes Use of them for this Purpose; No: The Lord will chuse Men who are Vessels made meet by the Operations of his blessed Spirit, for his sacred Use. And, as for my own Part, I would not lay Hands knowingly on an unconverted Man for ten Thousand Worlds.[7]

Despite the attitude here expressed (but not yet published) Boston and Whitefield continued to revel in each other. Early the following Sunday evening, October 12, Whitefield's farewell sermon reached some thirty thousand eager auditors.[8] With evident excitement and joy, Thomas Prince wrote that upon Whitefield's departure

great numbers in this town were so happily concerned about their souls, as we had never seen any thing like it before, except at the time of the general earthquake: and their desires excited to hear their ministers more than ever: so that our assemblies both on Lectures and Sabbaths were surprisingly increased, and now the people wanted to hear us oftener. In consideration of which, a public Lecture was proposed to be set up at Dr. Colman's church, near the midst of town, on every Tuesday evening . . . the first stated evening Lecture in these parts of the world. . . .⁹

Turning westward, Whitefield preached at Concord Monday, at Sudbury and Marlborough Tuesday, at Worcester and Leicester Wednesday, at Brookfield and Cold-Spring Thursday, and on Friday he arrived in Edwards' Northampton, where he spent the weekend. He regarded Edwards as a "solid, excellent Christian . . . I think, I may say I have not seen his Fellow in all New-England." Concerning the Sunday services which he conducted there, Whitefield wrote:

Dear Mr. Edwards wept during the whole Time of Exercise.—The People were equally, if not more affected, and my own soul was much lifted up towards God. In the Afternoon the Power encreased yet more and more. Our Lord seem'd to keep the good Wine till the last. I have not seen four such gracious meetings together since my Arrival. My Soul was much knit to these dear People of God, and, tho' I had not Time to converse with them about their Experiences, yet one might see, that for the most Part, they were a gracious tender People; and, tho' their former Fire might be greatly abated, yet it immediately appeared, when stirred up.¹⁰

The next day, October 20, 1740, Whitefield completed his tour of Massachusetts, moving south from Springfield to Suffield, Windsor, and Hartford where he aroused a "vast Concourse of people."¹¹ The weekend was spent in New Haven where he preached five times in three days. Departing Sunday evening Whitefield moved quickly through Milford, Stratford, Fairfield, Newark (Connecticut), and Stamford, preaching once in each parish. When he left Stamford Wednesday morning, October 29, his destination was Rye, New York. Before the day was over, the "Grand Itinerant" had completed his first and in every way most significant tour of the New England colonies.

To congregations accustomed to sermons stolidly read from closely written manuscripts, the free-flowing eloquence of the youthful and impassioned orator had much appeal. His sermons were simple, intrinsically logical, emotional, extemporaneous. His human sympathies real, his denominational prejudices negligible, and his superficial Calvinism adaptable and inclusive, Whitefield was admirably equipped to appeal to persons of widely divergent stations and loyalties. That keen observer of man and nature, Benjamin Franklin, set down his own valuable characterization of the evangelist:

He had a loud and clear voice, and articulated his words so perfectly that he might be heard and understood at a great distance, especially as his auditories observed the most perfect silence. . . . By hearing him often, I came to distinguish easily between sermons newly composed and those which he had often preached in the course of his travels. His delivery of the latter was so improved by frequent repetition, that every accent, every emphasis, every modulation of the voice, was so perfectly well turned and well placed, that, without being interested in the subject, one could not help being pleased with the discourse. His writing and printing from time to time, gave great advantage to his enemies. Unguarded expression, and even erroneous opinions, delivered in preaching, might have been afterwards explained or qualified; but *litera scripta manet*. Critics attacked his writings violently, and with so much appearance of reason, as to diminish the number of his votaries, and prevent their increase. So that, I am satisfied that if he had never written anything, he would have left behind him a much more numerous and important sect; and his reputation, in that case, would have been growing even after his death; because, there being nothing of his writing on which to found a censure and give him a lower character, his proselytes would be left at liberty to attribute to him as great a variety of excellences as their enthusiastic admiration might wish him to have possessed.[12]

It was clearly rather the printed than the spoken word which produced in New England the greater and more sustained attacks against Whitefield. Yet even with his preaching not all were equally impressed. When he left Boston, the *Evening-Post* (September 29, 1740) noted that "this Morning the Rev'd Mr. Whitefield set out on his Progress to the Eastward; so that the Town is in a hopeful way of being restor'd to its former State of Order, Peace and Industry." A "letter to the editor" of the *News-Letter* (October 2, 1740) bemoaned such an attitude on the part of the former paper, affirming that "the Generality of sober and serious Persons, of all Denominations among us (who perhaps are as much for maintaining Order, Peace & Industry as Mr. Evening-Post and Company) have been greatly Affected with Mr. Whitefield's Plain, Powerful, and Awakening Preaching. . . ." Though the second opinion probably represented the consensus, dissenters increased. By the middle of October six letters to Whitefield from the anti-Whitefield Reverend Alexander Garden of

South Carolina were printed and circulated in Boston,[13] while an attack on Whitefield, known as *The Querists* and originating in Pennsylvania, received Boston circulation. In November the *Evening-Post* published two sets of queries calling upon Whitefield to justify some of his remarks and to justify also the collections for his orphan house. In the same issue a letter pointing up the excesses of "Methodism" in England was craftily reprinted.[14]

The day that Whitefield left New England, he set down his reflections on the sojourn there.

I have now had an Opportunity of seeing the greatest and most populous Part of it [New England], and take it all together, it certainly on many Accounts exceeds all other Provinces in America, and, for the Establishment of Religion, perhaps all other Parts of the World. . . . Every five Miles, or perhaps less, you have a Meeting-House, and, I believe, there is no such Thing as a Pluralist or Non-resident Minister in both Provinces. Many, nay most that preach, I fear do not experimentally know Christ. . . . God has remarkably in sundry Times and diverse Manners, poured out his Spirit in several parts of both Provinces; and it often refreshed my Soul to hear of the Faith of their good Forefathers, who first settled these Parts. . . . The Ministers and People of Connecticut seem'd to be more simple than those that live near Boston, especially in those Parts where I went. But I think the Ministers Preaching almost universally by Note, is a certain Mark they have, in a great Measure, lost the old Spirit of Preaching . . . it is a sad Symptom of Decay of vital Religion, when reading Sermons becomes fashionable where extempore Preaching did once almost universally prevail. . . . As for the Universities, I believe it may be said, their Light is become Darkness, Darkness that may be felt, and is complained of by the most godly Ministers. . . . The Church of England is at a low Ebb, and, as far as I can find, had people kept their Primitive Purity, it would scarce have got Footing in New-England. . . . In short, I like New-England exceeding well; and when a Spirit of Reformation revives, it certainly will prevail more than in any other place, because they are simple in their Worship, less corrupt in their Principles, and consequently easier to be brought over to the Form of sound Words, into which so many of their pious Ancestors were delivered.[15]

When this Journal was printed the next year, anti-Whitefieldianism erupted in many quarters. Two groups in particular responded to the slap they had received: the New England ministers, the majority of whom "do not experimentally know Christ," and the New England colleges, whose "Light is become Darkness, Darkness that may be felt." Charles Chauncy,[16] one of those ministers of whose salvation Whitefield felt some doubt, in a letter to an Edinburgh minister asks "what was the great Good this Gentleman was the instrument of?"

In answer whereto, I freely acknowledge, wherever he went he generally moved the Passions, especially of the younger People, and the Females among them; the Effect whereof was, a great Talk about Religion, together with a Disposition to be perpetually hearing Sermons, to neglect of all other Business; especially, as preach'd by those who were Sticklers for the new Way, as it was called. And in these things chiefly consisted the Goodness so much spoken of. I deny not, but that there might be here and there a Person stopp'd from going on in a Course of Sin; and some might be made really better: But so far as I could judge upon the nicest Observation, the Town, in general, was not much mended in those things wherein a Reformation was greatly needed.[17]

Later when Chauncy reacted against the revival as a whole, the personal controversy between him and Whitefield continued. When Whitefield offered objections to certain passages in Chauncy's *Seasonable Thoughts*, the latter replied with *A Letter to the Reverend Mr. George Whitefield, Vindicating certain Passages he has excepted against in a late Book entitled, Seasonable Thoughts on the State of Religion in New England; and shewing that he has neither sufficiently defended himself, nor retracted his past Misconduct.*[18] Long before this, however, many others had taken up the cry against Whitefield. In October of 1742, the *News-Letter* published the following advertisement:

In a short Time will be Re-printed, upon proper Encouragement, A Warning against countenancing the Ministrations of Mr. George Whitefield, Published at the New-Church in Bristow. . . . Wherein are shewn, That Mr. Whitefield is no Minister of Jesus Christ: That his Call and Coming to Scotland are scandalous: That his Practice is disorderly and fertile of Disorders: That his whole Doctrine is and his, Success must be, diabolical; so that People ought to avoid him, from Duty to God, to Themselves, to Fellow-Men, to Posterity, and to Him. By Adam Gibb, Minister of the Gospel at Edinburgh. . . .

Timothy Cutler, now a rector in Boston, wrote a fellow Anglican that "Whitefield has plagued us with a witness."

It would be an endless attempt to describe the scene of confusion and disturbance occasioned by him: the divisions of families, neighbourhoods, and towns; the contrariety of husbands and wives; the undutifulness of children and servants; the quarrels among the teachers; the disorders of the night; the intermission of labour and business; the neglect of husbandry and the gathering of the harvest.

Our presses are for ever teeming with books, and our women with bastards. . . .[19]

Even the evangelist's clerical friends endeavored in a tactful way to rebuke him for his excesses.[20]

Meanwhile the two colleges smarted under Whitefield's totally unexpected and unwarranted attack. In April, 1741, two consecutive issues of the *Boston-Gazette* were comprised largely of a long letter by William Brattle, censuring the evangelist for his hasty and unfounded judgments. In July Whitefield sought to smooth the rough waters by writing a conciliatory, almost apologetic letter "To the Students, &c. under convictions at the colleges of Cambridge and New-Haven,—in New-England and Connecticut."[21] The ill feeling between these schools and Whitefield only grew, however, and by 1744 Harvard had drawn up a formal testimony against him, and Yale followed with its own the next year.[22]

When Whitefield left New England at the end of October, 1740, he felt that there was behind him much that was unfinished, indeed, much that was untouched. Enroute to Philadelphia he met Gilbert Tennent[23] at Staten Island and journeyed with him to New Brunswick. Before the trip was ended, Whitefield had urged Tennent to tour New England in order to carry on the "glorious work" that the former had begun. "After Prayer and some Arguments pro and con, we thought it the Will of God that Mr. Gilbert Tennent should go to Boston. He (diffident of himself) was at first unwilling, urging his Inability for so great a Work, but afterwards [was] convinced."[24] Two days later, Whitefield wrote to Governor Belcher:

This week Mr. Gilbert Tennent purposes to set out for Boston, in order to blow up the divine fire lately kindled there. I recommend him to your excellency as a solid, judicious, and zealous minister of the Lord Jesus Christ: he will be ready to preach daily: I suppose his brethren will readily open their doors. . . .[25]

From a Scotch-Irish Presbyterian background and environment, Tennent was the first ministerial candidate to receive a private education in the Middle Colonies.[26] Trained by his father, a graduate of the University of Edinburgh and founder of the famed Log College out of which the College of New Jersey (later Princeton) grew, Gilbert had a good knowledge of the classics, some knowledge of Hebrew, and a creditable understanding of the theological issues of the day. Hardly the rustic and unlettered peasant he is often portrayed to be, Gilbert Tennent was a worthy example of the prevailing Presbyterian concern for an educated ministry. In coming to Boston in December, 1740, Tennent inherited both the friends and the enemies Whitefield left behind. The *Weekly Post-Boy* printed a letter reproving him for leaving his own flock pastorless, vainly assuming that he could do more good than all the outstanding ministers of the area to which he came. ". . . was not the Reason of your travelling so many hundred Miles to preach the Gospel in this Place, founded upon the Insufficiency of the Ministers here for their Office? Why travel so far in such a rigorous Season to preach the Gospel, if the Gospel was really preach'd by the Ministers here? . . ."[27] Timothy Cutler, referring to Tennent as "a monster! impudent and noisy," noted that he told all his hearers "that they were *damned! damned! damned!* This charmed them; and, in the most dreadful winter I ever saw, people wallowed in snow, night and day, for the benefit of his beastly brayings; and many ended their days under these fatigues. . . ."[28]

The *Post-Boy* letter, obviously designed to create and foment opposition, had the effect of making sharper the distinction between those who favored and those who opposed the methods of Whitefield. As moderate and conciliatory statements from any sources became less frequent, description and discussion were metamorphosed into polemic and apologetic. Clearly in the apologetic class is Prince's characterization of Tennent.

He did not indeed at first come up to my expectation; but afterwards exceeded it. In private converse with him, I found him to be a man of considerable parts and learning; free, gentle, condescending: and from his own various experience, reading the most noted writers on experimental divinity, as well as the Scriptures, and conversing with many who had been awakened by his ministry in New Jersey, where he then lived; he seemed to have as deep an acquaintance with the experimental part of religion as any I have conversed with; and his preaching was as searching and rousing as ever I heard.

He seemed to have no regard to please the eyes of his hearers with agreeable gesture, nor their ears with delivery, nor their fancy with language; but to aim directly at their consciences, to lay open their ruinous delusions, shew them their numerous, secret, hypocritical shifts in religion, and drive them out of every deceitful refuge wherein they made themselves easy, with the form of godliness without power.[29]

Charles Chauncy, on the other hand, in a polemic and contrary account describes Tennent as

a Man of no great Parts or Learning; his preaching was in the extemporaneous Way, with much Noise and little Connection. If he had taken suitable Care to prepare his Sermons, and followed Nature in the Delivery of them, he might have acquitted himself as a middling Preacher; but as he preached, he was an awkward Imitator of Mr. Whitefield, and too often turned off his Hearers with mere Stuff, which he uttered with a Spirit more bitter and uncharitable than you easily imagine. . . .[30]

Tennent was himself relieved upon his departure. Unlike Whitefield he did not thrive on the arduous physical hardships attending an evangelistic tour. In 1743 he recalled his visit in these words:

I never undertook any Thing with a deeper Sense of my own Weakness, and a Sincerer Intention, to God's Glory and his Kingdoms Good; then [sic] my journey to New-England: And never underwent such hardships by Reason of the intense Cold, frequent Travel, and continual Labours as there. So that I am like to feel [sic] the Effects thereof to my Death, having thereby contracted a hardness of hearing, with other bodily Disorders. But that which comforts me under those Infirmitys is this, that the Eternal God was visibly with me in that Journey, in sealing my Labours with surprizing and manifold Successes. . . .[31]

After a tour of less than three months,[32] Tennent on March 2, 1741, left New England to its severe winter, returning home to face difficulties in his own communion.

Following his departure from the Boston area, Prince recalls there was "such a time as we never knew."

Both people and ministers seemed under a divine influence to quicken each other. The people seemed to have a renewed taste for those old pious and experimental writers, Mr. Hooker, Shepard, Gurnal, William Guthrie, Joseph Alein, Isaac Ambrose, Dr. Owen, and others; as well as later—such as Mr. Mead, Flavel, Shaw, Willard, Stoddard, Dr. Increase and Cotton Mather, Mr. Mather of Windsor, Mr. Boston &c. The evangelical writings of these deceased authors, as well as of others alive, both in England, Scotland and New England, were now read with singular pleasure; some of them reprinted and in great numbers quickly bought and studied. And the more experimental our preaching was, like theirs, the more it was relished.[33]

The Tuesday evening lectures were so crowded that in the middle of April Friday evening lectures began to be held at South Church. Nearly thirty private religious societies were formed, meeting one evening during each week; "so the people were constantly employing the ministers to pray and preach at those societies, as also at many private houses." In the first half of the year 1741, some sixty persons became members of Prince's church (South), and in the entire year over one hundred were admitted to New North. William Cooper (Brattle Street Church) remarked that in one week's time more people had come to him for advice about their salvation than in the preceding twenty-four years of ministry taken as a whole. John Webb (New North) testified that in the space of three months following Tennent's departure, he was visited by a thousand persons seeking spiritual counsel.

In a letter to Whitefield, dated April 25, Tennent tells of some of the results of his preaching outside Boston.[34] At Charlestown, "multitudes were awakened, and several had received great consolation, especially among the young people, children and Negroes." At Harvard there was a general "shaking among the dry bones," and the same was true in most of the towns that Whitefield had visited earlier. "The concern at New-port, was very considerable. Divers Quakers and children came to me, in distress about their souls, with others. At New-haven, the concern was general both in the college and town:—about thirty students came on foot ten miles to hear the word of God." Tennent reckoned that "by a moderate computation diverse thousands have been awakened." And throughout New England, other itinerant ministers had begun to follow the example of Whitefield and Tennent, while many resident pastors became zealous evangelists in and around their own respective parishes.

As Tennent's influence in New England continued to mount, his enemies sought ways in which to discredit him. For some months following his departure, there had circulated in New England rumors about and perhaps a few copies of Tennent's infamous sermon "On the Danger of an Unconverted Ministry." When in 1742 that sermon was reprinted in Boston, its title and Tennent's name became synonymous. On the whole, the harangue is not as poisonous and scathing as the number and heat of the references to it would indicate; yet its disruptive tendencies and unsoftened language furnished much ammunition for Tennent's enemies. Considering the proposition, "That the Case of such is much to be pitied, who have no other but Pharisee-Shepherds, or unconverted Teachers," Tennent declared that "natural men" have no call to ministerial work, that they delude the wicked into thinking they are saved, having "not the Courage, or Honesty, to thrust the Nail of Terror into Sleeping Souls," that they are only rarely instrumental in the conviction of sinners, and that unconverted ministers are very dangerous with respect both to doctrine and to morality. Because it was alarmingly dangerous the following counsel of Tennent's was vigorously, almost frantically, denounced: ". . . one who lives under a pious Minister of lesser Gifts, after having honestly endeavor'd to get Benefit by his Ministry, and yet get too little or none, but doth find real Benefit and more Benefit elsewhere; I say, he may lawfully go, and that frequently, where he gets most Good to his precious Soul. . . ." With many arguments from Scripture and from reason, Tennent labored to justify a person's going "a few Miles farther than ordinary, to enjoy those, which they profit most by. . . ."[35] All the church schisms, divisions, and separations, as well as the collapse of the traditional parish system, could now be laid at Tennent's door.

One of Tennent's shrewdest critics, John Hancock,[36] declared that it was the opinion of many that this single sermon had "sown the Seeds of all that Discord, Intrusion, Confusion, Separation, Hatred, Variance, Emulations, Wrath, Strife, Seditions, Heresies, &c. that have been springing up in so many of the Towns and Churches thro' the Province. . . ."[37] Though no scapegoat could bear all this sin, Tennent's sermon did injure the reputation and influence of its author, tending to place him among the radicals of Protestantism's and the revival's extreme left wing. When Tennent became aware of this danger, he took two corrective steps. He stigmatized the errors of the Moravian group whom in Pennsylvania he had come to know and to distrust, publishing a polemic against many features of their behavior which were not unlike those of which he had been accused.[38] His second move was an attempt to dissociate himself from another grand itinerant, James Davenport, archfanatic of the Great Awakening.[39]

In the *Boston Weekly News-Letter* of October 28, 1742, there appeared a letter charging Tennent, on the basis of the Nottingham sermon, with being even more unscrupulous than Davenport. Never, says the anonymous writer, has Davenport

in any Discourse of his, more warmly and strenuously inculcated the necessity of Ministers being Converted in order to their being useful; has never in stronger Terms, bewail'd the State of the Churches in the Land, on Account of the Want of unconverted Ministers; nor talk'd in a Strain that has a greater Tendency to make People discard Ministers sound in Principle and regular in Life, than Mr. T——t does in his above-mentioned Sermon.

Against such a charge Tennent was most anxious to defend himself. Why was the comparison with Davenport a brand of infamy?

Called to a church at Southold, Long Island, in 1738, Davenport had not long been settled there when the revival excitement reached him. In 1740 he attended a Synod meeting at Philadelphia, where he made the acquaintance of George Whitefield; in the summer of the same year he heard the thunderous preaching of Gilbert Tennent and Samuel Blair.[40] The ensuing summer Davenport set out for Connecticut,[41] adopting the pattern established by Whitefield and Tennent of preaching wherever an audience could be gathered. At Stonington, Westerly (Rhode Island), Branford, and New Haven he proclaimed a message of repentance with much fervor and enthusiasm, to the joy of many but to the dismay of more. In the latter part of July, 1741, a resident of Stonington wrote a letter expressing strong disapproval of Davenport's behavior—his invective, his preaching without preparation, his singing as he goes to the place of worship, and other infractions of decorum.[42] Later a New London layman recorded in his diary:

> I went to Town to Meeting to hear Mr. Davenport, but it was Scarcely worth the hearing. the praying was without form or Comelyness. it was difficult to distinguish between his praying & preaching for it was all Meer Confused medley. he had no Text nor Bible visable, no Doctrine, uses, nor Improvement nor anything Else that was Regular forenoon nor afternoon. . . . I cant Relate the Inconsistance of it.[43]

A detailed and illuminating letter in the *Post-Boy* (September 28, 1741), attempting to analyze "the Religious Commotions in the Colony of Connecticut," contains five lines favorable to the Awakening and about one hundred twenty-five against it. Davenport in particular receives dishonorable mention. Andrew Croswell, minister of Groton, endeavored to defend Davenport by rebutting this letter from Stonington. In three towns and within eight days, Davenport was instrumental, says Croswell, in bringing about the conversion of approximately one hundred persons. Croswell confidently asserts that there are other ministers who will speak up for Davenport's character; viz., Tennent, Whitefield, Owen (also of Groton), and Lord (of Norwich). This confidence was to be rudely shaken.

Davenport was, however, his own worst enemy. His unprovoked condemnation of Joseph Noyes, the minister of the First Church, New Haven, brought down upon Davenport the unbounded wrath of Yale's rector, Thomas Clap. Davenport moreover often treated his potential allies with the same disdain that he meted out to his professed opponents. Pretending to be able to distinguish infallibly and immediately the elect from the damned, he loudly and publicly greeted the former as brethren, the latter as neighbors. With a special vengeance he denounced his fellow ministers, calling them at random and without proof pharisees, unconverted men, blind guides, and wolves in sheep's clothing. He often revealed his view of a local minister by beseeching God, in a public prayer, to grant saving grace to this particular minister. With a martyr complex and a completely unpredictable fanaticism, Davenport soon repelled enemies and friends alike. In May, 1742, two laymen of Ripton parish in Stratford, Connecticut, filed with the General Assembly a complaint against James Davenport and Benjamin Pomeroy.[44] The preachers were charged with disturbing the peace and order of the town under the pretext of religious assemblies. Brought to trial, Davenport demonstrated a vehemence and belligerence that could not have better suited the purposes of the prosecutor. After a three-day trial the following judgment was passed on June 3, 1742:

> . . . This Assembly is of Opinion, That the Things alleg'd, and the Behaviour, Conduct and Doctrine advanced & taught by the said Davenport, do and have a natural tendency to disturb & destroy the Peace & Order of this Government: Yet it further appears to this Assembly, that the said Davenport is under the Influence of enthusiastical Impressions and Impulses, and therby disturbed in the rational Faculties of his Mind, and therefore to be pitied and compassionated and not to be treated as otherwise he might be. . . .[45]

The Assembly further decreed that "the said Davenport be forthwith transported out of this Colony to Long-Island, the Place from whence he came, and wherein he is setled." The following Thursday a boat sailed down the Connecticut River from Hartford, with Davenport under guard on his way to Southold. Pomeroy, who doubtless benefited by the comparison with Davenport, was at this time freed without any penalty being exacted.

Neither the judgment nor the involuntary exile sufficed to dampen the spirit of Davenport. In a few days, he set out for Massachusetts, arriving in Charlestown Friday, June 25, and in Boston the following Monday. To all he was most unwelcome. Those who favored the Awakening had more reason to fear him than did those who opposed it, for Davenport's behavior threatened to discredit the whole movement. The account of a contemporary witness explains in large measure the reaction against him.

> He has preached every Day since [his arrival] upon the Common, to pretty large Assemblies, but the greatest Part very far from admiring him, or being willing to give him any Countenance.—When he first ascends the Rostrum, he appears with a remarkable settled composed Countenance, but soon gets into the most extravagant Gesture and Behaviour both in Prayer and Preaching.—His Expressions in Prayer are often indecently familiar; he frequently appeals to God, that such and such Impressions are immediately from his holy Spirit, but especially his Sermons are full of his Impressions and Impulses, from God. He does not seem to be a Man of any Parts, Sprightliness or Wit. His Sermons are dull and heavy, abounding with little low Similitudes. He has no knack at raising the Passions, but by a violent straining of his Lungs, and the most extravagant wreathings of his Body, which at the same Time that it creates Laughter and Indignation in the most, occasions great meltings, screamings, crying, swooning, and Fits in some others. . . . Were you to see him in his most violent agitations, you would be apt to think, that he was a Madman just broke from his Chains: But especially had you seen him returning from the Common after his first preaching, with a large Mob at his Heels, singing all the Way thro' the Streets, he with his Hands extended, his Head thrown back, and his Eyes staring up to Heaven, attended with so much Disorder, that they look'd more like a Company of Bacchanalians after a mad Frolick, than sober Christians who had been worshipping God. . . .[46]

Clearly the Awakening had been brought to a sad pass. Thomas Prince, after describing the many successes of the revival, introduced the subject of Davenport's stay in Massachusetts in these words: "And then through the providence of the sovereign God, the wisdom of whose ways are past finding out, we unexpectedly came to an unhappy period, which it exceedingly grieves me now to write of. . . ."[47]

It so happened that when Davenport came to Boston, the association of Boston and Charlestown ministers was in session. Hoping to nip Davenport's fanaticism before it could bloom in the Massachusetts Bay area, the convening ministers testified that though Davenport appeared to be a truly pious man he was "deeply tinctur'd with a Spirit of Enthusiasm. . . . We judge also that the Reverend Mr. Davenport has not acted prudently, but to the disservice of Religion. . . . We judge it therefore to be our present Duty not to invite Mr. Davenport into our Places of publick Worship. . . ." This declaration, issued July 1, 1742, was signed by ministers who wrote, preached, and worked on behalf of the Great Awakening, even taking care at this time to testify "to the great and glorious work of God, which of his free grace he has begun and is carrying on in many parts of this and the neighboring provinces. . . ."[48]

This announcement James Davenport met in characteristic fashion: he pronounced the signers of the testimony unconverted and unworthy to be ministers, leading their people blindfolded into hell. Again to his defense came Andrew Croswell who struggled to answer each charge brought against Davenport.[49] Few were convinced. One of those ministers to whom Croswell had looked for support in defending Davenport, Gilbert Tennent, now lashed out with strong words against the Long Island itinerant. In a letter to Jonathan Dickinson,[50] Tennent wrote:

. . . As to his making his Judgment about the internal State of Persons, or their Experience a Term of Church-Fellowship, I believe it is unscriptural and of awful Tendency to rend and tear the Church. . . . The late Method of setting up separate Meetings is enthusiastical, proud, and schismatical. All that fear God, ought to oppose it as a most dangerous Engine to bring the Churches into the most damnable Errors and Confusions. . . . The Practice of openly exposing Ministers who are supposed to be unconverted in publick Discourse, by particular Application of such Times and Places, serves only to provoke them . . . and to declare our own Arrogance. It is an unprecedented divisial and pernicious Practice: It is Lording it over our Brethren, a Degree superiour to what any Prelate has pretended since the coming of Christ . . . the Pope only excepted; tho' I really don't remember to have read that the Pope went on at this Rate.

The sending out of unlearned Men to teach others upon the supposition of their Piety, in ordinary Cases, seems to bring the Ministry into Contempt; to cherish Enthusiasm, and bring all into Confusion: Whatever fair Face it may have, it is a most perverse Practice.

The Practice of singing in the Streets, is a piece of weakness, and enthusiastical Ostentation. . . .

I must also declare my Abhorence of all Pretence to immediate Inspiration, or following immediate Impulses, as an enthusiastical perillous Ignis fatuus.[51]

In August, the Grand Jury of Suffolk County exhibited to the "court of Assize and General Coal-Delivery" a bill of presentment charging Davenport with "many slanderous & reviling Speeches against the worthy and faithful Ministers of the Gospel in the Province."[52] After a warrant was issued, Davenport was apprehended and committed to jail. Several of the Boston ministers appealed to the court "that no Severities . . . be used on our Accounts" with the result that Davenport was declared *non compos mentis* and therefore not guilty. By October Davenport was back in Long Island to stand trial there for the neglect of his own parish.

After a final fulsome fiasco in New London during March of 1743, New England was free of Davenport's abnormalities.[53] A deliverance from much of his remaining pernicious influence was accomplished in a most unexpected way: Davenport retracted his errors. Through the brotherly but firm counsel of Solomon Williams and Eleazar Wheelock,[54] Davenport was convinced of that which he had already begun to suspect—that he was laboring with a misguided zeal and under a false spirit.[55] Like the fathers of the early church in its Donatian controversy, Williams convinced Davenport that a minister's being unconverted did not invalidate his ministry; furthermore, "It is beyond Contradiction that Practice [of pronouncing many ministers unconverted] has done much to hinder the Word of God." Wheelock's criticism was aimed primarily at Davenport's practice of sending out lay exhorters who usurped the authority and prerogatives of the standing ministry. In the summer of 1744, therefore, Davenport—penitent and of a more sober mind—published his *Confessions and Retractions*.[56] After specific admission to several of the charges most often brought against him, Davenport concluded with the hope that this full and voluntary adjuration would destroy those prejudices against Christianity in general and the "late glorious work of God in particular" that had been aroused chiefly by means of the very errors he now repudiated. By that time, 1744, the admissions could have no effect on the Awakening itself. It was a *late* glorious work of God; the divine showers had already been withdrawn.

But in 1741-1742, nearly everyone got wet.

CHAPTER 4

THE FLOOD, 1741-1742

THE REVIVAL WAS MUCH MORE THAN THE FIERY ministrations of Whitefield, Tennent, and Davenport. The Awakening was "Great" because it was general: none escaped its influence or avoided its controversy. In both coastal and frontier areas, within cities and rural communities, in churches and in open fields, people gathered to hear an earnest evangelistic gospel, be it preached by their own minister, a neighboring pastor, a trespassing itinerant, or an exhorter. Men whose words had never before been heeded now proclaimed, wrote, and published their zealous defense or their acrimonious contempt of the "present extraordinary work of God." New England's printing presses vastly increased their output, giving to religious subjects significant precedence. Executive, legislative, and judicial officials were obliged to note and to deal with this upsurge of religious interest. Over the most keenly intellectual or the most grossly credulous, the revival had its sway.

Contemporaries of the turbulent religious upheaval of 1740-1742 described it as a "great and general awakening." Later historians, less ready to admit either its greatness or its generality, have in concert described the revival as limited to this area or that, to this social class exclusive of that, and as arising from this or that socio-economic force. We have come a long way from what may be called "the economic interpretation of religion," when all felt obliged to excuse the obtrusion of churches and pious sentiments by explaining carefully that this sheep's clothing of religion concealed an economic wolf within. Yet the phenomenon known as the Great Awakening is of such proportions as once again to provoke the inclination to interpret it as something other than a religious movement.

It would be folly to suggest that the Awakening was completely divorced from the culture of eighteenth-century New England, from the shortage of specie, from the growth of trade, from the greater leisure and less crudity, from the vigilant struggles for popular representation and the increasing degree of political independence. This is, however, vastly different from cataloguing the revival as a "deep-rooted social movement," as a lower-class uprising, or as "a revolt of the backcountry producers." John Chester Miller viewed the movement as riding on the wave of hostility between rich and poor created by the Land Bank uproar, producing a full and permanent cleavage between the social classes. The uninhibited and fervent James Davenport, according to Miller, divided the "social classes much as during the Land Bank fervor. The Opposers were joined by more and more of the wealthy and educated as Davenport carried the Great Awakening down to a lower stratum and preached the gospel of discontent and levellism. . . . This conviction among the common people that they had been singled out by God for salvation and that the Opposers—the upper classes— were for the most part damned gave class feeling a new twist in Massachusetts."[1] Though this "new twist" probably serves as a useful counterweight to that other tenacious myth: that the elect and the elite were synonymous terms in colonial New England, it does not do justice to the historical evidence concerning the revival itself. Indeed, John Miller begins his discussion with a question that begs the question: "What caused the Great Awakening to split up the Congregational church and cut a swath between rich and poor, stimulating the hostility that already divided them?" This identification of the revival's opponents with the upper classes is followed by Perry Miller who declares the lists of subscribers to Chauncy's *Seasonable Thoughts* to be "a roster of antirevivalists and also a social register."[2] Eugene E. White writes of the revival as one of the "deep-rooted social movements" (p. 49), as a "social phenomenon" (p. 52), and as "confined to the cities and the settled areas of the East" (p. 51).[3] More recently, Richard D. Mosier views it as an affair not of the cities, but of the rural areas, as "a revolt of the backcountry producers from the stringent controls of the mercantile aristocracy which ruled from afar."[4] For the latter, the Awakening was also anticlerical and anarchial, "the first step in a movement which culminates in the American Revolution."[5] These statements of faith little resemble the historical situation.

There is, to the contrary, abundant evidence that this religious turmoil in New England was in fact "great and general," that it knew no boundaries, social or geographical, that it was both urban and rural, and that it reached both lower and upper classes. The geographical nonparticularity of the Great Awakening is readily established, though it is necessary to distinguish it, as we have done, from the earlier series of revivals emanating from Northampton. Beginning in 1734, and continuing for two or three years, these revivals were indeed largely a frontier phenomenon, concentrated along the banks of the Connecticut River from Northfield to Saybrook Point. To them, but alone to them, the term "frontier revivalism" can with propriety be applied, and not to the Great Awakening itself which began only after the earlier revivals were "very much at a Stop" and which in its initial phase was rather in the coastal than in the inland area.[6] It has already been shown that none of the grand itinerants limited himself to or was effective only in a single area. In the present chapter this geographical nonparticularity of the revival shall be further noted along with the diversified social strata of both the hearers and the heralds of the evangelistic Word.

Often referred to as the Whitefieldian revival, the Great Awakening in New England was as well the work of persons of little fame. For two or three years the light of obscure persons shone with startling brightness; suddenly God had thrust upon them grave responsibilities and great opportunities. Who has heard of Samuel Buell?[7] Yet young Buell, one year out of college and unordained, wrote to Eleazar Wheelock in 1742:

> I have Letters and invitations to Preach from all Parts . . . the world rages, hell trembles, heaven Rejoyces. . . . But my hands are full, Great numbers are Daily hanging about me for Some Spiritual morsle.
> . . . while thousands admire and flock with Delight to hear me, and thousands oppose me, may I Bee kept humble.[8]

As early as September of the previous year when he was licensed to preach by the New Haven association, Samuel Buell had become an instrument of the revival. In October he traveled from Fairfield, Connecticut, to Northampton, Massachusetts, preaching in nearly every parish along the way. So successful was his preaching in Northampton, where he spent a "fortnight or three weeks," that Edwards was moved to tears because his own ministry seemed by comparison so unprofitable.[9] Edwards advised Prince in December that "there were very extraordinary effects of Mr. Buell's labours; the people were exceedingly moved, crying out in great numbers in the meeting house, and great part of the congregation commonly staying in the house of God for hours after the public service."[10] An anonymous pamphleteer thought Buell unworthy of such honor: "He is not able to speak two sentences without transgressing the common Rules of Grammar. His Sermons were the most stupid Stuff that ever came from a Man's

Mouth."[11] But Buell nonetheless kept busy dispensing the "Spiritual morsle," the several contemporary references to him, favorable or otherwise, indicating the intensity and extent of his activities in the revival.

Eleazar Wheelock, better known than Buell but not because of his participation in the Awakening, was Connecticut's most energetic supporter of the movement.[12] He traveled extensively, argued boldly, and corresponded frequently in its behalf. Because he was the regularly ordained minister of the North Society of Lebanon and not a "foreigner or stranger" he was less often denounced than Whitefield, Tennent, and Davenport as an itinerant or "pretended apostle." The moderate criticism he received is, however, misleading with reference to the prodigious evangelistic labors he wrought. A popular and persuasive preacher, he itinerated widely during the Awakening, keeping a journal that reads much like Whitefield's.[13] Edwards, after urging Wheelock to go to Scantic or East Windsor where "they are wholly dead in this extraordinary day of God's gracious visitation," wrote:

Another thing that I desire of you, is, that you would come up hither and help us, both you and Mr. Pomeroy. There has been a revival of religion amongst us of late; but your labors have been much more remarkably blessed than mine; other ministers, as I have heard, have shut their pulpits against you; but here, I engage, you shall find one open. May God send you here with a like blessing, as he has sent you to other places: and may your coming be a means of humbling me for my barrenness and unprofitableness, and a means of my instruction and enlivening. I want an opportunity to concert measure with you for the advancement of the kingdom and glory of our Redeemer.[14]

Even in the first months of 1741 Wheelock had been energetically preaching in many places outside his own parish. In the fall of that year he began a tour which carried him eastward into Rhode Island and then into Massachusetts. He found the expectant interest still high, though it was now a year since Whitefield's visit. Although he was occasionally aware that "Satan is using many artful wiles to put a stop to the work of God," more often the great power of God was "much seen and many hopefully converted." In Voluntown, October 22, he

Preached twice with great enlargement, by Mr. Smith's barn to great assemblies. Many cried out; many stood trembling; the whole assembly very solemn, and much affection; four or five converted.[15]

When he left Voluntown, he set out over a newly opened road for Scituate, Rhode Island. After preaching there "to a considerable assembly," he continued east toward Providence, stopping along the way, for rest and refreshment, at "elder Fish's; found him a bigoted, ignorant Baptist; his wife soon shot her bolt and told us all what she was. She seemed to look upon baptism in their way as the only evidence to be relied upon of a safe estate."[16] In Providence Wheelock was invited by Josiah Cotton, first regular pastor of that city's only Congregational church, to preach in his pulpit.[17] After three sermons there, Wheelock was moved to remark: "O, the dreadful ignorance and wickedness of these parts; O what a burthen dear Mr. Cotton has daily to bear." But Wheelock was willing to help him bear it; returning from a suburban area the next afternoon, he

Preached to a full assembly: many scoffers present and one man hired for twenty shillings to come into the meeting-house and fall down, which he did and made a great disturbance; ordered all, who had a real concern for the salvation of their souls, to follow me to Mr. Cotton's in order to have a conference with them. A considerable number came, who seemed considerably moved.[18]

With great catholicity Wheelock preached in a Baptist meetinghouse on October 28 to the "poor, bigoted, ignorant prejudiced people," but was forced to conclude that "the principles of the separate Baptists are the most uncharitable, unscriptural, and unreasonable, that I have yet met with."

Wheelock traveled from Providence to Braintree and Boston, then to Dedham, Medfield, Bellingham, Uxbridge, and Windham. By December he was back in Lebanon, but even while reporting the blessings of heaven he was making plans for New England to receive more such blessing. He told Daniel Rogers,[19] Harvard tutor turned itinerant, that in Weathersfield "the whole town seams to be shaken."

Last Monday Night the Lord bowed the heavens and Came Down upon a Large assembly in one of the Parishes of the town the Whole assembly Seam'd alive with Distress the Groans and outcrys of the wounded here such that my Voice Co'd not be heard.[20]

He then urged Rogers to "Come into these parts I believe you might do much Service for the Lord here." Were it not that Wheelock had been constantly "full & Crowded with business" he would have returned to "Providence & the Narragansetts" before now. Perhaps he and Rogers could meet each other there. A letter to Stephen Williams in February disclosed Wheelock still acting as chief intelligencer of revival news. Breathless reports of the good work in Newbury, on Cape Ann, and elsewhere are thus concluded: "I have a thousand things to say but the bearer is in hast. We are all in a Moving State of Divine Goodness."[21]

Other men of little lasting renown saw to it that the world raged, hell trembled, and heaven rejoiced. Benjamin Pomeroy (1704-1784)[22] of Hebron, John Owen (1699-1753)[23] of Groton, Timothy Allen (1716-1806)[24] of New London, Nathanael Rogers (1701-1775)[25] of Ipswich, and William Shurtleff (1689-1747)[26] of Portsmouth are among those whose names in 1742 were known to all the clergy and many of the laity in New England, but were soon to be forgotten by both. Pomeroy was arrested by the civil officials of Connecticut for his vigorous revival activities,[27] while Owen was the instrument of an "extraordinary time" in his home parish.[28] Allen told of the "Sweet Season" in his New London school wherein "the Power, Grace & Love of God, are wonderfully Displayed. . . ."[29] Nathanael Rogers joined with his brother Daniel in a zealous and often tactless support of the revival that alienated and infuriated Theophilus Pickering, minister of the Second Society of Ipswich.[30] In Portsmouth the Awakening began on November 27, 1741, "the most remarkable Day that was ever known among us." This revival, for which Shurtleff had been fasting and praying, was so successful that Shurtleff became a thorough friend to the Awakening and to Whitefield whose "Travelling this Way" he regarded "as a favourable Providence, and that for which we owe abundant Thanksgiving to the God of all Grace."[31] Such men were the occasion of the Awakening's percolating down into every parish, becoming the concern of all the clergy and a reality to all the laity. These and others like them were the preachers whose contribution to history is found in the magnitude, the intensity, and the generality of New England's religious upheaval.

Revivalists and intellectuals tend in the present day to be of different camps. It was only long after the Awakening, however, that revivalism became the ally of an uneducated clergy. The great revival in New England was not anti-intellectual nor were its chief defenders obscurantist. Harvard and Yale had been needlessly alienated from the revival by the blundering, if pious, slander of Whitefield. Even with this handicap, there was no rising gradient of erudition as one moved from revivalist into antirevivalist circles. Jonathan Edwards of Northampton and Benjamin Colman of Boston were intellectuals who had no superior in New England; and both were firm, capable friends of the Awakening.

Like many ministers of the revival, Edwards was often called upon to preach in other parishes than his own. Speaking in strange churches and towns—by invitation only—he exercised a direct influence outside Northampton in person as well as by pen. The most famous sermon of New England colonial history was preached by Edwards at the height of the religious upheaval. To Enfield Jonathan Edwards came on July 8, 1741, to speak at an announced evening lecture. His listeners, characterized as "very secure, loose and vain," knew of Edwards and were confident of hearing from him something more than the impromptu pretentious rantings of immature exhorters.[32] Taking his text from Deuteronomy 32:35, "Their foot shall slide in due time," Edwards first observed that "there is nothing that keeps wicked men at any one moment out of hell, but the mere pleasure of God."[33] Preaching with a vigor and clarity that commanded not only attention but also comprehension, Edwards aroused the emotions of his hearers to such an extent that he had to pause to request that they restrain their groans and weeping so that he could continue. He then drew a picture of

. . . the dreadful pit of the glowing flames of the wrath of God; there is hell's wide gaping mouth open; and you have nothing to stand upon, nor any thing to take hold of. There is nothing between you and hell but the air; it is only the power and mere pleasure of God that holds you up.

The congregation, not surprisingly, was "deeply impressed and bowed down with an awful conviction of their sin and danger." From nothing which Edwards said would the majority of his fellow divines have dissented. There was nothing in the manner in which it was said that could be censured or described as enthusiastic or irregular. Remote and shadowy theological notions he had translated into immediate and concrete empirical scenes. Though some might question his motive, none could doubt his meaning. When Edwards sent the sermon to the printer later in the year, he entitled it "Sinners in the Hands of an Angry God."

At New Haven in 1741 Edwards delivered a significant discourse on *The Distinguishing Marks of the Spirit of God, Applied to that uncommon Operation that has lately appeared on the Minds of many of the People in New-England: With a Particular Consideration of the extraordinary Circumstances with which this Work is attended.*[34] This work placed him at the head of the apologists for the revival and served as a model for other proponents of the movement. Early in 1743 Edwards was again traveling in Connecticut preaching at Lebanon while Eleazar Wheelock was at Northampton. He wrote his wife that "many ministers have been urging me to go to New-London, but I refused unless a number of them would go with me: and last night Mr. Meacham, Mr. Williams & Mr. Pumroy agreed to go down with me the next week, to endeavour to reclaim the People there from their Errours."[35]

A modern historian remarks that "for fifty years after the tremendous enthusiasms of the Great Awakening religion was tired in New England. . . ."[36] From this point of view, one would expect to find Northampton winded by 1740. Even before Whitefield's coming, however, Edwards reported that "there was a visible Alteration: There was more Seriousness, and religious Conversation, especially among young People. . . ." Following the visit of the English evangelist, the tempo of religious agitation increased.

The Revival at first appear'd chiefly among Professors, and those that had entertained the Hope that they were in a State of Grace, to whom Mr. Whitefield chiefly address'd himself; but in a very short Time there appeared an Awakening and deep Concern among some young Persons that looked upon themselves as in a Christless State; and there were some hopeful Appearances of Conversion, and some Professors were greatly revived. In about a Month or six Weeks there was a great Alteration in the Town, both as to the Revivals of Professors, and Awakenings of others. By the middle of December a very considerable Work of God appeared among those that were very young; and the Revival of Religion continued to increase; so that in the Spring, an Engagedness of Spirit about Things of Religion was become very general amongst young People and Children, and religious Subjects almost wholly took up their Conversation when they were together.[37]

In the spring and summer of 1741 such manifestations as jerking, fainting, and crying out appeared in the Northampton meetinghouse. Indeed, the revival was distinguished from the one five or six years earlier, said Edwards, by the fact that now

Conversions were frequently wrought more sensibly and visibly; the Impressions stronger, and more manifest by external Effects of them; and the Progress of the Spirit of God in Conviction, from Step to Step, more apparent; and the Transition from one State to another more sensible and plain; so that it might in many instances, be as it were seen by By-standers.[38]

Edwards, philosopher and theologian, was not ashamed of the gospel, even when it came in power and in might.

The senior pastor in Boston at this time was Benjamin Colman of Brattle Street Church.[39] Respected for his learning, Colman was known in England and Scotland both because of his sojourn abroad and because of his many, able writings. A great friend to institutions of higher learning, he had bestowed upon him in 1731, by Governor Belcher, the degree of Doctor of Divinity from the University of Glasgow. Though he preached and wrote on a great many subjects, "above all Jesus Christ and the Covenant of Salvation through him was his grand and favourite Subject, and most usual Topick. . . ." With respect to his manner of preaching

although in general his Voice might be said to be soft and still, and that "his Speech and Doctrine dropt as the Dew, and distilled as the small Rain upon a tender Herb," yet when occasions for it occurred he could notably imitate a Boanerges, and play the Artillery of Heaven against the hardy Sons of Vice, and uncover the dreadful Pit.—With what Light, and Flame, and Power have we sometimes known him dispense the Word, and by the Terrors of the Lord perswade Men in the Applications of his Discourse? Yet he was ever careful to observe a just Decorum and Behaviour, and spake as became the Oracles of God.[40]

Colman is certainly to be classified as a constant friend of the Awakening, though just as certainly he is to be excluded from the ranks of Davenport, Croswell, Rogers, and Paine. His position was one not of moderation but of discrimination. With much zeal and sincere concern, he favored and furthered the revival, taking care, however, to define the movement in such a way as to make the excesses and abnormalities no proper part of it. Colman was the first New England minister to correspond with Whitefield, and was instrumental in bringing about the latter's visit to New England. He showed great interest, moreover, in the earlier Northampton revival, corresponded regularly with Edwards and others connected with it, passed on to his friends abroad news of religious awakenings in the colonies, and urged Edwards to write the *Faithful Narrative.*

Immediately after Whitefield's visit to Massachusetts, Colman preached in his own church Boston's first evening lecture, October 21, 1740, in which he entreated that the interest shown during the evangelist's visit not be allowed to expire.

Our dear People, Your Ministers have with Pleasure seen you in the Weeks past, Old and Young, Parents and Children, Masters and Servants, high and low, rich and poor together, gathering . . . to the Doors and Windows of our Places of Worship. . . . The Fame of a singular servant and holy Youth, an extraordinary Servant and Minister of Jesus Christ . . . had prepar'd you for his Visit. . . . God gave him a wonderful Manner of Entrance among us . . . and we were sometimes melted together in Tears. . . . And now our beloved Brethren and Sisters, you and your Children, we are going to prove, confirm and increase, by the Will of God, the seeming good Dispositions begun or revived in You, toward Christ and his Word, in a just and reasonable pious Care and Sollicitude for your Salvation.

* * *

. . . nor let us have Cause to say by and by, "It was vain Curiousity, Novelty, the Fame and Face of a Stranger. . . ." Walk not your own Ministers in the same Spirit, in the same Truth, in the same Wisdom and Grace of God! and share they not in the same Care, Desire and Zeal for your Souls? Have they not shown it by receiving Him gladly in the Lord, who lately came to you in his Name and Power? Why did we so receive him, encourage his Heart and strengthen his Hands in Preaching to you, after the wondrous unfainting Manner he did? Was it not for your sake, that you might be quickened, and more roused up to a Care for your selves?[41]

Colman concluded this lecture-sermon with an appeal that those now partially aroused and awakened continue their interest in the things of God until conversion is experienced.

We have seen of late many greatly affected under the preaching of the Word; now Cherish your Convictions, and beg of God, by the Power of the Holy Spirit, to fasten 'em deep in your Souls. . . . Improve the little Heat and Life you feel, and pray for a thorow saving Conversion. . . . We have admir'd to see how many of you have been of late affected! we shall admire more, wonder and be asham'd and griev'd, if we see your Affections cool and go off! if Sabbaths and Ordinances are neglected as heretofore, or formally attended. If you have "begun in the Spirit, take heed that it end not in the Flesh."[42]

In 1741 Colman was exuberant in his correspondence with Whitefield about the sweeping force of the revival. "The Work of God with us goes on greatly . . . our crowded serious Assemblies continue, and great Additions are made to our Churches. Yesterday no less than nineteen. . . ." The following year his enthusiasm had abated little as he wrote Whitefield that even Harvard had been touched.[43] He closed a lecture given in April, 1742, by giving Glory to God for the Great and good Work of his Grace, which He has so visibly begun, spread and is carrying on, in every Part almost of our Provinces.[44]

Colman, scholarly author and outstanding liberal, did not hesitate to "play the Artillery of Heaven against the hardy Sons of Vice." Among the established ministry of New England in 1741, he was second to none in influence and prestige. Because the Awakening enjoyed the benefits of this influence and prestige, it not only drifted down to the masses but was lifted up where even gentlemen could behold.

One is obliged to conclude that it is not possible to divide New England society horizontally, indicating this stratum which felt the Awakening's effect, and that stratum which was untouched. Many of Boston's converts, Colman announced, were "among the Rich and Polite of our Sons and Daughters."[45] Neither is it possible, moreover, to establish vertical partitions, separating this area which was flooded from that which remained dry. There were of course inequities, and the revival appeared in varying form and degree. Yet the frontier was not now as in 1734-35 the stronghold of a movement which left the cities untouched. Nor did the coastal areas alone enjoy the showers from heaven, while the religious life of less accessible towns withered away. Whether the population was dense or sparse, the mode of living primitive or moderately luxurious, the class high or low, the economy agricultural or mercantile, the revival was there.

In Middleborough, Massachusetts, where Peter Thacher (1688-1744) had been pastor for over thirty years, the church seemed to be too dead even to respond to the living waters of the Great Awakening. The growth of irreligion and immorality within the congregation was "a constant heavy Weight" upon Thacher's "tender heart." He refrained from leaving his congregation, he confided to Thomas Prince, only because he could not find a suitable text for a farewell sermon. After Tennent came to Middleborough in the spring of 1741, the people "were more inclined to hear," so that Thacher added a weekly public lecture. Then, with the visit of his neighboring minister, Josiah Crocker of Taunton, suddenly on November 23, 1741, all heaven broke loose. "I have written Accounts of seventy-six that Day struck, and bro't first to inquire what they should do to escape condemnation."

From this Time, there was an uncommon Teachableness among my People: Scarce one Word of Counsel seemed lost, or a Sermon in Vain. From this Time, they must have four Sermons in a Week, two Tuesdays, two Thursdays: The Word of the Lord was very precious in those Days.— In a few Days from that 23d of November, so greatly to be remembered, there appeared to be above two Hundred awaken'd. . . .[46]

Peter Thacher had no time now to search for an appropriate farewell sermon text. At the time of his death, 1744, the church at Middleborough had three hundred forty-three members. Of that number, one hundred seventy-four had joined during the Great Awakening.

In the small town of Harvard, about forty miles west of Boston, a revival appeared under the pastor, Joseph Seccomb, even before the arrival of Whitefield in New England:

And after he preached in New-England very few of this People did ever hear him. But God was pleased to make Use of the usual Means; to rouze and awaken sleepy Sinners by the small Voice; and as before observed by some of the very same Sermons that made no impression before.[47]

That "this Reformation hath not been carried on violently, nor by Strangers" Seccomb regarded as proof of its being from God. The other criterion was the "good Fruits and Effects" of it. In December, 1739, four young men "who had been of too loose a Life & Conversation in Times past" were converted, and from that time on "there was scarce a Sacrament pass'd (which is with us once in eight Weeks) without some Additions to the Church . . . tho' twelve is the greatest Number that has been receiv'd at once." This "great Shaking among the dry Bones" produced better husbands, wives, children, masters, and servants. Proud of the orderliness with which all this had been accomplished, Seccomb, moved even to admit that he was using old sermons, boasted that there had been little censoriousness, and that "none have cried out under the Word but once, and then but five or six." In Harvard, the gentle showers from heaven never became a torrential rain.

A revival occurring in a given area often reached many who lived far from that area. Persons traveled to the main crossroads to hear a Whitefield or a Wheelock and returned to spread the good news. John Porter, minister of Bridgewater, went to Braintree to attend Whitefield's preaching and reported that he had not known true grace until he heard "that Man of God."[48] Wheelock recorded in his journal that one woman came from Kingston, Rhode Island, to hear him preach at Voluntown, Connecticut (a bumpy ride of more than twenty miles); she "came out clear, and went away rejoicing in God, longing to have her husband and others taste and see with her."[49] But the classic example of "itinerant listeners" is Nathan Cole, farmer in Kensington, Connecticut, whose eager, almost frantic efforts to hear Whitefield vividly reveal the trembling excitement of the day. Having heard of Whitefield's preaching "like one of the old aposels" in the Middle Colonies, Cole found himself "more & more hoping soon to see him."

but next i herd he was on long iland & next at boston & next at northampton & then one morning all on a Suding about 8 or 9 oClock there came a messenger & said mr. whitfeld preached at hartford & weathersfield yesterday & is to preach at middeltown this morning at 10 o clock   i was in my field at work   i dropt my tool that i had in my hand & run home & run throu my house & bad my wife get ready quick to goo and hear mr. whitfeld preach at middeltown & run to my pasture for my hors with all my might fearing i should be too late to hear him   i brought my hors home & soon mounted & took my wife up & went forward as fast as i thought the hors could bear, & when my hors began to be out of breath i would get down & put my wife on the Saddel & bid her ride as fast as she could & not Stop or Slak for me except i bad her & so i would run untill i was almost out of breth & then mount my hors again & so i did several times to favour my hors we improved every moment to get along as if we was fleeing for our lives all this while fearing we should be too late to hear the Sarmon for we had twelve miles to ride dubble in littel more then an hour. . . . when i came nearer it was like a stedy streem of horses & their riders scarcely a horse more then his length behind another all of a lather and fome with swetther breath rooling out of their noistrels in the cloud of dust every jump every hors seemed to go with all his might to carry his rider to hear the news from heaven for the saving of their Souls it made me trembel to see the Sight how the world was in a strugle i found a vacance between two horses to Slip in my hors & my wife said law our cloaths will be all spoiled see how they look for they was so covered with dust that that looked allmost all of a coler coats & hats & shirts & horses We went down in the Streem i herd no man speak a word all the way three mile but evry one presing forward in great hast & when we gat down to the old meating house thare was a great multitude it was said to be 3 or 4000 of people asembled together   we gat of from our horses & shook off the dust and the ministers was then coming to the meating house i turned and looked toward the great river & saw the fery boats running swift forward & backward bringing over loads of people the ores roed nimble & quick every thing men horses & boats all seamed to be struglin for life   the land & the banks over the river lookt black with people & horses all along the 12 miles i see no man at work in his field but all seamed to be gone. . . .[50]

Cole arrived in time; he heard; and later he, like Whitefield, reacted against the cold formality and authority of the established churches.[51]

So the multitudes came, from all parts of New England, from all stations of society, to receive the sweet dews of heaven. Benjamin Colman
had thrilled to see "in the Weeks past, Old and Young, Parents and
Children, Masters and Servants, high and low, rich and poor together,
gathering . . . to the Doors and Windows of our Places of Worship
. . ."[52] It was a general awakening.

Boston, with its population of about five thousand families,[53] was
the cultural, economic and political center of New England in the
eighteenth century. It affords full evidence of the presence of the
Awakening in areas removed from the dangers and deprivations of
frontier life, and removed as well from the indebtedness or illiteracy
of rural life. There was without question opposition in the city, but it
appeared only after the Awakening had been in progress for some time.
Even as the revival declined, the majority of Boston's ministers continued to speak in its favor. Though Buell wrote in April of 1742 that
"opposition increasis So fast here in Boston," he reported at the same
time, "I have Preach'd 5 time in Boston Publickly, to Vast Assemblies
—my Labours have been attended with Great Success throu the Blessing
of God."[54]

In Boston the established ministers who resisted the Great Awakening were outnumbered three to one. The unevenness was aggravated by
the fact that of these three divines hostile to the revival, only one,
Charles Chauncy, was active in his opposition.[55] The other two, both
of the Mather family, published nothing concerning the religious excitement, though they privately expressed their disdain of the whole affair.[56]
Samuel Mather, son of Cotton Mather, was ordained in 1732 as Joshua
Gee's associate in Second Church.[57] In 1741 he was dismissed from
that relationship because, among other reasons, of his attitude toward
the Awakening and his reluctance to participate in the furtherance of
it. Before a church council which had been called to reconcile the differences between Mather and Gee, and between Mather and many of the
congregation, the former vowed to "endeavour to be more frequent and
distinct in preaching on the nature, and pressing the necessity, of regeneration by the Spirit of grace," and to "endeavour to beware of any
thing in my sermons or conversation which may tend to discourage the
work of conviction and conversion among us. I shall be cautious and
watchful in this respect; and, in public and private, encourage the said
good work of God."[58] If Mather's pledges were satisfactory, his allegiance to them was not, and on December 21, 1741, he was dismissed
from the church.[59] Mather Byles, grandson of Increase Mather and first

pastor of the Hollis Street Church, succeeded in avoiding any public controversy related to the revival. Though publishing a sermon in 1741 on "Repentance and Faith The Great Doctrine of the Gospel of Universal Concernment," Byles' position—religious and poltical—was carefully conservative, and his sympathies were thoroughly Old Light.[60] For the most part whatever strong feelings against the Awakening either Samuel Mather or Mather Byles had, they were willing to let those feelings be expressed by Charles Chauncy.

The proponents of the revival in Boston were more numerous and more diffuse: Benjamin Colman was ably reinforced. Brattle Street Church was ministered to by William Cooper as well as by Colman. Cooper in 1715 was ordained as the latter's associate, and continued in that capacity until his death in 1743.[61] Before Whitefield's arrival in New England, Cooper had preached and published four sermons on "The Doctrine of Predestination unto Life, Explained and Vindicated." Illuminating because they reveal how a rigid Calvinism can still be evangelistic, they also indicate Cooper's concern with the matter of salvation.[62] Early the next year, Cooper's evangelistic solicitude became even more pronounced as Whitefield and Tennent fanned sparks of interest into flames of enthusiasm. In Old South Church, Cooper spoke on March 22 on the subject "One shall be taken, and another left." He permitted no idle conjecture concerning the relevance of his sermon to the revival then in progress.

I make no doubt but all of you think what has led me to these Words at this Time; the remarkable Work of Grace begun, and I hope going on amongst us; the eminent Success which God has been pleas'd to give to his preached Gospel of late; the surprizing Effusion of the Holy Spirit, as a Spirit of Conversion to a blessed Number, I doubt not; as a Spirit of Conviction unto many. I would therefore hasten to improve the Words in an Application to three sorts of Persons.—To those that have been taken in the Gospel Net, and upon Scriptural Grounds may be thought to be converted. —To those who are at present only under Convictions, and so are in a hopeful Way to be converted, tho' not yet got through the strait Gate.— And to those who are yet unawaken'd, and left to remain in carnal Security.[63]

Recognizing the danger of Whitefield-worship, Cooper advised those who have been converted during the revival not to ascribe too much to him who was the means of their conversion. Bless God for him, but "don't look so much at the Instrument, as to over-look the Efficient." When Cooper observed the pervasive anxiety, the fearful uncertainty, he informed his hearers that they are "under convictions" and that it is by this means that Christ "prepares the Way for his own Entry into Souls of Sinners."

Therefore cherish them, labour to promote the Vigour of them, and watch against every thing that tends to deprive you of them, or render them ineffectual or unsuccessful.—If your Convictions are but superficial, beg of God to make them deep. If they are but transient, beg of God to fasten them as a Nail in a safe Place.—And whatever your Convictions be, don't rest in them. Don't stop at Convictions. But seek the holy Spirit as a Spirit of Regeneration. Labour after a compleat Conversion to God, a saving Close with the Lord Jesus Christ.[64]

Cooper together with Colman made Brattle Street Church, Boston's most liberal church at the time of its founding, a significant center of revival activity and promotion.

Charles Chauncy was the most persistent but not the only voice emanating from First Church, Boston. Thomas Foxcroft, senior pastor since 1725, experienced a paralysis in 1736 which hampered but did not arrest his activities.[65] He heard Whitefield with much satisfaction in the fall of 1740. Convinced that this sort of gospel was just the thing that Boston needed more of, he took as his subject for the Thursday lecture, October 23, "Evangelistic Preaching; its Nature, Usefulness and Obligation." Acclaiming the Apostle Paul as the great example of "gospel preaching," Foxcroft avowed,

And I can't forbear observing here, We have in a fresh Instance seen this Pauline Spirit and Doctrine remarkably exemplify'd among us. We have seen a Preacher of Righteousness, fervent in Spirit, teaching diligently the Things of the Lord. . . . And as for us, we have been surpriz'd—We have been pleas'd—And shall we not now strive to imitate![66]

Joseph Sewall, sharing with Thomas Prince the ministerial labors at Old South Church, believed that the Great Awakening was itself a means and not simply an occasion of grace.[67] While the Holy Spirit is the author of every work of conviction, there are three means, stated Sewall, that the Spirit uses to bring about a conversion: first, the Word of God; second, "providential dispensations," particularly those that bring distress and affliction; and third, "His own Works of Grace." The revival was thus elevated to a means ordained of God for bringing men to salvation.

God is pleas'd to pour out his Spirit upon his People, and then his Works of Grace, are as the Light which goeth forth. Many ask the Way to

Zion, with their Faces thitherward, and not a few declare God's Works of Grace towards them with rejoicing. Convictions and Conversions become more frequent and apparent. . . . Persons that were before quietly in their Sins and unconcerned, are so awakened that they can't stifle their Convictions nor conceal their Distress. . . . The Ministers of Christ will be encouraged and enlivened in their Work, and such as are under Convictions will be awakened to a more diligent Attendance on the Word and Ordinances. Now such things as these . . . must have an happy tendency to rouse the sleepy and secure Sinner. . . . And thus the holy Spirit maketh use of the Works of his Grace to convince Men of their Sin and Danger. . . .[68]

Like most of the standing ministry who supported the revival, Sewall had by 1742 begun to recognize and inveigh against "every Thing that hath a Tendency to quench his Spirit, and obstruct the Progress and Success of his good Work." The Old South minister summarized his warnings thus:

In a Word, Let us be zealous for God, and good Works and at the same Time beware of the dangerous Extream of Enthusiasm. . . . May we, in the critical Conjuncture, walk circumspectly, not as Fools, but as Wise! It is my Judgment that the prudent Regulation of our religious Commotions, is of great Moment in order to our defending and preserving the Work of God, as we are unworthy Instruments in his Hand.[69]

Thomas Prince, Sewall's colleague and scribe at the 1743 assembly "occasioned by the late happy Revival of Religion in many parts of the Land," was Boston's foremost reporter of the Great Awakening.[70] From his *Account of the Revival of Religion in Boston* many quotations have already been given. More than simply a witness to Prince's own prorevivalism, it is the best single piece of narration on the Great Awakening in New England. Prince was also in large part responsible for the disorganized but important *Christian History,* the first specifically religious magazine in the colonies.[71] Since it was the avowed purpose of the magazine to give instances of the "surprizing and . . . extensive Revivals" of religion, its reports are invaluable in revealing the nature and extent of the movement.[72] Ostensibly edited by Thomas Prince, Jr., the magazine's enemies were probably correct in declaring the elder Prince to be the power behind the pen. But even before the *Christian History* made its appearance, Boston had been thoroughly drenched by the heavenly flood.

John Webb,[73] senior minister at New North, caught up in this sweet season of wetness, delivered in Brattle Street Church, October, 1741, a lecture in which he described Christ in this time of great concern beseeching those still without grace to receive the divine gift of salvation.[74] Webb's associate, Andrew Eliot,[75] ordained in the New North Church in 1742, signed the testimony of 1743 favoring the Awakening,[76] with some critical reservations concerning itineracy. A similar testimony was made by Samuel Checkly,[77] pastor of the New South Church from which Whitefield had in 1740 been obliged to lead an uproarous congregation.[78]

The division of Boston's Congregational clergy in this turbulent period was thus as follows: nine prorevivalist, three antirevivalist, and three neutral.[79] Five churches fully supported the Awakening (Brattle Street, Old South, Second, New North, and New South), while one, Hollis Street, was opposed to it. New Brick and West were neutral, First was divided. The city's one Presbyterian church, pastored by John Moorhead,[80] was as determined in its support as the one Baptist church was in its opposition. One segment of Boston society did hold aloof from the revival: namely, that which was encompassed in the city's three Anglican churches.[81] But Anglicanism, in eighteenth-century New England at least, was not wholly identical with respectability. In the metropolis, as on the frontier, many sought the way to Zion.

William Cooper with happy vigor eulogized New England's religious flood which had indiscriminately swept all before it.

But what a dead and barren time has it now been, for a great while, with all the Churches of the Reformation? The golden Showers have been restrained; the Influences of the Spirit suspended; and the Consequence has been, that the Gospel has not had any eminent Success: Conversions have been rare and dubious; few Sons and Daughters have been born to God; and the Hearts of Christians not so quickened, warm'd and refreshed under the Ordinances, as they have been. . . .

And now,—Behold! The Lord whom we have sought, has suddenly come to his Temple. The Dispensation of Grace we are now under, is certainly such as neither we nor our Fathers have seen; and in some Circumstances so wonderful, that I believe there has not been the like since the extraordinary pouring out of the Spirit immediately after our Lord's Ascension. The Apostolical Times seem to have return'd upon us: Such a Display has there been of the Power and Grace of the divine Spirit in the Assemblies of his People, and such Testimonies has he given to the Word of the Gospel.[82]

This was not pious hyperbole. There had been nothing like it before in New England and there was to be, despite the ecclesiastical engineering of Lyman Beecher, nothing quite like it again. From Stamford, Connecticut, to York, Maine, from Danbury to Northfield (the New England Dan to Beersheba), from James Davenport to Jonathan Edwards, there had been a great and general awakening.

In the months of the revival's intensity, New England joyfully received news of evangelism whether among the followers of Zinzendorf, Francke, Wesley, Whitefield, Finley, Watts, Frelinghuysen, or Brainerd; and whether among the United Brethren, Quakers, Presbyterians, Anglicans, Baptists, or Indians. The revival of piety was everywhere—England, Europe, America. God's mercies, so evident at home, were likewise being abundantly poured forth abroad. It was a mighty consummation, a climax in the history of redemption! Works on salvation and conversion, of any age and from any convenient source, were revived and reprinted.[83] In the attestation to Jonathan Dickinson's *A Display of God's Special Grace*,[84] Boston ministers Colman, Sewall, Prince, Webb, Foxcroft, and Gee expansively declared: "He must be a Stranger in Israel, who has not heard of the uncommon religious Appearances in the several Parts of this Land, among Persons of all Ages and Characters."

But then the six clergymen wrote:

This is an Affair which has in some Degree drawn every One's Attention, and been the Subject of much Debate both in Conversation and Writing. And the grand Question is,—Whether it be a Work of God, and how far it is so?

When the loyal supporters of the revival paused long enough to ask and to consider calmly this grand question, the decline of the Great Awakening in New England had begun.

CHAPTER 5

THE EBB, 1742-1743

THE SUDDENNESS WITH WHICH THE BLESSINGS OF heaven fell on New England soil in 1741 is comparable only to the abruptness with which those showers were withdrawn. And the ending appeared as inexplicable as the beginning. Of the latter, it has already been noted that "this great and surprizing Work does not seem to have taken its Rise from any sudden and distressing Calamity or publick Terror. . . ."[1] Conversely, the quick decline in "People's Engagedness in Religion" did not lend itself to any simple explanation. In both the middle and southern colonies, revivalism sputtered on through much of the eighteenth century. But in New England, that flood of religious anxieties, interests, reformations, excesses, exhortings, and conversions known as the Great Awakening lasted something less than two years. Its effects, to be sure, were felt in theology, denominational structure, education, and even politics into the nineteenth century. The "great and extraordinary Work of God" itself, however, was powerfully and speedily accomplished. The dramatic quality of the New England Awakening is due in large part to the very swiftness with which it moved, as a great flood: in, all over, and out.

From our vantage point, no special perspicacity is required to conclude that the religious intensity of 1741 could not long be maintained. The dreadful concerns, the traumatic awakenings, the accelerated devotion—these by their nature are of limited duration. The fever pitch must soon pass, else the patient dies. Even some of the revival's keener contemporaries recognized the inevitability of its decline. Early in 1741, William Cooper of Brattle Street Church observed:

The present Season is indeed extraordinary. We have enjoy'd some new, powerful, and impressive Means of Grace. Many have been wro't upon. There are many Examples of Persons in Concern for their Souls, and striving after Salvation. Religion, and especially the Nature and Necessity of Conversion, is now much more the Subject of Conversation than has been usual. But as these things become more familiar, and the Occasion begins to grow Old, it may be expected the Concern of some will abate; and their Convictions, tho' now seemingly great, will gradually decay, and at length go off; and they will appear to be such Manner of Persons as they were before. I tell you of this before it comes to pass, that you may not be offended. . . .[2]

The ebb of this flood of revivalism would seem then to require no elaborate explanation: it declined simply because it had to, because society could not maintain itself in so great a disequilibrium. The puzzle remains, however, that if the cessation of intense Awakening was normal and expected, was even openly predicted, why was it in fact accompanied by such noise and clamor, bitterness and schism? Flood waters normally display all their vengeful fury as they advance, while their retreat is chastened and still. But in New England, the religious "Broyls" were far more in evidence as the Great Awakening departed than as it entered.

In the midst of a partisan campaign, it is often difficult to perceive the issues through the murky atmosphere of epithets, scare words, heresy hunts, and villainous oversimplification. That protagonists and antagonists of the revival, alike, indulged in obfuscation is monotonously apparent in the fecund pamphleteering of the period. The antirevivalists saw the Awakening as throwing New England into "Convulsion and heat of Contention,"[3] as endorsing and encouraging persons who "are subversive of Peace, Discipline and Government," as causing the churches to become "Dens of Disorder, Confustion, Noise and Clamour,"[4] and as sowing the seeds of "Discord, Intrusion, Confusion, Separation, Hatred, Variance, Emulations, Wrath, Strife, Seditions, Heresies, &c."[5] The proponents of the revival, on the other hand, viewed this religious concern as a "Sweet Season" wherein "the Power, Grace & Love of God, are wonderfully displayed,"[6] as an occasion for "giving Glory to God for the Great and good Work of his Grace, which He has so visibly begun, spread and is carrying on,"[7] and as a means whereby "diverse thousands have been awakened."[8]

The vehement denunciations and equally vehement defenses of the revival, however much they fail by their immoderation to inspire credence, do show the hardening alignment of opposition forces, the growing bitterness among the clergy, and the very real threat to New England's religious homogeneity. As the declension became more pronounced, the question "Whether it be a Work of God, and how far it is so?" was asked with greater urgency and frequency. And the year

1743 seemed to be a time for evaluation, retrospection, exultation, and recrimination. The *Christian History*, which began collecting its materials in 1743, did by the word "history" imply that now it was time to read about the conversions and praise God for them. Most blatant of all, the Massachusetts clergy in public convocation voiced clearly contrary views of the Awakening and its effects. The clergy had long striven, for the most part with success, to present a united front in any crisis and to keep any disagreements which might arise as private as possible. But in 1743 that long record of ministerial unity was broken, warning of the theological and ecclesiastical schisms that were soon to follow.

In May of that year, the ministers of "the Province of Massachusetts-Bay" testified at their annual meeting in Boston "Against several Errors in Doctrine, and Disorders in Practice, Which have of late obtained in various Parts of the Land."[9] Thus began the open warfare among the New England divines. This testimony was not unopposed during the framing or after its publication: it almost certainly represented a minority opinion.[10] That it called attention to and disapproved of many errors and disorders was not the principal point of contention. The objection was rather to its failure to offer any words of praise or thanksgiving for the genuine good done by the revival, thereby tacitly declaring that there had been no real Awakening. Upon the insistence of Joseph Sewall, the following phrase was reluctantly inserted in the last paragraph of the final draft: "and where there is any special Revival of pure Religion in any Parts of our Land, at this time, we would give unto God all the Glory." This compromise clause still did not declare, however, that there was, in fact, a revival in any parish. Joshua Gee of Boston's Second Church, in a letter to the moderator of this convention, Nathanael Eells of Scituate, stated that the promoters of the revival acknowledge that in the religious upheaval there have been errors and are concerned about the elimination of those errors.

But yet they did not think they should be faithful to the Doctrines of Grace, and serve the cause of real and vital Religion among us, if they voted for a *Testimony against Several Errors and Disorders*, unless it might be amended and enlarged by an open Acknowledgment of the late remarkable Effects of a gracious Divine Influence in many of our Churches.[11]

Gee further objected that the title page under which the testimony was issued was grossly misleading. In using the words "the Pastors of the Churches in the Province of Massachusetts-Bay in New England at their Annual Convention in Boston," at least three misconceptions are created. In the first place such a statement would lead many to believe that the assembly had some power or authority, like a provincial synod. As a matter of fact, this "Annual Convention," notes Gee, is only an occasional, voluntary assembly of those pastors who happen to come to Boston on the annual occasion of the General Assembly's election of counselors for the ensuing year. Its pseudo-official character is probably not understood abroad, and therefore such a testimony as the group issued substantiates the absurd and fallacious accounts of the state of religion in New England by "A. M." and John Caldwell, discrediting the revival movement everywhere.[12] Furthermore, the reference to pastors in Massachusetts-Bay is misleading, for " 'Tis well known, that others were admitted to vote, who are Pastors of Churches beyond the Bounds of this Province."[13] Finally,

I judge it necessary the publick should know, and would have it published to the world, as undeniable Matter of Fact,— 1) That scarce one Third Part of the Pastors of the Churches of the Province of the Massachusetts-Bay were present at the late Convention. 2) That of those who were present, it was but a small Majority [thirty-eight out of about seventy] that voted the last Article or Paragraph, which caused such Debates about an Attestation to the Work of God's Grace appearing of late Years in a remarkable Revival of Religion among these Churches.[14]

If one wishes to ask why these misconceptions were not clarified, or the minority voice not more in evidence, it is, writes Gee, because the friends of the revival were not allowed to testify in its behalf, but were stifled in "Clamour and Opposition."

Viewed as a whole, the *Testimony* of May, 1743, could only have a grave number of ill effects, according to Gee. Benjamin Prescott of Salem, replying to Gee's letter and this charge, announced that the only bad effect of the *Testimony* was Gee's letter which it apparently provoked.[15] Prescott then claimed that the much-contested last paragraph did certainly contain an acknowledgment of the revival and of its validity, but so much effort and vigorous language was required of Prescott to substantiate this claim that he succeeded only in revealing its absurdity. The reasons given for the convention's omitting an attestation to the good done by the revival were poor and inconclusive. By way of summary, Prescott attempted to discount all of Gee's charges with the affirmation that they were wholly the result of a personal grudge against Chauncy.

It was time for the other side to summon its warriors to the defense. Near the end of Gee's letter to Eells, he called for all ministers "of the country" to meet in Boston the day after the Harvard commencement for the purpose of framing a more satisfactory testimony concerning the recent Awakening. In the *Boston Gazette* for May 31, 1743, the following announcement appeared:

It is desir'd and proposed by a Number of Ministers both in Town and Country, that such of their Brethren as are persuaded there has of late been a happy Revival of Religion, thro' an extraordinary divine Influence, in many Parts of this Land, and are concern'd for the Honour and Progress of this remarkable Work of God, may have an interview at Boston, the Day after the approaching Commencement; To consider whether they are not called to give an open conjunct Testimony to an Event so surprizing and gracious; as well as against those Errors in Doctrine and Disorders in Practice, which thro' the permitted Agency of Satan have attended it, and in any measure blemish'd its Glory and hindered its Advancement: And also to consult the most likely Methods to be taken, to guard People against such Delusions & Mistakes as in such a Season they are in Danger of falling into, and that this blessed Work may continue and flourish among us. . . .[16]

Thus on Thursday, July 7, about ninety New England ministers gathered, and "being persuaded there has of late been a happy Revival of Religion," proceeded to choose a committee "to consider the Promisses and make a Report to Morrow Morning at nine of the Clock."[17] The report which was submitted by the committee and adopted by this "counter-convention" after discussion and amendment occupied the next five issues of the *Christian History*.[18] It was called

The Testimony and Advice of an Assembly of Pastors of Churches in New-England, At a Meeting in Boston July 7, 1743. Occasion'd By the late happy Revival of Religion in many Parts of the Land. To which are added, Attestations contain'd in Letters from a Number of their Brethren who were providentially hindered from giving their Presence.[19]

Bearing sixty-eight signatures, the testimony was augmented by the favorable witness of forty-three ministers who sent in their accounts, so that the views of one hundred eleven New England divines are here represented. Fifteen of the sixty-eight subscribed to the substance of the testimony "excepting against that Article of Itinerancy, or Ministers, and others, intruding into other Ministers Parishes without their Consent, which great Disorder we apprehend not sufficiently testify'd against, therein."[20] The July meeting, though clearly as much in favor of the revival as the earlier group was opposed to it, did include two pages of testimony against the extravagances and irregularities accompanying it. Since there is great similarity between the errors censured by both groups, the failure of the earlier convention to admit that good has been mixed with the error appears to have been the real provocation of the "counter-convention" and of the ministerial schism.

The spectacle of New England's ministers publicly and widely divided, issuing conflicting testimonies and ascribing to God dissimilar things, was a new experience for the colonists. Minor disagreements—minor from the viewpoint of the issue or the number of controversialists—there had been often before. But on this occasion, the established ministry was badly and palpably split. Ezra Stiles reckoned that of the four hundred ministers in New England in 1743, one hundred thirty ardently supported the revival.[21] The raucous discord struck at clerical prestige and at Congregationalism's integrity. In September a disrespectful tirade was published, being "Address'd to the Pastors of New-England." In imitation of the form used by the July assembly, the title "The Testimony and Advice of a Number of Laymen respecting Religion, and the Teachers of it" was affixed to what was probably the work of only one individual. Yet the publication of so irreverent, facetious, and sarcastic a tirade against the clergy connected with the Awakening was itself an indication of the hurt resulting from the division. Describing the present state of religion, the author(s) writes:

Now let any One who knows any Thing of the State of Religion before and since the coming of the grant Itinerant [Whitefield] and his Second [Tennent] into this Province, recollect & compare them together: For Party Zeal and Rage were almost entirely subsided and worn off among the Laity before they came here; but while they were here and since their Departure, they have been higher than ever was known in this Country. Formerly the Laity were not remarkable for their spiritual Pride and Ostentation; but they have obtained very much of late. Formerly the People could bear with each other in Charity when they differ'd in Opinion, but they now break Fellowship and Communion with one another on that Account . . . every unprejudic'd Person must easily and certainly see, that pure Religion and undefil'd before God and the Father flourish'd more, and that Disorders, Divisions, Errors, Confusions, and an antichristian and uncharitable Spirit prevail'd less formerly, than they do now.[22]

The decline of the Awakening, inevitable, normal, and anticipated though it had been, promoted sharper factions and wider schisms.

As parties crystallized, each minister found himself drawn away from a comfortable neutrality to one of the opposing poles. Revivalists were collectively designated New Lights, while the adversaries of the Awakening were Old Lights. "Such distinguishing names of reproach, do as it were divide us into two armies, separated, and drawn up in battle array, ready to fight one with another; which greatly hinders the work of God."[23]

Few New Lights, despite Old Light zeal in pointing out the extravagances of the revival, were unwilling to admit that much which went under the name of godly zeal was more nearly devilish enthusiasm. Prominent revival leaders early counseled against the disorders and errors of the time. Colman in the first days of 1742 spoke of the dangers of itinerary and of leaving one's own minister to hear another, while in the previous September Edwards had carefully demonstrated that all the emotional extremes and physiological effects in the revival were not essential to the converting work of God. Jonathan Parsons of Lyme preached February 4, 1742, on a "Needful Caution in a Critical Day," warning such who are either opposed or indifferent to the revival not to "stumble or cavil at the work of God's rich and free grace manifest at this day, from those errors and irregularities visible in the happy subjects of it," and freely admitting that the questionable behavior of some of the new converts was a matter of "shame and deep abasement."[24] Tennent strongly condemned the misguided zeal of Davenport, urging all God-fearers to "rise up and labour to crush the enthusiastical Cockatrice in the Egg. . . ." And even Davenport, at last, had been led to admit that much chaff had been mixed with the wheat.

One of the most important "self-critics" of the Great Awakening was Jonathan Dickinson, zealous Presbyterian and able theologian of Elizabethtown, New Jersey.[25] In 1742, he published in Boston, anonymously at first, *A Display of God's special Grace* to which was affixed an attestation by Boston ministers Colman, Sewall, Prince, Webb, Cooper, Foxcroft, and Gee. Written in the form of a dialogue, the treatise adequately conveyed Dickinson's belief that a great deal of "Human Infirmity" had been mixed with the genuine operation of the Spirit of God. Though Dickinson justified fainting, crying out, "frights and terror" as natural and inevitable concomitants of an effectual conviction, he spared no severity in denouncing those who, like Davenport and Whitefield, publicly condemn or cast suspicion upon persons visibly leading a good life. Such zealots "set at Naught their

Brother," quotes Dickinson. If one have apprehensions concerning the true state of a professing Christian, these suspicions "should either be concealed in our own Breasts; or else (if we have Opportunity for it) privately, charitably, and affectionately communicated only to the Person concern'd, for his best Good and Advantage." It is equally dangerous and erroneous to pronounce any person to be positively of the elect, argued Dickinson, who proceeded logically from this point to an attack upon any manifestations of the ugly specter of antinomianism.[26]

This dialogue, while clearly defending the Awakening, was carefully aimed at the revival extremists, and even in the eighteenth century the hit dog howled. Andrew Croswell, whose boiling point was very low and whose acumen was even lower, regarded Dickinson's *Display* as an attack upon the whole revival movement and therefore to be publicly denounced as quickly as possible.[27] Since Dickinson's intention, as well as the intention of the seven Boston ministers who endorsed the treatise, was only to defend, purify, and justify the revival, the New Jersey theologian in some amazement protested Croswell's charge.

I was so far from entertaining the least Thought, of bringing a Slur or Reproach upon the Work of God, which has been so conspicuous of late in our Land, or upon any that are zealous for it, in any Part of that Dialogue, that I was acted by directly contrary views, in the whole Undertaking. Tho' I must also declare, that I then did, and still do think, that some zealous and godly Brethren, who are earnestly and sincerely engaged in that Cause, have run into very great Irregularities; and have thereby been accidentally very injurious to it, in their Endeavors to promote it; and that others (the Antinomians in particular) may pretend the Cause of God, when they are in a most direct and immediate Manner, subverting and undermining it. Upon these Accounts, I could not but hope, it would be of some Service to the Interest of Christ's kingdom to set that Cause in a proper Light; to shew the Opposers of that miraculous Work of divine Grace, the dreadful Danger of their Case; to convince some of our godly Brethren, of the ill Effects of their mistaken Conduct; and to detect, and if possible prevent the progress of those mischievous Errors, which so openly appear among us, and would take Sanctuary under a pretense of the Cause of God and Religion. This, Sir, is a plain and faithful Account of my Motives to that Work. . . .[28]

Dickinson also cleared himself of errors of which Croswell had accused him, indicating where the latter had exaggerated and grossly misrepresented him. The straw man was quickly blown down.

Others such as Nathanael Appleton of Cambridge and Ebenezer Turell of Medford, repelled by the extravagances of Davenport, Buell, and Croswell, sought, while not wholly discounting the Awakening, to criticize some of the personalities and practices connected with it.[29] And a torrent of denunciation, as was noted in an earlier chapter, fell upon Whitefield and Tennent as individual performers—apart from their share of responsibility for the total upheaval, the "unnatural Heat" of the day. There was also a subtle criticism which took the form of publishing excerpts from a respected divine (such as Richard Baxter) on a sensitive subject like lay preaching.[30] By the end of 1743, it was evident that the New England clergy was divided not on the question of whether there were errors in doctrine and disorders in practice attending the revival, but on the question of whether, notwithstanding these errors and disorders, the revival was a work of God.

The Old Light answer was losing all evidences of moderation and ambiguity, as by this date the antirevivalist attitude became one of deliberate, unflinching, indiscriminate opposition. Before 1743 the Great Awakening had by nearly all been regarded as at least in part a divine operation.

But that was at a Time when the superstitious Pannick run very high, and bore down every body that was not well fixed and established either by a natural Steddiness of Temper, or by strong Reason and Reflection. But as soon as the Passions of the People subsided, and Men could coolly and calmly consider, almost every one of but tolerable Sense and Understanding in religious Matters, in great Measure changed their Opinions of the Spirit that prevailed here, and had been raised by Whitefield and Tennent.[31]

The extravagant beliefs and actions were not of a "different and contrary nature and tendency" from the entire revival, nor were they but appendages to it. Rather they indicated that there was nothing of God in it. The author of *An Impartial Examination of Mr. Davenport's Retractions*, after lamenting "that this Confession is neither so full nor so early as might have been expected," observed,

Neither Mr. Davenport, nor any other of the late Tribe of Itinerants, had one single Reason to think themselves called of God, and sent on an extraordinary Work, as they all at Times pretended. . . .

If Mr. Davenport or his Friends hope, to re-establish the Credit of the chief Workers in this late Work, as really sent of God, they must necessarily be disappointed, the confessing and giving up such Things as were indisputably owing to a false Spirit will never establish the rest. Enthusiasts must never retract any Thing any more than the Pope, if they once give up their Infallibility they are infallibly gone; And from thence it came to pass that ever since that fatal Distinction of Appendages and essential Parts, the whole Work has been at an awful Stand.[32]

It could not be that truth and error coexisted; one pinch of antinomianism ruined the whole loaf.

The bulk of this positive, organized antagonism against the Awakening revolved about five topics: itinerant preaching, lay exhorting, censoriousness, church divisions and separations, and doctrinal errors. Besides creating jealousies and threatening prerogatives, itineracy flaunted the Congregational theory of the ministerial office. The Puritan minister had not been elevated to a rank that was universal and permanent; he was not a minister at large, but only of a particular congregation. Hooker's advice that there be no ordination of a "Pastor without a People" had been generally followed; few New England divines of the colonial period were ordained until called to some church. Ministers did of course preach away from their own pulpits, but only by invitation of the minister or ministers into whose parish or meetinghouse they entered. Anyone leaving his flock was further obliged to see that it was well cared for during his absence. In the many vitriolic verbal attacks on itineracy, if names were mentioned at all, it is noteworthy that the itinerants who violated these conditions bore the brunt of the attack.[33] Men such as Brainerd and Buell received ordination from Presbyterian bodies before they were settled over a church. Croswell, Pomeroy, Wheelock, Tennent, and Davenport, each of whom had his own church, were often charged with neglecting their responsibilities while infringing on those of others. On such a charge Davenport was brought to trial after his return from Massachusetts to Southold, while Whitefield's connection with his Georgia parish was by many considered rather an excuse than a reason for traveling. On the other hand, the itinerants regarded themselves as missionaries of a gospel of salvation that could recognize no bounds. And in many a sparsely settled parish, the meetinghouse might be fifteen or twenty miles from some of the parishioners. Could there be any harm in bringing light to these dark places?

To those who saw in such zeal a grave threat to New England ecclesiastical order, the only possible answer was an affirmative one. Wrote Samuel Niles in 1745:

. . . Now 'tis easy to point out the Troublers of our Peace and former happy Union. Every Man that will judge impartially and free from design, knows that the Rev. Messirs Whitefield, Tennent, Davenport and other Itinerants, with the many Exhorters under their Influence, have thrown us into this Convulsion and heat of Contention.[34]

At Rumford, New Hampshire, Timothy Walker resurrected a dilemma with which Catholic controversialists had confronted the irregular Protestant ministers of the sixteenth century. Ministers could only be chosen in one of two ways: by the usual and orderly method of the laying on of hands by proper authorities, or by the direct and immediate authority of Christ in which case, stated Walker, "we may justly demand of them a Confirmation of their Mission by the Seal of Miracles, which is always expected and granted in that Case." Since the ordination of many of the itinerants or "pretended apostles" was irregular or at least suspect, and since the performance of miracles did not generally comprise a part of their repertoire, itinerant ministers often found themselves impaled on the horns of this dilemma. Complained Walker, ". . . the old Divinity, which has stood the Test of above seventeen hundred Years, is become stale and unsavory, to many wanton Palates; and nothing will please them but new Preachers, new Doctrines, new Methods of Speech, Tone, and Gesture."[35]

John Hancock of Braintree, ever ready to strike at the Awakening in general and at Tennent in particular, published, in answer to Tennent's outburst at Nottingham, a sermon entitled *The Danger of an Unqualified Ministry*.[36] The Novice or unqualified minister is a danger to himself, because he becomes a prey to pride. He is likewise a danger to every church officer who authorizes his mission and to every soul that is led by him. In short, his ministry "is of very dangerous and destructive Tendency to the True Interest of Religion." Hancock could only agree with Walker that "the Itinerants of the present Day . . . are no ministers of Jesus Christ."

> Their greatest Success has always been by drawing Crowds of the unguarded Populace around them; who are but poorly furnish'd with the Christian Armour; who are utterly unacquainted with the surprising Effects of Error & Enthusiasm in all Ages & Countries; who have many Times weak Understandings and strong Passions, and are therefore apt to take zeal for Argument, and Rapture and Extasy for Demonstration.[37]

A correspondent to the *Boston Weekly News-Letter* urged that as there is "a very wholesome Law of the Province to discourage Pedlars

in Trade" so it is now "Time to enact something for the Discourage-
ment of Pedlars in Divinity also; for I apprehend the latrer [*sic*] are
become as common as the former and more prejudicial to the Commonwealth. . . ."[38] Revivalists attempted to parry at least a portion of
these many attacks, even by referring to Christ as the first itinerant,[39]
or by attributing the success of the Reformation to itinerants.[40] Yet
itineracy was the one ecclesiastical disorder which rankled in the
breast of many of the revival party and which in July of 1743 caused
the only major difference of opinion among the friends of the
Awakening.[41]

There were itinerant exhorters as well as itinerant ministers, but
exhorters were objects of scornful criticism whether they itinerated or
not. The exhorter, unordained and usually uneducated, posed a new
and pernicious threat to the New England clergy.

> There is a Creature here whom perhaps you never heard of before. It is
> called an Exhorter. It is of both Sexes, but generally of the Male, and
> young. Its distinguished Qualities are Ignorance, Impudence, Zeal.
> Numbers of these Exhorters are amongst the People here. They go from
> Town to Town, creep into Houses, lead Captive silly Women, and then
> the Men. Such of them as have good Voices do great Execution; they move
> their Hearers, make them cry, faint, swoon, fall into Convulsions.[42]

This creature assumed no ministerial function except that of preaching,
and even in this activity some strove valiantly to distinguish nicely
between exhorting and preaching. But the Old Lights were not to be
duped by a subterfuge of this sort. If the speaking was more than a
quiet conversation among family and intimate friends, then it was
preaching! By April of 1742, Gilbert Tennent was clearly convinced
of the danger "of Lay-Mens being sent out to exhort and teach, sup-
posing they to be real Converts." To a minister friend in Connecticut
he wrote:

> . . . I cannot but think that if it be encouraged and continued it will be
> of dreadful Consequence to the Churches Peace and soundness in Principle.
> I will not gainsay, but that private Persons, may be of Service to the
> Church of God, by their private, humble, fraternal Reproofs and Ex-
> hortations . . . ; but in the mean time, if Christian Prudence, Meekness and
> Humility do not attend their Essays, they are like to be very prejudicial
> to the Churches real Weal. But for ignorant young Converts to take upon
> them authoritatively to instruct and exhort Publickly, tends to introduce
> the grossest Errors and the greatest Anarchy and Confusion. . . . It is bare

Presumption (whatever Zeal be pretended notwithstanding) for any
Person to take that Honour to themselves, unless they be called of God . . .
thro' their Imprudences and Enthusiasms the Church of God suffers.[43]

When about a year later, even the pugnacious Andrew Croswell admitted to Prince that he had now "seen Reason to alter my Judgment,
particularly with reference to Exhorters," it could safely be concluded
that little was being said in favor of lay preaching. Croswell confessed,

> For tho' I was the first in New-England that set them up, I now see (too
> late) that the Tendency of their Ways is, to drive Learning from the
> World, and to sow it thick with the dreadful Errors of Anabaptism,
> Quakerism and Antinomianism.[44]

Finally, Davenport in 1744 recognized that he had "done much hurt
to religion, by encouraging private persons to a ministerial and authoritative kind or method of exhorting. . . ."[45] The complete abandonment
of the exhorters by both friends and foes of the revival is eloquent
testimony to the avalanche of criticism under which they were buried.[46]

The revival was roundly denounced further for the brusque spirit
of many of its proponents, for its moving in neither meekness nor love,
for its "censoriousness." New Lights were given to rash judging and
frequent condemning, were always emphasizing if not creating differences, and in general were promoters of disharmony and mutual
suspicions. The most infuriating feature of this censoriousness was
the ready and repeated stigmatizing of ministers who did not fully
join in the revival as "opposers" or more generally as carnal and sinful
men. Much support or at least friendly neutrality was lost to the movement by an unnecessary and unattractive pettiness and peevishness.
Toward the end of 1741, when Jonathan Ashley preached on "The
Great Duty of Charity" from I Corinthians 13:1-3, William Cooper
interpreted the sermon as being an attack on the Awakening![47] With
discriminating care and eminent fairness, Ashley had called attention
to certain of the revival's liabilities, while assuring his hearers that
these disorders did not invalidate the whole movement. After Cooper
published his objections, the author of a tract advised him that "Whatsoever Work cannot bear the Encouragement and Practice of Charity
in all it Branches . . . cannot be a good Work."[48] Long after the
Awakening had passed, complaints were still heard of and events still
evidenced the pervasive censoriousness of 1741-42.[49]

The greatest threat of this censoriousness was its manifest tendency to promote separations. These were of all ecclesiastical disorders the most serious and enduring. Before the end of 1741 this schismatic proclivity was already in evidence. A general consociation of Connecticut ministers was called at Guilford in December to consider

> what is proper to be done in these Times, particularly, in order to prevent Division in Churches, and to heal such as have already arisen by means of Mr. Davenport's Preaching; and a few others of his Followers, whose Zeal wants a little Regulation. . . .[50]

By the time of the annual election the following May, the situation in Connecticut was viewed with alarm and governmental aid was sought. Isaac Stiles in a sermon preached at Hartford at the time of election asked,

> Can nothing be done to heal our unhappy Divisions? To put a stop to, and prevent Unscriptural Separations & Disorderly Practises of various kinds, which have a direct Tendency to, and by a natural Causality necessarily do, disturb the Peace of this our Jerusalem, and greatly weaken the Wall of it? . . . Mark them which cause Divisions & Offences, contrary to the Doctrine which ye have learned, and avoid them. . . . A Church-rending, Unpeaceable, Party Spirit, is certainly a bad Spirit. . . . To me it plainly appears . . . that diverse things relating to, and transacted in, these Separate Meetings, are a great Blemish to the Christian Name and Profession, directly contrary to the Religion of the Bible; particularly to that Apostolick Rule, I Corinthians 14, 40. Let all things be done Decently & in Order. That they are subversive of Peace, Discipline & Government: Lay open the Sluices & make a Gap to let in a Flood of Confustion & Disorder; and very awfully portend the Ruin of these Churches, unless a Stop be put to them. . . . Wherefore let us beware lest . . . our Houses of Prayer be haunted with Evil spirits, & turn'd into Dens of Disorder, Confustion, Noise and Clamour; or into Dens of Thieves & Robbers: And lest . . . our whole Land should become an Aceldama, a Field of Blood & Slaughter on account of Religion. . . .[51]

Stiles' fears were shared by so many that the General Assembly that month passed a law whose purpose was "regulating abuses and correcting disorders in ecclesiastical affairs," the effect of which was sharply to reverse the trend toward greater religious freedom in Connecticut.[52] Connecticut ministers were restrained from entering other parishes than their own by the threat of having their salaries withdrawn; that is, they shall be "denied and excluded the benefit of any law in this colony, for the encouragement and support of the gospel ministry."

Under the terms of this provision, Benjamin Pomeroy was legally deprived of his salary for seven years; his congregation, however, made voluntary contributions that alleviated his financial difficulties. Whee-lock wrote to Clap that he too was "Deprived of my Living, at Least of the Benefit of a Law to secure it to me (with how much Justice & Righteousness the World will See another Day) Whereby [I] have Suffered much already & am Like to Suffer more as Religion declines among us."[53] For ministers not of Connecticut, the "foreigner or stranger," a further provision decreed that such persons if they "shall presume to preach, teach, or publicly exhort, in any town or society within this colony, without the desire and license of the settled minister and the major part of the church" shall be arrested as a vagrant person and sent "from constable to constable, out of the bounds of this colony." Not only Davenport was sent down the Connecticut River under this provision, but Samuel Finley, later president of the college at Princeton, was in the fall of 1743 also ejected from the colony.[54] The stringent law in addition provided a fine and, in the event of re-peated offense, a jail sentence for any laymen who did "publicly teach and exhort the people" without the proper invitation and authorization. Interpreting the Saybrook Platform as binding on all established churches, the law drove many New Light churches into the Baptist or Presbyterian folds, for these groups now enjoyed more freedom than the nonconforming Congregationalists. This law of 1742 indicates the strength and the position of Connecticut orthodoxy in the mid-eighteenth century.

The Connecticut law was more successful in dealing with individual offenders than with recalcitrant church groups. Late in 1742 the *News-Letter* received reports from "a Gentleman of Veracity in Connecticut" that "religious Broyls are in *Statu quo,* and the Separation in several Places still continues and at present there is no Prospect of an Ac-comadation. . . ."[55] In some cases the "Broyls" arose from Old Light censoriousness, as when Philemon Robbins of Branford preached in 1742 by invitation to a "Baptist" group in Wallingford, Connecticut.[56] As in Finley's case, Robbins went only where he was invited, but again the invitation was not from a properly authorized person. The New Haven Association, which in a previous affair had already developed a dislike for Robbins, found him disorderly for not having obtained the permission of the established minister, Samuel Whittelsey, Sr., and expelled him from the council. Struggles between Robbins and the New Haven ministerial body continued for years. As bitterness mounted, Robbins was moved to observe that he would rather be under a bishop than an association.[57]

The more liberal colony of Massachusetts was not without its difficulties of this nature, though for the most part they did not reach the extreme of definitive separations until a few years later. There was an extended controversy at Middleborough following the death of Peter Thacher.[58] At Ipswich, New Lights withdrew from the Second Church to ordain John Cleaveland as their pastor.[59] A prorevival majority in Hull forced the dismissal of their conservative pastor,[60] and at Grafton an ecclesiastical council labored to prevent a separation.[61] In Exeter, New Hampshire, prompt and forceful council action effected the healing of a schism.[62] In the period of decline now under consideration, however, the Awakening in Massachusetts was hurt, not so much by actual separations as by the frictions within the churches and among the clergy which posed the ever-vexing threat of division. Samuel Mather and party had removed from New North for reasons which in part stemmed from the revival, and this object lesson would not readily be forgotten. Parsons' sermon in September of 1742 at First Church must have confirmed the fears of many ministers that to support the Awakening was to promote separations.

I'm perswaded that Separations are warrantable and highly necessary where the Ministry is corrupt in those things mentioned in the Sermon, unless it can happily be redress'd a better Way.[63]

Beware of that ministry, Parsons advised, which teaches unsound doctrines such as "Free-Will in Opposition to the absolute Sovereignty of God; Election from Faith foreseen; good Works before Justification, &c," and of that ministry which neglects to preach the important gospel doctrines of repentance, faith, and grace, and of that ministry which "expressly denies or plainly endeavors to hide the glorious Work of divine Grace under the Filth of human imprudences." Such divines like to think that they have a "Right to censure, where they have no Heart to assist."[64] A sermon of this type, "full of Design, Wrath and Virulence" and tending "to promote Separation, and to banish the little Remains of Christian Benevolence, & brotherly Love that are left among us,"[65] demonstrated the path censoriousness was most likely to follow and inevitably evoked a healthy distrust of the revival. Divided congregations and church fractures represent the ultimate of the "Disorders in Practice" that brought about the decline of the Awakening.

Coupled with the accusation of disorder was the companion charge that the revival sheltered and fostered doctrinal error. In the treatises, sermons, narratives, and testimonies of the period, the phrase "Disorders and Errors" repeatedly occurs. But though each ecclesiastical disorder was often treated separately and denounced in considerable detail, the doctrinal errors were usually alluded to without elaboration or specification.[66] Frequently there appeared the simple statement that the revival was contrary to "True Religion." There were, however, two words commonly used to refer to the miscreance of the New Lights: enthusiasm and antinomianism. The latter term had since Anne Hutchinson's day been a harsh and dreaded epithet in New England, a brand reserved for those who opposed orthodoxy in belief and behavior and whose presence was deemed a threat to society. In general, the term carried with it at this time little of the moral odium associated with it abroad, though New Englanders felt that antinomianism long tolerated would surely lead to moral anarchy. More theological than moral, the charge, when it was specific, dealt with the revivalists' emphasis upon the doctrine of justification by faith at the expense of the doctrine of sanctification as an evidence of that faith.[67] The Awakening, accompanied as it was by Edwards' resurrection of a purer Calvinism, did turn many toward a re-examination of the work of God in the salvation of man. In discounting the efficacy of good works and of a moral character in attaining divine grace, the revival party was certain to be charged with antinomianism; its accusers were just as certain, however, to be charged with Arminianism. And if the New Lights were libertines, the Old Lights were Pharisees.

The antinomian could be sure that faith without the law was enough to save him, and could be positive concerning his own election because of his personal liaison with God. God would assure such a person of his salvation, and He might go so far as to inform him of others who lacked that salvation. There was therefore a natural kinship between antinomianism and enthusiasm, to the extent that the two might coalesce. Enthusiasm, when the word was carefully used, meant the divine impulses and visions, the special calls from God, the particular inspirations.[68] These personal revelations, beyond and perhaps contrary to scripture, were to be accepted as sufficient basis for any kind of behavior. They were the "new light" by which the zealots claimed to be led and for which they were contemptuously named. Ebenezer Morton, a Middleborough layman, contributed the following doggerel:

Whate'er Men speak by this New-Light
Still they are sure to be in the right:
'Tis a dark Lanthorn of a Spirit
Which none see by but those that bear it:
A Light that falls down from on high
For Spiritual Trades to cozen by:
An *Ignis Fatuus* that bewitches,
And leads Men into Pools and Ditches.[69]

To most of New England's standing ministry, of the revival party or not, any such "new light" was a manifest heresy, a pernicious threat to orthodoxy and to society. There were, however, among the revivalists sufficient tendencies toward enthusiasm to make the charge uncomfortably effective.

In 1742 Chauncy cautioned against enthusiasm,[70] while the same year William Hooper advised all to "Be upon your Guard against Infidelity and Enthusiasm. I know not which of these is the greatest Enemy to true Religion."[71] One of the outstanding treatises produced in the Awakening period was *An Enquiry Into Enthusiasm* by Benjamin Doolittle of Northfield.[72] Defining enthusiasm as "strong Fancy, Imagination or Conceit of having large Communications from or Participations with the Deity," Doolittle traced its origin to the Garden of Eden. When the forbidden fruit was eaten, Adam and Eve displayed a proud desire to know more about and be greater than God. "Thus Enthusiasm was man's first, or original sin. . . . 'Tis therefore no Wonder that all Mankind are so fond of it, and so ready to fall in with it." In a Chauncylike style and with careful organization, Doolittle described the effects of enthusiasm on its victims. It produces in them (1) a contempt for all reason and argument, (2) faith without foundation, (3) blind obedience to impulses and "heated imaginations," (4) great and sudden joy, (5) contempt of all not wholly in sympathy with their position, and (6) a spirit of persecution against all who differ, to the limit of their power; yet they will "bawl out Persecution, as loud as they can roar" if the "least Restraint" be put upon them. Not to Doolittle alone did the charge of enthusiasm have all these connotations; to denounce the revival as enthusiastic was to encumber it, therefore, with a web of doctrinal delinquencies. In the aftermath of the Awakening, with the growth of separate schools of thought, other theological vagaries may be laid at the door of the New Lights of 1741-1742.[73] But in the year of decline, 1743, it was antinomianism and enthusiasm, vaguely defined and loosely held, which were responsible for the criticism and fear that the Awakening was an enemy of orthodoxy.

By the end of 1743 all the principles, even most of the details, of criticism of the revival had been established. The Great Awakening was dead, although many were trying to force air into its lungs while others were still hacking at the corpse whenever possible. The Whitefield controversy sputtered on, seemingly without end. In 1744 the *Evening-Post* printed everything that anybody thought or said against Whitefield or against his orphan house, which one day was declared to have no orphans and the next was reputed to be filled with starving children. When the following year Whitefield returned to New England for his second visit, he found few available pulpits and mostly adverse declarations and testimonies. In September of 1744 Gilbert Tennent preached at Philadelphia on "The necessity of studying to be quiet and doing our own Business."[74] In 1746 Thomas Prince discoursed on "The Salvation of God," but the salvation he referred to was the restoration of peace between Prussia, Saxony, and Hungary, the victories of Great Britain and Hungary, the debilitation of the French army, and the death of the king of Spain.[75] In 1747 Thomas Foxcroft published a seventy-six page booklet in commemoration of the times when God worked wonders of "Creation, Redemption, and Providence."[76] On page 57 the Great Awakening was mentioned.

CHAPTER 6

CASCADES:
CHAUNCY and EDWARDS

HUMAN EXPERIENCE IS COMPLEX. AND THE ATTEMPTS
to explain it, if they honor the integrity of that experience, are similarly
complex. Having forsaken the hope and even the desire to reduce the
universe to a common denominator of fire or water, earth or air, modern
man slowly recognizes that no segment of that universe or of life lends
itself to such Milesian simplification. A historian of science has recently
well written, "The common belief that we gain 'historical perspective'
with increasing distance seems to me utterly to misrepresent the actual
situation. What we gain is merely confidence in generalizations which
we would never dare make if we had access to the real wealth of contemporary evidence."[1] Every age is one of decision and complexity to
those who live in it; the alternatives are seldom but two, the dilemmas
are many-horned, and the causes as well as the effects of a given event
display maddening multiplicity.

Those who with greatest sagacity sought to explain that cataclysm of
human experience in eighteenth-century New England made no attempt to gainsay its complexity. Jonathan Edwards may have wished he
could ingenuously declare that all was of God, but he wrote:

It is a hard thing to be a hearty zealous friend of what had been good
and glorious, in the late extraordinary appearances, and to rejoice much
in it; and at the same time to see the evil and pernicious tendency of what
has been bad, and earnestly oppose that. But yet I am humbly, but fully
persuaded, we shall never be in the way of truth . . . till we do so.[2]

Charles Chauncy in 1742 declared that "there are, I doubt not, a number in this land, upon whom God has graciously shed the influence of
his blessed Spirit. . . ."[3] He may have preferred to dismiss the whole
movement as satanic seduction, but he cautioned that insofar as a true
work of God

appears in this or any other Place, I am, if I know myself, in a Disposition to rejoice in it, and thank God for it; And instead of saying any Thing to oppose it, would do all in my Power, to encourage and promote it. But 'tis easy to observe, a Work of God may be thought to consist in those Things in which the Bible does not make it to consist; and great Stress may be laid upon such Appearances as are no sure Characteristicks of a saving Change in Men's Hearts. . . .[4]

While Edwards labored long and well to defend the Awakening, Chauncy concentrated his effort on "Faithfully pointing out the Things of a Bad and Dangerous Tendency, in the late and present, religious Appearance, in the Land." Although both he and Edwards were concerned with separating the wheat from the chaff, the attention of one was fixed on the wheat, the other on the chaff. And to winnow rightly was indeed "a hard thing."

Edwards and Chauncy, respectively, stood out above the other apologists for, and antagonists of, the revival. As we have seen, however, they did not stand alone in this mid-century battle of ideas, for many had been profoundly moved, this way or that, in 1740 to 1742. Even more significant perhaps is the fact that neither the Boston liberal nor the Northampton Calvinist stood alone historically. For the battle which they fought was part of an ancient war that gave no sign of imminent abatement. The protracted struggle between enlightenment and piety, between reason and faith, had through familiarity lost none of its zest. Old, it somehow always seems new. The challenge is just as great, the prizes of war just as precious in the last campaign as in the first. Though the terrain and matériel do from time to time vary, the battle plan is nigh inflexible. It goes something like this. On the one hand the forces of reason, clarity, humanism, logic, liberalism, naturalism, and modernism are deployed. Against these time-honored stalwarts stand the ranks of revelation, mystery, theism, emotion, conservatism, supernaturalism, and medievalism. The latter stubbornly refuses to yield an inch of territory, while the former amiably seeks, not unconditional surrender, but only a small strip of land here or a free corridor there—suggesting that it really does not make much difference to anybody. As the conflict begins, the orthodox army closes its ranks, presenting to the enemy a solid, implacable, immovable phalanx. The forces under rationalism's banner, however, are widely dispersed, they may even seem disorganized. Unready and unwilling to fight a pitched battle, they dispatch sorties toward the opposite camp, deftly probing for weakness or vulnerability in the imposing line. They attack swiftly;

never in force; retreat and attack, first here and then there, again and again; until finally, a small opening is made, the solid line cracks, the enemy breaks through. Now it is orthodoxy which retreats, not in haste but orderly and en masse, either to some more defensible battle line or to a small, impregnable fortress in which case rationalism is granted the run of the land. And rationalism runs, and rules, until it grows soft or tired or afraid. The tide of the battle then turns once more. But the war never ends.

A single campaign can be won in a decade; it may take a generation or even much longer. As the Reformation by dividing Christendom made possible a more rapid intrusion of rationalism, so the Great Awakening through its divisiveness similarly hastened the collapse of orthodoxy. Of course reason's trumpet had for some time been blowing in New England; a little more heavy marching around the walls and a few more powerful blasts should do the trick. Edwards sadly recognized that the revival had divided "us into two Armies separated and drawn up in Battle-array, ready to fight with one another. . . ." However deplorable this effect might be, Edwards, in accepting it, put on the whole armor of God sagaciously to lead his fervent followers. Chauncy, by 1743, was prepared to accept any challenge thrown down and to sneer at any formation of the forces which he would someday defeat. Thus the battle began in Oriental fashion with the mightiest warriors dueling first (the melee would come later). Chauncy lived to help direct most of the wider struggle that followed, but Edwards died before many of the great battles were fought—though he had thoughtfully stored ammunition in gratifying quantity. How much of the full fight is foretold in the preliminary skirmishes of the early 1740's? And what in this instance were the peculiarities of matériel and terrain?

Before answering these essential questions, it may be well to justify the division of forces. Was not Edwards rather than Chauncy the peerless wielder of logic, the epitome of clarity, the champion of reason? In a recent exceedingly valuable study of Edwards, the philosopher-revivalist is acclaimed as "intellectually the most modern man of his age" and indeed "much ahead of his time."[5] Jonathan Edwards' intellectual prowess needs no defense; nevertheless, it is Charles Chauncy and not Edwards who in the post-revival period stands firm in the fore-guard of the modern disdain for the inscrutably supernatural and the modern penchant for the pragmatically reasonable. New England's anxious and declining religious establishment was comparable to Europe's Protestant scholasticism of the seventeenth century; in both instances, there were increasing concessions to formal orthodoxy and accelerated withdrawals to speculative irrelevancies. The numerous intellectual fences built and guarded by these theologians were as objectionable to Edwards as to Chauncy. But Chauncy tore those fences down by seeking truth in common sense and natural philosophy, while Edwards wrecked them by seeking truth in a revelation revived by religious experience. For Edwards this did not mean revolting against or ignoring reason; reason was to be boldly used, but it was not to be glorified.

Augustine's God was also Edwards', and Augustine's "faith seeking knowledge" is an intellectual biography of his New England counterpart. However much knowledge one searches for and finds, it is with faith that one begins. The theocentricity of Edwards' private, pastoral, and philosophic life, readily and repeatedly admitted by him, places him in the center of the tradition of evangelical piety. To be sure, Edwards used the most "enlightened" intellectual tools available, in some cases seizing newer and better ones than any of his contemporaries and wielding them with consummate skill, but with all he was fashioning a philosophy based on an absolutely sovereign, personal yet transcendent, essentially inscrutable God. If God and his ways were not altogether past finding out, it was only because of his revelation which reason is permitted to interpret. Doctrines seemingly irrational and absurd were soberly defended; defended, it is granted, with great logic, a greater logic in fact than most could muster in any age. It was, however, the logic of one concerned to show the finite littleness of man, the infinite bigness of God, and was less a harbinger of Channing than a reminiscence of Aquinas.

While Edwards' use of reason was humble both before God and the data of experience, Chauncy's—like his successors'—was humble before neither. It was Chauncy who in his fondness for cultured mankind in general and for Tillotson in particular ushered in and embodied the later age. Revelation was not cast aside, not yet; but in that ever-delicate balance between revealed and natural theology, the latter for the Old Brick Bostonian weighed more heavily. Natural laws, natural truths, and natural religion were respectable and acceptable because, by definition, they harmed not a single ratiocination. Insights, like those from a mystical experience, not verifiable in the public court of reason, were thrown out. Emotions, "passions," were suspect. Christianity, "not mysterious," was indeed as "old as creation," while religion was to be "explained and defended," not necessarily believed and felt. Reason was queen, theology the handmaid. Following the Awakening, Chauncy adopted and abetted the growing allegiance to common sense in New England, helping it a measure of the way toward its certain and ultimate end, which was not Arminianism nor even Unitarianism, but humanism.

When the revival began, neither the thirty-seven-year-old Edwards nor the thirty-five-year-old Chauncy was conscious of standing in any tradition other than that of the reformed Christianity which they shared. In the early phases of the upheaval, each was feeling his way—the sentiments of the two are at times almost indistinguishable—before from the heat, the smoke, and the flames diverging pathways appeared.

By the fall of 1741 Edwards was ready, more ready than any Old Light, to dismiss a great deal of the concomitants of the revival as irrelevant to any objective evaluation of it. Years before the Great Awakening, the Northampton preacher was by virtue of his *Faithful Narrative* well-known as a friend to revivalism. His labors and his evident sympathies were by many regarded as in some measure responsible for this later and much larger religious freshening. In the days of the earlier revival along the Connecticut River valley, people were eager to hear what was happening, to have a description of how and where the Spirit of God worked. By 1741 an interest not in the events *per se* but rather in their source and significance had arisen, so that Jonathan Edwards in September of that year received an invitation to preach at the Yale commencement. Yale, unready and unwilling to hear a "foreigner or stranger," consented to listen to one of her own sons, not certain whether she would be scorched as had the Enfield citizenry only two months earlier. But Edwards went to New Haven to make converts of a slightly different sort from those he sought at Enfield; he hoped to save these hearers not so much from the fiery pit of hell as from an icy indifference toward the revival.

He spoke on *The Distinguishing Marks of a Work of the Spirit of God, Applied to that uncommon Operation that has lately appeared on the Minds of many of the People in New England . . . ,*[6] a sermon that no one but Edwards could at this time have delivered; for the revival was then still at flood tide, when no spokesman would publicly condemn it as a whole and few would impartially examine it. So overawing and rapid had been its rise, so manifest its power and mysteriously contagious its energies, so sure and joyful its promoters that none dared, if they could, to resist the sweeping force. To Edwards, furthermore, an opportunity had been granted for long study of revivals and their effects, while to most of his listeners at New Haven, revivalism was less than a year old. In a position to render the Awakening a unique service, Edwards preached a sermon, echoes of which were heard in many places, particularly as the revival became less intense and criticism correspondingly safer.[7]

It would not be correct to assert that Edwards here spoke with complete impartiality; he did champion the cause of the revival, earnestly pleading its validity and divinity. Yet even in these exciting days of 1741 a power of discrimination is evident in Edwards which later was given fuller and freer expression. In *Distinguishing Marks*, Edwards dismissed as irrelevant such things in the revival as its extraordinary intensity, its effects "on the bodies of men," its showy, noisy religiousness, its effects upon men's imaginations, and the irregularities, disorders, and errors of some who were associated with it. These things may, we know from Scripture, accompany a divine work; on the other hand, Edwards stated, they have appeared in situations that were not of God's doing. They are then not trustworthy criteria by which one may judge the contemporary religious scene. Arguing closely from his text, I John 4, Edwards presented a positive statement of valid criteria. The "distinguishing marks" were five: a true revival (1) will cause a greater esteem for Jesus (I John 4:2), (2) will operate against the interest of Satan (4:4, 5), (3) will cause a greater regard for scripture (4:6), (4) will lead persons to truth, convincing them of those things that are true (4:6), and (5) "operates as a spirit of love to God and man" (4:7 f). From his "trial of the spirit" then rushing throughout New England, Edwards judged "that the extraordinary influence that has lately appeared causing an uncommon concern and engagedness of the mind about the things of religion, is undoubtedly, in general, from the Spirit of God."[8] Extended among so many places and over so many months, the revival cannot be a pretense or delusion. As far as the Northampton experiences are concerned, "we must throw by all talk of conversion and Christian experience; and not only so, but we must throw by our Bibles, and give up revealed religion; if this be not in general the work of God."[9] In view of this judgment, the commencement speaker warned all "by no means to oppose, or do any thing in the least to clog or hinder, the work; but, on the contrary, do our utmost to promote it." In the coldest, darkest corner of New England, by New Light standards, Edwards had defended the Great Awakening and had spoken harsh words to any that tried to thwart it. He was never invited back.

The same day that Edwards spoke at the Connecticut college, Charles Chauncy delivered at Boston's First Church the Thursday lecture on the topic, "An Unbridled Tongue a sure Evidence, that our Religion is Hypocritical and Vain."[10] To consider this message in its proper context it is necessary to take notice of some words spoken at a Thursday lecture three months earlier:

> There is nothing betwixt you and the place of blackness of darkness, but a poor frail, uncertain life. You hang, as it were, over the bottomless pit, by the slender thread of life, and the moment that snaps asunder, you sink down into perdition. . . . Who has bewitched you, O sinners, that you are thus lost to all sense of your own safety and interest! Be convinc'd of your danger. You are certainly in a state of dreadful and amazing hazard. You are the person mark't out . . . for an exclusion from the kingdom of heaven: And if you live and die in your present condition, you will surely be made miserable without mercy or remedy. 'Tis no tale I am now telling you; No, but the very truth of the true and faithful God. O realise it to be so! and awake out of your security. Awake thou that sleepest, and call on thy God![11]

Incredible as it now seems, the author of these words is Charles Chauncy. In 1741 Chauncy, allowing himself to be carried along in the main current of the revival, described in this sermon the change which takes place in a new convert as great and momentous, almost sudden. "Light is not more contrary to darkness, nor heaven to hell, than the lives of these persons now are to what they once were."[12] The First Church minister did not denounce the great terrors and sorrows that accompany conviction and salvation, but like Edwards stated only that they were not *essential* to salvation. Some are "recovered to God, in a more mild, and kind, and gentle manner" while some are wrought upon speedily, having great terrors of conscience and strong agonies and convulsions of soul.[13] Again like Edwards, Chauncy concluded that no one type of manifestation was necessary to a divine work, that the only *sine qua non* was a "real and effectual renovation of heart and life. . . ." He advised new converts to beware of spiritual pride, to avoid becoming too presumptuous, too secure, unteachable. "Take care to keep your zeal under the government of sound judgment."[14] Or, as Edwards had said, avoid "managing the controversy . . . with too much heat, and appearance of an angry zeal."

By September Chauncy, less enthusiastic about the present work of God, had by no means abandoned his evangelistic endeavors.[15] In the Thursday lecture given the day Edwards was trying to win Yale's official blessing—which when added to God's would save any cause— Chauncy, though seeking converts, did go out of his way to reprove those who spoke evil of their neighbors. Unbridled tongues, running in any direction, were bad—lying, flattering, filthy speaking; but censoriousness needed special attention. A little later, in December, Charles "Old Brick" tried to correct the critical attitude on the part of the laity toward some of the clergy, pointing out that not all ministers were equally or similarly endowed, but that God in his wisdom and "for your benefit, has distributed so great a variety of gifts to ministers. . . . And bear with me, while I go on to caution you against such an itch after other preachers, as may lead you to forsake your own ministers on the Lord's-day, to the breaking in upon the good order in the Town."[16]

At the end of 1741, there was thus no sharp clash between Edwards and Chauncy and no "distinguishing names of reproach" had yet been invented. Chauncy was concerned with good order and Enlightenment; Edwards, with holy affections and piety; but the battle lines were still to be taken. In 1742-43, however, their views of the revival were refined, clarified, and more fully expressed. Properly speaking, there was no "great debate" in the sense of a series of published attacks and counterattacks. Only Chauncy's *Seasonable Thoughts* (1743) was a direct refutation of Edwards, and only the latter's *Religious Affections* (1746) squarely faced Chauncy's position. Each champion recognized, however, the worthiness and stature of his opposition.

In July, 1742, on the Sunday following the Harvard commencement, Chauncy took a more direct aim at the revival, describing enthusiasm and cautioning against it. Though he singled out Davenport as "the occasion of my studying, and preaching, and afterwards giving way to the publication" of this sermon, Chauncy denounced all excesses carried on under cover of divine inspiration. In sending Davenport a complimentary (?) copy of the sermon, Chauncy wished that "it may be of service to you, as I hope it will to others, guarding themselves against the wilds of a heated imagination." The sermon proper equated enthusiasm, "a kind of religious Phrenzy," to antinomianism and all the horrors pertaining thereto.

No greater mischief has arisen from any quarter. It is indeed the genuine force of infinite evil. Popery it self han't been the mother of more and greater blasphemies and abominations. It has made strong attempts to destroy all property, to make all things common, wives as well as goods.—It has promoted faction and contention; filled the church oftentimes with confusion, and the state sometimes with general disorder.—It has, by its pretended spiritual interpretations made void the most undoubted laws of God. It has laid aside the gospel sacraments as weak and carnal things; yea, this superior light within has, in the opinion of thousands, render'd the bible a useless dead letter.—It has made men fancy themselves to be prophets and apostles; yea, some have taken themselves to be Christ Jesus; yea, the blessed God himself. It has, in one word, been a pest to the church in all ages, as great an enemy to real and solid religion as perhaps the greatest infidelity.[17]

The Great Awakening, of course, had not brought all these plagues. Here, however, was what one could expect if the affair was further encouraged. Chauncy enjoyed a good fight, but he did not like being a martyr. The attack was fun, especially if a counterattack could be avoided. Near the end of his sermon against enthusiasm, he exhorted,

> Let us esteem those as friends of religion, and not enemies, who warn us of the danger of enthusiasm, and would put us on our guard, that we may not be led aside by it . . . they run the hazard of being call'd enemies to the holy Spirit, and may be expected to be ill spoken of by many, and loaded with names of reproach: But they are notwithstanding the best friends to religion. . . . They have been stigmatised as Opposers of the Work of God; but 'tis a great mercy of God, there have been such Opposers: This land had, in all probability, been over-run with confusion and distraction, if they had acted under the influence of the same heat and zeal, which some others have been famous for.[18]

Chauncy was not without a spiritual pride of his own.

It was not pride, but timidity, which led Chauncy to attack the Awakening obliquely in 1742, partly by writing an anonymous letter, mostly by acting as literary editor for all antagonists of the revival.[19] In his letter to George Wishart, an Edinburgh minister, describing the "State of Religion in New-England"[20] Chauncy spoke more boldly than in any of his public utterances up to that time. ". . . there never was such a Spirit of Superstition and Enthusiasm reigning in the Land before; never such gross Disorders and barefaced Affronts to common Decency; never such scandalous Reproaches on the Blessed Spirit, making him the Author of the greatest Irregularities and Confusions. . . ."[21] Characterizing the "Goodness that has been so much talked of" as, in general, "the Effect of enthusiastick Heat" and "a Commotion in the Passions," the letter won the enmity of the revival party who deeply resented any discrediting abroad of the New England Awakening. An attack on the revival even more crafty and furtive was the publication at Boston in 1742 of an account of the infamous "French Prophets" of the Cevennes.[22] The account was devoid of subtlety in its attempt to damn by association, for the French Prophets were the epitome of enthusiasm, as Munster was of anabaptism. New England would, if the New Lights were not put out, become a land seething with Methodists,[23] Familists, Antinomians, wild prophets, Quakers, and the like. To Chauncy, mostly by default, this work has been attributed. Yet no more than the appendix can possibly be his, the main letter of over ninety pages originating from New Haven.[24] Chauncy is, however, probably responsible for the editing and publication of the entire account and must therefore be credited with a share of the effect of this damaging, if indirect, calumny. Before 1743 arrived Chauncy had thus assumed a place of leadership, somewhat uncomfortably at times, among those of strangely unheated imaginations. He was, however, still fighting to a great extent under cover or with benefit of camouflage, not openly throwing down or accepting any public challenges.

In March, 1743, there was issued at Boston a broadside entitled *The Late Religious Commotions in New-England considered. An Answer to the Reverend Mr. Jonathan Edwards's Sermon Entitled, The distinguishing Marks. . . .*[25] Generally, though erroneously, attributed to Chauncy, it was probably the work of Chauncy's classmate, William Rand.[26] As a direct attack on Edwards' defense of the Awakening, it was, however, only the initial phase of a full offensive. For when this polemic appeared it was almost immediately out of date. Late in March, Edwards, having greatly expanded and altered his New Haven sermon, published *Some Thoughts Concerning the Present Revival of Religion in New-England*. Chauncy, recognizing that the volume must be answered in kind, quickly wrote to his cousin, the Reverend Nathanael Chauncy of Durham, Connecticut, as follows:

Mr. Edwards' book of 378 pages upon the *good work* is at last come forth; And I believe will do much hurt; and I am the rather inclined to think so, because there are some good things in it. Error is much more likely to be propagated, when it is mixed with truth. This hides its deformity and makes it go down the more easily. I may again trouble myself and the world upon the appearance of this book. I am preparing an antidote, and if the world should see cause to encourage it, it may in time come to light.[27]

What was the poison Edwards administered to New England, that required of Chauncy an immediate antidote?

Edwards, having viewed the attacks on particular aspects of the Awakening—itineracy, enthusiasm, Whitefield, censoriousness—and the equally specific counterattacks, decided that it was time that "something should be published, to bring the affair in general, and the many things that attend it, that are subjects of debate, under a particular consideration." It would be more fitting, conceded the thirty-nine-year-old author, if "some elder minister had undertaken this . . . but I have heard of no such thing a doing, or like to be done. I hope therefore I shall be excused for undertaking such a piece of work."[28] Not only has Edwards here amplified his earlier sermon, but he has also altered the tenor of his remarks. In September, 1741, opposition to the Great Awakening was manifest chiefly by a reluctance to join in a promotion of the revival. Edwards therefore defended the revival with the hope of persuading the hesitant to approve and support it. At the end of 1742, however, the ranks of active, deliberate antirevivalists were beginning to form, and at those as yet disorganized forces Edwards directs the first half of his treatise. The initial proposition is an uncompromising, categorical assertion "that the extraordinary work that has of late been going on in this land, is a glorious work of God." Many denounce the Awakening because they judge the work *a priori*, looking rather at its source (Whitefield and other young itinerants) than at its effects (changed lives). There are also those whose consideration of the work is based upon a philosophy that precludes or disparages emotion. This was a new argument, and one which lay very close to Edwards' ultimate defense of the revival. It also lay close to the essence of Edwards' differences with Chauncy. "All will allow that true virtue or holiness has its seat chiefly in the heart, rather than in the head: it therefore follows . . . that it consists chiefly in holy affections [i.e., emotions]. The things of religion take place in men's hearts, no further than they are affected with them."[29] With an image of persons such as the staid, prosaic, stolid, rational, deadly serious Chauncy in mind, Edwards rebuked those who "reject such and such things as are now professed and experienced, because they never felt them themselves." God beckons, but some will not hear; the Spirit powerfully moves, yet there are those who will neither bend nor budge. "At a time when God manifests himself in such a great work for his church, there is no such thing as being neuters." To civil authorities and ministers Edwards speaks sharp words of rebuke for their indifference toward the revival, an indifference that is preventing the New England revival from becoming world-wide.[30]

And I humbly desire that it may be considered, whether we have not reason to fear that God is provoked with this land, that no more notice has been taken of this glorious work . . . by the civil authority; that there has no more been done by them, as a public acknowledgment of God in this work, and no more improvement of their authority to promote it, either by appointing a day of public thanksgiving to God . . . or a day of fasting and prayer, to humble ourselves . . . or so much as to enter upon any public consultation, what should be done to advance the present revival of religion. . . .

But above all others, is God's eye upon ministers of the gospel, as expecting of them, that they should arise, and acknowledge and honor him in such a work as this, and do their utmost to encourage and promote it: for to promote such a work, is the very business which they are called and devoted too . . . to awaken and convert sinners. . . .

. . . a time of glorious out pouring of the Spirit of God to revive religion, will be a time of remarkable judgments on those ministers that do not serve the end of their ministry.[31]

Finally, "every living soul" is obliged to acknowledge the present revival as the work of God.

Before braving the wrath and wisdom of the Old Brick valiant, Edwards sought to dampen the enemy's powder by confessing that there was much in the Awakening which he would not attempt to defend. There was an obligation, he believed, nonetheless to discriminate carefully between the good and the bad. "They that highly approve the affair in general, cannot bear to have anything at all found fault with; and on the other hand, those that fasten their eyes upon some things in the affair that are amiss and appear very disagreeable to them, at once reject the whole." Neither attitude is justifiable. Edwards, therefore, though clearly approving "the affair in general," devoted a full section of this treatise to a careful, candid, and detailed examination of the errors accompanying the revival, conceding to the "Opposers" that there had been both ecclesiastical disorders and doctrinal aberrations. In reality Edwards was further from Davenport and Croswell than from Hancock or Chauncy, and closest to Dickinson, Colman, and Prince Croswell was unable to discriminate; Chauncy, after 1743, unwilling; while Edwards for over a decade and a half labored to distinguish meticulously the good from the bad. This was the more difficult since the palpable works of the flesh so often obscured the finer fruits of the Spirit.

If Old Lights took time to read the fourth part of Edwards' treatise, they found most of the wind taken from their sails. Edwards acknowledged and excoriated the spiritual pride of so many New Lights, which pride he regarded as a major cause of error in the Awakening. Vilification, abusive and censorious judgments and language arise from this sin. "Spiritual pride is very apt to suspect others: whereas a humble saint is most jealous of himself, he is so suspicious of nothing in the world as he is of his own heart."[32] A second major cause of disorder is error in belief, such as (1) that immediate revelation, contrary to Scripture, is right, (2) that specific prayers are invariably answered, (3) that any act bringing immediate benefit should be performed regardless of future consequences, (4) that God's approval of persons or things can with certainty be known, and (5) that external order in religious matters, notably education of the ministry, is of little importance. A third source of evil is a failure to observe the counterfeits of genuine spiritual experiences, to discriminate carefully, to guard against satanic wiles. Christians and especially new converts must recognize the mixture of the corrupt and the divine in their own experience, and must not slavishly imitate others' experience. Three particular errors of the revival Edwards strongly, unflinchingly condemned. ". . . censuring others that are professing Christians, in good standing in the visible church, as unconverted" is, he laments, "the worst disease that has attended this work."[33] Pronouncing with certainty on the state of a person's soul is improper, while abusing public prayer by making it an occasion of passing judgment on others is inexcusable. Lay exhorting, furthermore, has been a grave disorder when it has become more than simply conversation. Authoritative full-time teaching and preaching are to be restricted to a properly ordained and educated ministry. With a suspicious eye on New Haven, Edwards advised ministers to be trained in colleges that are nurseries of piety.[34] Despite these full concessions—and they did not distract Chauncy for one moment— Edwards had indeed administered a strong and large dose; the antidote would have to be powerful and quick. It was already amixing.

The week before the publication of Edwards' treatise was announced in the *Boston Weekly News-Letter*, Chauncy, who must have seen an advance copy of the book, published the title page, i.e., the table of contents, of his *Seasonable Thoughts on the State of Religion in New-England, A Treatise in Five Parts*.[35] And in the next two issues of the *News-Letter*, advertisements of the publication of Edwards' volume appeared just above the announcement of the forthcoming *Seasonable Thoughts*.[36] This juxtaposition of the two great treatises on the New England Awakening, hardly coincidental, served to manifest the precise nature of Chauncy's refutation. His five-part treatise was patterned after Edwards' five-part work, point by point. It was not until September that the details of the ready-made outline could be filled in, and *Seasonable Thoughts* concluded.[37] And not until then did Chauncy publicly disavow the Awakening *as a whole* and refute Edwards in particular.

In the manner of the *Account of the French Prophets*, Chauncy damned the revival by identifying it with the enthusiasm and antinomianism of New England's earlier history. This uncomplimentary comparison "will not only prepare the Reader for what he may meet with in the following Sheets, but powerfully tend to undeceive him, if he has entertain'd a good Opinion of such Things as have once already, raised Disturbances in the Country. . . ." Of the almost numberless errors that went under the name of antinomianism in the seventeenth century Chauncy selected sixteen as those "which might be thought to bear a Resemblance to the unsafe Tenets of the present Day."[38] Even as Eck tried to dismiss the Protestant Reformation by comparing it with the Hussite movement, so Chauncy labored to prejudice his readers against the Awakening by treating it in terms of earlier antinomianism, libertinism, and enthusiasm.

The major share of Chauncy's efforts, however, both in research and in writing, was directed toward a meticulously specific examination of the revival whose decline had then begun. To combat Edwards' reports of "surprising conversions," Chauncy spared no trouble to amass reports of "shriekings and Screamings."

I have been a Circle of more than three hundred Miles, and had, by this Means, an Opportunity of going thro' a great Number of towns in this, and the neighbouring Government of Connecticut, and of having personal Conversation with most of the Ministers, and many other Gentlemen, in the Country, and of settling a Correspondence with several of them, with a particular View to know, as nearly as might be, the Truth of Things, upon better Evidence than that of meer Hear-say.[39]

The Awakening was characterized as a time when there was "flocking after some particular ministers, and glorifying in them as though they were Gods rather than Men." It was a time when "Men's Professions and Affections rose" high and numerous conversions were "much boasted of." This spiritual condition of persons has everywhere been judged with too much haste and positiveness, and few have paused to consider "how precarious that Religion must be, which has its Rise from the Passions, and not any thorow Change in the Understanding and Will."[40] If not in New, at least in Old England, Chauncy's statement would be received with grateful sobriety. To call this crude excitement of 1740-42 a work of God is to misname it, Chauncy affirmed, for the converting work of divine grace is a secret thing, the same at all times and in all places, and invariably productive of the fruits of the spirit: righteousness and holiness. The grand question was still the same: was the revival, after all, a Work of God?

Most of Chauncy's labor in *Seasonable Thoughts*, three hundred and thirty-two pages out of four hundred and twenty-four, was devoted to a discussion of "Things of a bad and dangerous tendency" in the Awakening. That this was not the real issue did not matter; that it dealt only with the symptoms of the revival and rejected Edwards' waiving of their prime relevance was apparent. Chauncy, however, found in these discrediting reports the major justification for his work, believing them to be the real and urgently necessary antidote. His wide mouth must have been firmly set as the vials of his wrath poured out against that disastrous practice, itineracy. Whitefield and Tennent were treated with special venom, but all itinerants, named or unnamed, born or unborn, were—if words can damn—consigned to perdition. His large head must have wagged in anguish and his small body tensed with nervousness as he denounced with detestation those "great terrors of conscience, strong agonies and convulsions of soul" which in July, 1741, he had found acceptable.[41] No longer to be tolerated is the awful terror which produces "strange Effects upon the Body such as a swooning away . . . Shriekings and Screamings; convulsion-like Tremblings and Agitations, Strugglings and Tumblings, which in some Instances have been attended with Indecencies I shan't mention."[42] Any average imagination could appreciate and successfully embroider such a description. On the other hand, there were those strange persons who during the revival flood were not terror-stricken, but joyful and enraptured. This, however, was no better. That sudden light and joy which comes to many is not a truly religious joy, for instead of making men better Christians—the function of true joy—it expresses itself in "extasies," laughing, kisses of congratulation, and the like. So whether one was filled with fear or with delight, the results, to Chauncy, were about the same. Chauncy of course does not altogether rule out emotional reactions in conversion, but it is instructive to note that he defines true religious joy as essentially sober and dutiful Christian living.[43] Whereas Edwards had written, "Our people do not so much need to have their heads stored, as to have their hearts touched. . . ,"[44] Chauncy had declared that the revivalists "place their Religion so much in the Heat and Fervour of their Passions, that they too much neglect their Reason and Judgment."[45] The battle formation was becoming discernible—but Charles Chauncy was not yet through.

There was this matter of rash and uncharitable judging which many, including Edwards, had strongly condemned but which none resented more bitterly than Chauncy. Highly sensitive to criticism—Part III of *Seasonable Thoughts* is devoted in its entirety to "Shewing, in many Instances, wherein those, who have appear'd against the Disorders prevailing in the Land have been injuriously treated"—Chauncy simply could not forgive this cutting censoriousness, seeing in Whitefield the first, formal, and efficient cause for the presence in New England of this unlovely spirit. "The only thing I can say in Excuse for Mr. Whitefield is, that he was young in Years and Christian Experience, as well as of raw Acquaintance with Divinity. . . ."[46] Taking all things into consideration, one can only conclude that the "new light" philosophy is fallacious, heretical, dangerous; the impulses and impressions, the heated imaginations, the "Aptness to take the Motion of their own Minds for something divinely extraordinary"—these are clearly of a bad and dangerous tendency.[47] And the "enthusiastical Spirit," more than anything else, is a great danger for " 'Tis indeed the true Spirit of Quakerism; the Seed-Plot of Delusion. . . ."[48] The final danger against which Chauncy warned his reader was that of doctrinal error. Not satisfied to clothe this accusation in the ambiguity of a word like "antinomianism," he specified several types of New Light unorthodoxy or heresy overrunning and overwhelming the land.

In the first three hundred pages, Chauncy gave the results of his observations and travels with the expectation that these results when published would invalidate the revival. In much of what he found to censure he had been anticipated by Edwards. But whereas Edwards and Chauncy agreed on many of the disorders and errors, they did not agree on the conclusions to be drawn therefrom. Recognizing this significant discrepancy, Chauncy sought to refute some of Edwards' theses.[49] The latter had argued that these "bad things" in the present day are, taken collectively, only accidental effects of a good work. Chauncy, however, regarded the frequency and uniformity of these evils as sufficient evidence that they are not accidental but natural parts of the upheaval. Agreeing with Edwards that mistakes and excesses are to be expected when the passions are raised, Chauncy stated significantly that the fallacy lay in ascribing the rise of emotions to the influence of the divine spirit. Whereas Edwards claimed that the Great Awakening was unique and that there were no rules for it, Chauncy retorted that the phenomenon was not unique and that there were quite enough rules, including biblical ones, by which it should be governed and judged. To Edwards' assertion that superstition and intemperate zeal always accompany great revivals of religion, Chauncy answered that indeed they do, but that such qualities appear in the ungodly, not, as Edwards had claimed, in the true converts. Edwards had attempted to excuse or at least explain the Awakening's errors in terms of the ministry of many young converts. But whose fault was it that young converts were permitted to preach? If they were unfit vessels, argued Chauncy, their preaching should have been prohibited. (With this, Edwards, but not all New Lights, had agreed.) The Northampton minister had asserted that when the convert discovers his own danger and depravity, the preciousness of his soul, the greatness and excellence of God, it is then "no Wonder that now they think they must exert themselves, and do something extraordinary. . . . 'Tis a Wonder, if they don't proceed without due Caution, and do Things that are irregular, and will, in the Issue, do more Hurt than Good." In reply to this, the Old Brick pastor is richly sarcastic. " 'Twould be no Wonder, if those who had *extraordinary* Discoveries of God, were to an *extraordinary* Degree, filled with Lowliness and Humility, and such an Awe and Reverence of the divine Majesty, as would make them *eminently* circumspect in their whole Deportment towards him. . . ."[50] Edwards had defended the revival in general as of divine origin. In a rare display of humor, Chauncy wryly observed that indeed it was from God and the punishment no more than was deserved.

With the conclusion of the first part of his treatise Chauncy had finished his work. In order to maintain the effect of complete refutation of Edwards' treatise, Chauncy rounded out *Seasonable Thoughts* with four additional sections, offering, however, little that was novel or significant or even particularly seasonable. The final topic of both treatises was a consideration of how best to promote true religion. This part, Chauncy acknowledged, "would have required Enlargement, but that many Things are well said upon it by Mr. Edwards, in his late Book; which, if He, and I, and Others, would carefully attend to, it might do much towards putting an End to our present Difficulties."[51]

The case had been stated at length for both sides. There was to be no series of petty rebuttals nor prolonged cross-examinations. The points of agreement were no less evident than the contrary convictions tenaciously held. When, after still further reflection on the religious turbulence of his day, Edwards again took up a defense of the revival, there was no discussion of itineracy, censoriousness, antinomianism, or even of *Seasonable Thoughts*. The issue lay in a reckoning of the proper balance between logic and emotion, experience and reason. Chauncy thus summarized his case: "There is the Religion of the Understanding and Judgment, and Will, as well as of the Affections; and if little Account is made of the former, while great Stress is laid upon the latter, it can't be but People should run into Disorders."[52]

Calvinism is often thought of as an *a priori*, dogmatic system, but in Edwards it was, though still dogmatic, clearly empirical, *a posteriori*. Edwards frequently appealed to experience, his own or another's, as convincing evidence of the validity of a position—as when he offered the spiritual ecstasies of his own wife to dispel all possible doubt concerning the efficacy of the revival. For him the Great Awakening was a large and timely laboratory of experience, experience that could not be ignored, controverted, or denied. A great deal had happened; lives had been changed; sleepy saints had been stirred. Whatever had been the extravagances of Davenport, the blunders of Whitefield, or the telling charges of Chauncy, there was a residual good—the revival of the unconcerned and the conversion of the unredeemed—that Edwards could not betray and would not disavow. Here he drew his line of defense and from it he never retreated.

In 1746, Edwards published his final philosophy of the Awakening, *A Treatise Concerning Religious Affections*,[53] which became in America a philosophy for future revivalism as well. This psychological study of religion stands, moreover, unrivaled in its field until William James published his *Varieties of Religious Experiences* in 1902. It was Edwards' conviction and his principal contention that "true religion, in great part, consists in holy affection." Chauncy, it will be remembered, had charged that this was precisely where the fallacy lay—in ascribing the rise of affections to the divine spirit. If that be fallacy and delusion, Edwards was willing for the land to be filled with this kind of madness. To demonstrate the integral part that emotion plays in the religious experience, in all true religion, Edwards pointed out to Chauncy and all of like opinion that there is not a "Religion of the Understanding and Judgment, and Will" and a religion "as well of the Affections." Rather, religious experience, like all experience, is an organic whole. For Chauncy, the faculties of the mind were separate entities, and it was clearly up to judgment and will, sitting in the chariot seat, to hold a tight rein on the pawing, restless steeds which are the emotions. Edwards granted the existence in the mind of only the understanding and the will, emotions being simply the "more vigorous and sensible exercises" of the will. And the ascription of the rise of emotions to divine promptings is so far from being fallacious that it is indeed ridiculous to assume that God can move men at all without raising their affections. "The things of religion are so great, that there can be no suitableness in the exercises of our hearts, to their nature and importance, unless they be lively and powerful." Religion involves powerful emotions; it does not and cannot subsist on indifference, or on weak, dull, lifeless wishes. The person who "has doctrinal knowledge and speculation only, without affection, never is engaged in the business of religion." Religious alterations of any import and conversion itself become possible only as the emotions are aroused. Hear ye, all dull and detached, casual and pedantic. "I am bold to assert, that there never was any considerable change wrought in the mind or conversation of any person, by any thing of a religious nature, that ever he read, heard or saw, that had not his affections moved."[54] The Scriptures (if Chauncy wanted to play the game according to the biblical rules) offer ample evidence of the proper place of the emotions, often urging a fear of the Lord, or an earnest care or a tender love. The religious duties which God commands—praying, singing, observing the sacraments, preaching—are purposely designed to influence the emotions. Prayer, writes Edwards, sounding strangely like a twentieth-century Protestant liberal, is not for the purpose of moving or inclining the heart of God; its purpose, rather, is "suitably to affect our own hearts with the things we express, and so to prepare us to receive the blessings we ask." Singing of hymns or praises must be specifically designed to excite and express the religious affections. The sacraments, moreover, are sensible representations of divine truths, which, being sensible, affect us more readily than would their abstract counterparts. Likewise preaching is ordained specifically for the purpose of impressing divine things on the hearts and affections of men. While commentaries may give one a good doctrinal understanding of divine things, they are insufficient and inferior to preaching for they have not an equal tendency to impress their truths upon one's affections. The emotions were thus for Edwards an essential part of all significant experience, and experience was a wide, palpable path to truth.

Jonathan Edwards thought it worth while further to note the evidence in Scripture that sin consists very much in a denial of these religious affections. Many times the hardness of heart of individuals and of groups is denounced as gross sin (Mark 3:5; Ezekiel 3:7; II Chronicles 36:13; Hebrews 3:8, 12, 13).

Now by a hard heart is plainly meant an unaffected heart, or a heart not easy to be moved with virtuous affections, like a stone, insensible, stupid, unmoved, and hard to be impressed. . . . Since it is so plain, that by a hard heart . . . is meant a heart destitute of pious affections, and since also the Scriptures do so frequently place the sin and corrupton of the heart in hardness of heart; it is evident, that the grace and holiness of the heart, on the contrary, must in a great measure consist in its having pious affections, and being easily susceptive of such affection.[55]

Perry Miller described *Seasonable Thoughts* as "a classic of hard-headed, dogmatic rationalism,"[56] but Edwards would probably have preferred "hard-hearted" as a characterization of both the work and its author. Chauncy, who had written that "an enlightened Mind, not raised Affections ought always to be the Guide of those who call themselves Men," was no disposition to see in swoonings and tremblings the moving of a divine spirit. And Edwards, who could conceive of God as powerfully reviving men in no other way than by raised affections, felt Chauncy's heart to be scarcely less obdurate than that of Pharoah in Moses' day.

Edwards concluded this final apologia with a second attempt to arrive at the "distinguishing signs of truly gracious and holy affections." At New Haven he had, following the text of the day closely, observed that an esteem for Christ, a hatred of Satan, a belief in the Bible, and a love of God constituted the distinguishing marks of a work of the spirit of God. Now, following reason more closely than Scripture, and dealing only with the the saving work of the Holy Spirit, Edwards tremendously broadened the range of activity and heightened the significance of religious affections. In order to accomplish this task with a swift sureness, it was still necessary to know how holy emotions are to be discerned from unholy ones, and whence the former arise.

Holy and gracious affections arise, Edwards declares, from influences that are supernatural and divine, from the spirit of God which dwells within the elect as a new principle.

> . . . those gracious influences which the saints are subjects of, and the effects of God's Spirit which they experience, are entirely above nature, altogether of a different kind from any thing that men find within themselves by nature, or only in the exercise of natural principles; and are things which no improvement of those qualifications, or principles that are natural, no advancing or exalting them to higher degrees, and no kind of composition of them, will ever bring men to; because they not only differ from what is natural, and from every thing that natural men experience, in degree and circumstances, but also in kind; and are of a nature vastly more excellent. And this is what I mean, by supernatural, when I say that gracious affections are from those influences that are supernatural.
> From hence it follows, that in those gracious exercises and affections which are wrought in the minds of the saints, through the saving influences of the Spirit of God, there is a new inward perception or sensation of their minds, entirely different in its nature and kind, from any thing that ever their minds were the subjects of before they were sanctified.[57]

The new principle of which Edwards writes is a new disposition, a new spiritual sense, a new kind of exercise of the faculty of the understanding. In an earlier sermon, Edwards had called it "A Divine and Supernatural Light"[58] and often referred to it elsewhere as a "sense of the heart."[59] This new sense is not to be confused with conscience, inspiration, or a special "feeling" for things religious. It is Calvin's "new eye," Wesley's "organ of faith," William James' "knowledge by acquaintance"; it is a "true sense of the divine excellency of the things revealed in the word of God, and a conviction of the truth and reality of them thence arising." By ordinary and natural means one may believe that God is glorious; but he who has this spiritual light "has a sense of the gloriousness of God in his heart." The former is "merely speculative and notional," the latter is a "sense of the heart." The former concerns only understanding and judgment, the latter concerns the will, inclination, or heart. "Thus there is a difference between having an opinion, that God is holy and gracious, and having a sense of the loveliness and beauty of that holiness and grace. There is a difference between having a rational judgment that honey is sweet, and having a sense of its sweetness."[60] To Chauncy this "sense of the heart" might at first appear tolerable, but only until he considered how readily the divine and supernatural light of Edwards could become the pernicious and pretentious light of Davenport.

Summing up the theme of the treatise and of much of its author's experience, Edwards offered this definition of religion: "The essence of all true religion lies in holy love; and in this divine affection and an habitual disposition to it and that light which is the foundation of it and those things which are the fruits of it, consists the whole of religion."[61] Religion was intrinsically emotion, not reason. It was an affair of the heart, experiential, personal. Based on a mystical, yet also noetic experience, it expressed itself in noble, consistently moral living. It affected not alone man's understanding, but also his will, that is to say, his whole being. Edwards could heartily assent to the venerable words, "Therefore if any man be in Christ, he is a new creature; old things are passed away; behold, all things are become new."[62] Miller has written that it is "utterly incorrect" to call Edwards a mystic, "at least, in any sense that would imply the merging of the finite individual with a distinctionless divine."[63] A mysticism of this type—rather more to be found in the Eastern than in the Western tradition—is not to be found in Edwards. He was, however, a mystic in an accepted sense of the word, for he was one of that company who believe themselves to have had an experience of God and for whom that experience is the most absolute, certain, and joyful source of knowledge and basis for behavior. To Chauncy the experience was denied. He could challenge Edwards only with a reason removed from experience and a religion devoid of feeling.

In 1741 Edwards and Chauncy did not greatly differ either theologically or in their attitudes toward the young revival. Basic differences of temperament were present, however, precluding a continued harmony between the two men. Their separation, partially evident in 1742 and fully apparent in 1743, took first the form of a contrary view of the Awakening, that upheaval that disturbed men's minds as well as their hearts. But Chauncy had not yet been led, by way of Arminianism, to Universalism; nor had Edwards yet, by abandoning Stoddardeanism, embraced an unyielding Calvinism. The intellectual bifurcation, begun as a dispute over the significance and propriety of "Shriekings and Screamings," was soon to become a contest over the nature of God and the constitution of man. The public duel of the two great champions was over; the noise of preparation for battle could be heard.

CHAPTER 7

INSTITUTIONAL EFFECTS
of the GREAT AWAKENING

EVEN AS THE GREAT AWAKENING OVERFLOWED THE confines of Congregationalism into New England's other religious groups, so its effects were felt not alone in religion but in all phases of subsequent American life. Political, social, and intellectual life bear evidence of its powerful sweep. The revival determined the rise of Connecticut's political parties, exercising thereby an effect of great proportion and enduring significance.[1] It made possible an accessible, earnest, evangelistic gospel for the frontier of that and of later times. It brought into being well-defined schools of thought, a new and noteworthy phenomenon in New England religious history, and contributed to the establishment of three notable institutions of higher learning. Richard Niebuhr observes that America "cannot eradicate, if it would, the marks left upon its social memory, upon its institutions and habits, by an awakening to God that was simultaneous with its awakening to national self-consciousness."[2] While Niebuhr refers here to the Awakenings in all the colonies, it may be said with accuracy that the effects of the New England revival alone were limited neither to religion nor to New England. In this study, however, attention is centered upon the religious effects, institutional and theological, of those memorable years, 1741 and 1742.

In 1743 there was manifest disagreement over the validity of the revival.[3] In 1745 there was a clash, equally evident, concerning the effects of that great upheaval.[4] William Shurtleff of Portsmouth who saw the revival as a vessel of blessing resented the testimony of anti-Whitefieldians that religion in 1745 was in poorer condition than in 1740.

As People long'd more to hear; so Ministers lov'd more to preach than they used to do, and usually spoke with greater Power. Some of them that were Strangers to true and vital Piety before, became now acquainted with it; and others that were grown in a great Measure dead and formal, were quicken'd stir'd up, and had new Life put into them. Some great and important Doctrines that before, if not wholly omitted, were but gently touch'd; were now more largely insisted on, more clearly unfolded, and more warmly press'd. Our Assemblies were vastly throng'd; and it was rare to see a careless and inattentive Hearer among them all. Their thirsty Souls seem'd greedily to drink down every Word that drop'd from the Preacher's Lips.

All this and more, Shurtleff declared, followed in the wake of Whitefield and Tennent's coming to New England.[5] The voice of the opposition was stronger and more strident. Ministers who convened in New Haven in February, 1745, summarized the effects of the Awakening as follows:

Antinomian Principles are advanc'd, preach'd up and printed;—Christian Brethren have their Affections widely alienated;—Unchristian Censoriousness and hard judging abounds, Love stands afar of [sic], and Charity cannot enter;—Many Churches and Societies are broken and divided;— Pernicious and unjustifiable Separations are set up and continued. . . . Numbers of illiterate Exhorters swarm about as Locusts from the Bottomless Pit:—We think upon the whole, that Religion is now in a far worse State than it was in 1740.[6]

Nearly two decades after the Awakening, Ezra Stiles looked back upon it as a time when "Multitudes were seriously, soberly and solemnly out of their wits."[7]

The revival had set off explosive effects: that much was clear.[8] But were the effects for good or ill? It was within Congregationalism that the aftermath was first and most keenly felt. The most immediate result of the revival was the making of new converts: this awakening power was sufficiently evident to win for the movement the name by which it is known. Nevertheless, an attempt to estimate the number of "new births" in the period is fraught with difficulty. Later writers are content to state simply and vaguely that "thousands" were added to the churches at this time,[9] while earlier writers took refuge in that biblical generality, "multitudes." In the *Christian History*, statistics of the number of persons becoming full church members are seldom given. Where they are given, however, they reveal that the Great Awakening was not a mass movement of repentant sinners clamoring for acceptance by the churches. During 1741 and for some years after, the *Boston Gazette* noted the number of additions to the Boston churches during the preceding week. Since the total weekly number for all the churches hovered around ten or twelve during the height of the revival, it is evident that the crowded "sawdust trails" of later revivalism were absent. Joseph Seccombe, who in 1744 acclaimed the "good Fruits and Effects" of the revival in his parish at Harvard, Massachusetts, noted that since 1739 there had been nearly one hundred additions to his church, a yearly average of about twenty. At the height of the excitement Seccombe wrote, "scarce a Sacrament pass'd (which is with us once in eight Weeks) without some Additions to the Church . . . tho' twelve is the greatest Number that has been received at once."[10] In East Lyme, which parish "consists of betwixt 60 and 70 Families, leaving out the Churchmen and Baptists," one hundred white persons and thirteen Indians were admitted to the church between April, 1741, and January, 1744. In the most successful month, July, 1741, there were thirty-two additions.[11] Successes of similar proportion were attained in Groton, North Stonington, and Franklin, Connecticut.[12]

Much more numerous and more frequently mentioned than the conversions were the signs of repentance and concern. William Cooper of Brattle Street Church remarked that in one week, at the height of the revival, more persons came to him in anxiety and concern than in the preceding twenty-four years of his ministry.[13] Meanwhile, John Webb of New North Church declared "that he had five Hundred and Fifty Persons noted down in his Book (besides some Strangers) that have been with him in their Soul Troubles within a Quarter of a Year."[14] This concern might fully awaken the sinner and it might also revive the saint. Prince noted that many of those coming to confer with their ministers about the state of their souls "had been in full communion and going on in a course of religion many years."[15] The recurrent phrase "especially among young people," in connection with this visible concern for religion, suggests that many converts were formerly in the Half-Way Covenant. Depending upon the practice of each church, such a convert might or might not be reckoned a new church member. Visiting preachers or itinerant evangelists, as a rule, ventured only to indicate the numbers "under great Concern for their Souls," recognizing that longer observation was needed to determine the true conversions—if indeed such a determination was possible at all. It was at least apparent to most of the standing as well as to the traveling ministry that the anxiety was extensive and that many were asking, "What must I do to be saved?"

This concern, manifesting itself in more conspicuous ways than pastoral consultations and anxious queries, provoked a deeper loyalty to the externals of religion. Church attendance increased, while many agitated for more church services. If the meetinghouses did not open their doors with a frequency sufficient to satisfy the zealous and earnestly desirous, then religious exercises would be held in private homes. Cooper noted that

Religion is now much more the Subject of Conversation at Friends Houses, than ever I knew it. The Doctrines of Grace are espoused and relished. Private religious Meetings are greatly multiplied. . . . There is indeed an extraordinary Appetite after the sincere Milk of the Word.[16]

An enterprising pastor would move from one private society to another, offering here a prayer or there a few words of exhortation. Young people formed their own groups for "Prayer and reading Books of Piety." "If at any Time Neighbours met, the great Affairs of Salvation were the Subject of Discourse."[17] Weekly lectures, i.e., sermons on a weekday, were added to the schedule of many churches, Chauncy reporting in 1742 that "Evening-lectures were set up in one Place and another; no less than six in this Town, four weekly, and two monthly ones. . . ."[18] The Massachusetts General Court responded to public interest by enforcing a more strict observance of the "Lords-Day."[19] The concern of many young converts did not end with the reading of good and proper literature, but expressed itself in an earnest, if often unguided, evangelism. Itineracy and lay preaching with all their patent defects did much to destroy "puritan tribalism." When a church or minister refused to become evangelistic, a schism or secession would often result, this leading to the formation of a new and fervent group or to an alliance with some already existing ecclesiastical body whose missionary concern was obvious. Thus cells of self-commissioned ambassadors for Christ increased. The long-neglected Indian now received more attention both on the frontier and in the settled areas, two of the outstanding missionaries to the Indians being earnest friends of the revival. These were David Brainerd who labored effectively though briefly among the Indians of New Jersey, and Eleazar Wheelock whose Indian School at Lebanon was later moved to New Hampshire where it became Dartmouth College. In the days that followed the Awakening, people were not simply inquiring about salvation: they were striving to become both recipients of and agents for that gift of grace.

Had the Great Awakening never occurred, it is doubtful that Edwards would have written *An Humble Inquiry into the Rules of the*

Word of God, concerning The Qualifications Requisite to a Complete Standing and Full Communion in the Visible Christian Church.[20] This treatise was Edwards' public confession of a conviction he had long harbored: that none but the converted should be permitted to share in the privileges of full church membership and to receive communion. Reflection upon regeneration and conversion during the years of the Northampton and the New England revivals forced upon Edwards the revolt against Stoddardeanism, whatever the effects of such a revolt might be on "my own reputation, future usefulness, and my very subsistence." As he "became more studied in divinity" and "improved in experience," he grew convinced that only a negative answer was proper to the question: "Whether any adult persons but such as are in profession and appearance endued with Christian grace or piety, ought to be admitted to the Christian Sacraments; particularly whether they ought to be admitted to the Lord's Supper."[21] Thereafter, those who presented themselves for church membership at Northampton were to be required to sign a confession of faith and to acknowledge their personal experience of divine grace.

The major result of this important step taken by Edwards is that it represented a return to the "sect ideal." To primitive Congregationalism, the church was a group of believers separated from the world, regularly purified through a careful discipline, emphasizing personal achievement in religion and in ethics. It was a "holy community," which should not lower its standards or erase its requirements in order to include the whole of society. The Cambridge Platform had without equivocation declared that "the matter of a visible church are Saints by calling."[22] With reference to the admission of members, it decreed that "the things which are requisite to be found in all church members, are, Repentance from sin, & faith in Jesus Christ. And therefore these are the things whereof men are to be examined. . . ." Churches should exclude from their fellowship those who do not continue to live as saints.[23] And the sacrament of communion was the keystone in the structure of a pure church, for its observance was an occasion when strict examination of the communicants was possible and excommunication, if necessary, forthcoming. To achieve a visible church that conformed as nearly as possible to the invisible one was, beneath all the bitterness, self-righteousness and censoriousness of the New Lights, a major purpose of their separations. To purify the parish church and to alter its status from an established church for all society to a holy community for saints alone was the aim of the Humble Inquiry.

The campaign for the abandonment of the Half-Way Covenant thus auspiciously launched was continued by Edwards' theological heirs, principally by Joseph Bellamy, Chandler Robbins, Stephen West, and Nathanael Emmons. Their insistence upon a church membership of the regenerate only and upon a service of communion restricted to the visible saints evoked sharp outcries from such Old Lights as Moses Mather and Moses Hemmenway.[24] John Devotion of Saybrook wrote in obvious dismay that "Bellamyan Notions are that no Child receive Baptism but of Parents in full Communion, and such as come to Communion must have Assurance of Regeneration. . . ."[25] Despite an angry opposition, Old Light churches, under the continuing influence of "the New England theology"[26] and of a new series of widespread revivals, had generally ceased by the turn of the century to admit any but the converted to full membership. It cannot be said, however, that the basic premise of the Half-Way Covenant, the identification of religion with moral improvement, was abandoned. It was clearly preserved in New England Unitarianism, and was later through the labors of Horace Bushnell restored to Congregationalism. Yet even in the eighteenth century it was to be found among the Old Light churches; the Half-Way Covenant was more easily deserted because visible sainthood was more readily allowed. On occasion it was even confused with visible morality. As full membership became less difficult, half membership became less necessary, and the new wine of moral sincerity was poured into the old skins of divine grace.

In addition to having the tempo of their religious activities greatly accelerated, ministers were otherwise influenced by the revival. Sermon style, primarily by reason of Whitefield's example, was altered to a looser, more extemporaneous delivery. Those who continued to read from their manuscripts did so self-consciously and often, as in Chauncy's case, apologetically. The content of preaching became generally more theological, less moral, more a propagation of a network of conviction—a conscious Calvinism or a conscious rationalism of an Arminian-Universalist type. The office of the ministry was more carefully scrutinized as many, without proper ordination by men to confirm the call by God, took upon themselves the functions and prerogatives of clergymen. While the newly converted lay preachers were instrumental in sustaining an evangelistic emphasis, they by abundant disorder and studied tactlessness aroused determined opposition. By way of reaction against this professional invasion, the standing ministry tightened the requirements for ordination and decided as far as possible what persons should train for the ministry.

This clerical discipline took the form chiefly of a firmer control of the agencies of education. Those who in Connecticut withdrew from the regular churches (Separates) were not allowed to attend the established schools; moreover, they could not start their own school without a special license from the General Assembly, which license would certainly not be granted. The same law provided that "no Person who has not been educated or graduated at Yale College, or at Harvard College in Cambridge, or some Foreign Protestant College or University, shall be allowed the special Privileges of the established Ministers of the Government."[27] The sole attempt to overcome the deficiency in New Light ministerial education during the Awakening was Timothy Allen's infamous and ephemeral "Shepherds Tent." Set up first in New London, this hastily organized seminary boasted in February, 1743, an enrollment of fourteen;[28] it stood there shakily a few months before it was removed to Rhode Island, where it soon expired.[29] Of much greater importance are three schools whose founding, though approximately a generation after the Awakening in New England, is directly related to influences arising from it. Dartmouth College, incorporated in 1769, was an outgrowth of New Light Eleazar Wheelock's Indian School that had been founded in Lebanon, December 18, 1754.[30] The movement, begun in 1739 to establish in New Jersey a college comparable to Harvard and Yale, was resumed in 1745 under the initiative of the newly formed, prorevivalist Presbyterian Synod of New York. This college which opened at Elizabethtown in May, 1747, is of course more directly a result of the Middle Colony revival; yet New Englanders of New Light persuasion were of influence, both immediate and remote, in the presbyteries of which the New York Synod was comprised.[31] The College of New Jersey, or Princeton as it was later called, served as a "nursery of piety" not only for Middle Colony Presbyterians but also for New Lights of Congregational and Baptist persuasion; seventeen of its first sixty-nine graduates served as ministers in New England.[32] Among Baptists there was agitation for a college to train and educate its ministry. James Manning, member of the Princeton class of 1762, was chosen as President of New England's third college, chartered in 1764 and first located at Warren, Rhode Island. In 1770 it was moved to Providence where in 1804 it received the name of Brown University.[33]

Where indifference to religion is widespread, tolerance is no problem; but when religion becomes intensely vital, bigotry becomes more pervasive. In Connecticut the immediate effect of the Great Awakening on religious liberty was detrimental. Elsewhere democracy and individualism in religion sprang ahead, and ultimately even in the land of steady habits, religion was made free. In the 1720's Connecticut had granted a measure of toleration to Anglicans, Quakers, and Baptists, allowing them freedom of worship and, upon proper registration, exemption from the support of any other form of worship. When in the divisive days of 1741 and after, Presbyterians and Congregationalists withdrew from the established churches to form new ones, they expected like other dissenters to be permitted to support their own ministry and to be released from the public taxation for support of the standing ministry. But the General Assembly, now acting in such a way as to make the Saybrook Platform obligatory, ruled "that those commonly called Presbyterians or Congregationalists should not take the benefit of that Toleration Act."[34] When New Lights started changing the names of their churches to "Baptist" in order to come under the terms of the Toleration Act, that act was repealed. Other laws, already noted, provided for the arrest and punishment of New Light itinerants, and restricted ordination of ministers to graduates of approved schools, while New Light civil officials were deprived of their offices.[35]

To Solomon Paine, the radical preacher of Canterbury, this alliance of church and state was all wrong.

The cause of a just separation of the saints from their fellow men in their worship, is not that there are hypocrites in the visible church of Christ, *nor* that some fall into scandalous sins in the Church, *nor* because the minister is flat, formal, or even saith he is a minister of Christ, and is not, and doth lie; but it is their being yoked together, or incorporated into a corrupt constitution, under the government of another supreme head than Christ, and governed by the precepts of men, put into the hands of unbelievers, which will not purge out any of the corrupt fruit, but naturally bears it and nourishes it, and denies the power of godliness, both in the government and gracious effects of it.[36]

The Separate church gathered at Preston March 17, 1747, characterized the church from which it withdrew as one

which caled it Self Partly Congregational & Partly Presbyterial; who submitted to the Laws of the Government to Settle articles of faith; to govern the Gathering of the Church & Settlement & Support of its ministers building of meeting houses, Preaching Exhorting &c . . .[37]

The Opposers, or Old Lights, were not everywhere, if anywhere, the leading exponents of a free and catholic spirit.[38] The standing ministry was for peace, to be sure, wrote Reuben Fletcher, "an Independant," but

upon the same terms that the Pope is for peace, for he wants to rule over all Christians throughout the whole world, and they want to rule from one town to another, throughout the whole country. If they could have their wills, separates and Baptists would have no more liberties here than the protestants have in France or Rome. What tyrant would not desire peace on the same terms that they do?[39]

A generation after the revival Ezra Stiles was still justifying the despotism of Congregationalism in Connecticut.[40]

These stern and passionate words, though palpably extreme, nonetheless reveal a significant and growing impatience with the alliance of church and state. Puritanism recognized a co-operating church and state as a happy, desirable entente, but insofar as New England Puritanism was characterized by pietism, thus far it contained within itself the acids of dissolution. The Great Awakening, by increasing piety, increased proportionately the dissatisfaction with rigid and especially political control of spiritual affairs. Pietism is invariably associated with that which is voluntary and personal, as it is antagonistic toward that which is compulsory and cultural—in the name of Christ. As a corollary to this developing resistance to the state-church intimacy, the reviving pietism, by making the distinction between elect and the reprobate once more an issue, raised again the question of political suffrage. Even in the seventeenth century there had been some embarrassment concerning limitation of political participation to church members. By the second quarter of the eighteenth century, few defended such restriction. So long as religious stratification was not rigid, political suffrage related to ecclesiastical status worked no great hardship. But with the dogmatic claims and intense disputes now arising, the only plausible and acceptable step seemed to be to sever this knot of the ecclesiastical-political tangle.

Even though in Connecticut the government continued for decades to interfere in ecclesiastical affairs, religious liberty was to some extent advanced by a debilitation of the ecclesiastical structure itself. The consociations, through a combination of causes, gradually lost their authority over the local congregations, so that by 1768 a Saybrook minister sorrowfully observed, "We are breaking to pieces in our Churches very fast in Connecticut."[41] The growing democratic restlessness together with the party schisms that followed the revival made an authoritative, presbyterian control infeasible. Old Lights lost their enthusiasm for powerful consociations when, as was the case in New Haven, New Lights obtained a controlling majority. The significant controversy in Wallingford in 1758 over the ordination of James Dana was between an ecclesiastical council and the New Haven Consociation, both of which claimed jurisdiction in the matter. The latter intervened on behalf of a minority of the church which had protested the settlement of Dana, whom they believed to be infected with Arminianism. The council, comprised of Joseph Noyes, Isaac Stiles, the Whittelseys and other Old Lights, proceeded with the ordination of Dana in defiance of an explicit prohibition by the Consociation. They were consequently pronounced "disorderly persons, and not fit to sit in any of our ecclesiastical councils, until they shall clear up their conduct, to the satisfaction of the consociation of New-Haven county. . . ."[42] For the Old Lights it was a new experience to be condemned by that very ecclesiastical structure which they had so long defended and by a weapon they had so often used. The General Association of the whole colony passed under New Light influence at this time.[43] Old Lights met this reversal by undermining the consociations' basis for power. Consociations have a right of jurisdiction, wrote William Hart, "only of such ecclesiastical or spiritual causes as are of a criminal nature; only in cases of heresy or scandal . . . they have no stated times of sitting . . . they have no power of convening themselves, undesired by those who, by our constitution, have a right to call them into business. . . ." Consociational power was being turned into tyranny and slavery introduced into the place of liberty.[44] Other Connecticut Old Lights came to believe that "Lord Bishop is more palatable with many now than Lord Consociation."[45] Chauncy Whittelsey found it not surprising, in view of "the high Claims of the Consociation and the Dissentions occasioned thereby," that the "Chh of England, gradually gains upon us."[46]

While Old Lights thus backed away from strong interchurch control, New Lights revealed an increasing affinity for the Presbyterians. From 1766 to 1775 delegates from the New York and Philadelphia synods met with the "Congregational Associations of Connecticut." Their mutual interests as well as their close resemblance led in 1801 to a "Plan of Union,"[47] by which the missionary expansion of the two denominations was for a time to be directed. While this intimacy with Presbyterians suggests a tightening of church government in Connecticut, the joint assembly actually did not attempt to control the Congregational churches. Within these churches local loyalties were of more importance than denominational ones, and the conflict over theological issues prevented either centralization or workable control. Church councils and even the consociations tended to represent a faction, not a denomination, while each church was jealous of its own beliefs and rights, and suspicious of other churches' orthodoxy and power. Church councils, less powerful and less permanent than consociations, tended moreover to be substituted for the latter. Whereas before the Awakening ordinations were generally performed by the appropriate consociations or with its explicit approval, they now gradually became the work of an informal and sympathetic council. In 1762 Whittelsey observed that "Among the People thro' the Colony, the Ballance is plainly in favour of Liberty. . . . They may possibly uphold Consociation Ordinations in the County [New Haven] for a Season, but they will not obtain, I think, in any District to the Eastward or Northward of us."[48] Presbyterianizing died hard in Connecticut, but it died. In 1784 the Saybrook Platform was repealed, and though complete disestablishment was not achieved until 1818, long before that time both the government and the consociation had ceased to be ruling powers in local church affairs.[49]

The problem of ecclesiastical freedom was not so complicated in Massachusetts where a more liberal charter and a more vocal Anglican minority precluded—even before the Awakening—an effective partnership of church and state. Though church schisms were not so plentiful in Massachusetts, theological division in the Bay colony was sharper than elsewhere. This diversity here as in Connecticut prevented rigid control by consociations. Finally there was in Massachusetts a strong voice for congregational polity. Nathanael Emmons, of Edwards' theological school and of the tradition of John Wise as well, strenuously opposed any step which seemed to compromise the autonomy of the local congregation. He resisted even the establishment of an association of the Massachusetts churches, concerning which he is reported to have said: "Associationism leads to Consociationism; Consociationism leads to Presbyterianism; Presbyterianism leads to Episcopacy; Episcopacy leads to Roman Catholicism; and Roman Catholicism is an ultimate fact."[50] Over a century later, the Congregational historian Leonard Bacon rejoiced that in this period the churches learned to content themselves "with the simple and Scripture policy which rejects all ecumenical, national, provincial, and classical judicatures ruling the churches of Christ, and recognizes no church on earth save the local or parochial assembly and fellowship of believers. . . ."[51]

With reference to freedom within the local church, the change is more difficult to trace. Several factors suggest, however, that even as greater liberties were enjoyed by the churches, so were the parishioners under less restraint. The emphasis upon a personal religious experience had then, as always, the effect of making converts less dependent on external authority—scriptural or ecclesiastical. Those to whom religion in the 1740's had suddenly become meaningful knew that the kingdom of God was within them; their private divine vocation, be it called new light, inner light, or sense of the heart, was their ultimate and occasionally their only appeal. To them only one covenant was of pressing significance: the covenant of grace. The church covenant was important, but secondary. Mediation was unnecessary, priesthood was universal. The civil covenant was obsolete, and society was shattered, but into members not classes.

Religious democratization of this sort found fullest expression, of course, in New Light churches. But in Old Light communions too the "power of the keyes" rested ultimately in the pew instead of in the pulpit, or even in an aggregate of pulpits. The breaking up of the prevailing parish system further weakened intrachurch discipline as well as interchurch control. After the Awakening it was possible, even fashionable, to leave the established church to join a separate society, a Baptist or Anglican church, or perhaps to hold religious services in a private home. Church minorities were now more outspoken than ever before, and could generally muster a council or committee that shared its ecclesiastical or more often its theological position. And, as Ezra Stiles ingenuously remarked, ". . . such are the circumstances of our churches, so intermixt with sects of various communion, that it is impolitic to use extreme and coercive measures—since universal liberty permits the oppressed to form into voluntary coalitions for religious worship."[52] The "circumstance of our churches" together with the abundance of immediate personal religion in some of the churches promoted greater individual freedom from ecclesiastical control.

The bitter party spirit or "censoriousness" of which the Old Lights had complained in 1743 continued to prevail in New England. Councils were frequently called in an attempt to settle controversies within the churches. As early as September, 1742, the following advertisement appeared in the *Boston Weekly News-Letter:*

A Proposal

To be printed by Subscription the celebrated Mr. Lock's *Letter concerning Toleration;* as being very seasonable to check the Spirit of Persecution rising up among us . . .[53]

But not even Locke could quench this spirit. In 1749, Samuel Dunbar, who found it appropriate to preach at Medfield on *Brotherly Love, The Duty and Mark of Christians*, exclaimed:

> Look abroad, my Christian Brethren, see what a sad Declension of Love there is among the People of God! See how they separate themselves from one another! Hear how they censure one another! Are not these the loving Names they have given each other, Opposers, Carnal, Unconverted, Pharisees, Dead, Hypocrites, New Lights, Enthusiasts? What! . . . Are they that have entered into solemn Covenant to walk together in Love?[54]

While this conspicuous absence of brotherly love tended to divide Christians into two hostile camps, it also formed a third camp of those "who have no great Opinion of the Work, nor are violent Opposers of it" and who may "be tempted to lay aside all Religion, and even the Profession of it as a meer Farce."[55]

The most obvious effect of this party spirit, if not of the Awakening as a whole, was the creation of new churches. Not all of the new churches of this period, however, resulted from schisms and separations. Stiles estimated that in New England during the era of revivals there was "an augmentation of above 150 new churches . . . founded not on the separations, but natural increase into new towns and parishes."[56] And when a church was brought into being by a separation, it was not always the New Lights who withdrew. William Shurtleff pointed out that

> this dividing Spirit is not confin'd to those that are Friends to what we esteem as a remarkable Work of God's Grace that has been going on among us. No; those that have been disaffected to this Work have, in sundry Instances, withdrawn from their Ministers, for their firm and conscientious Attachment to it; and where they have set up a separate Congregation, if I have been rightly inform'd, have been encourag'd and assisted in it by such as have made the loudest Complaints of the like Disposition in others.[57]

Ecclesiastical separation was, moreover, the vogue in the years immediately following the Awakening, regardless of whether the issue at hand pertained to the revival. Even where there had been long-standing grievances, not until after many New Lights had set the example did other disaffected groups have the temerity to withdraw.

Accepting these reservations, it remains true that separation by New Lights was the chief cause of new churches arising at this time and was the most conspicuous institutional effect of the Great Awakening. These separations destroyed the traditional New England parish system, weakened the structure of establishment, and undermined the Saybrook Platform. Members of the schismatic churches challenged the propriety of public taxation for ministerial support, violated the traditional rules of ordination and "right hand of fellowship" association, protested against admitting the unconverted to communion, objected vigorously to cold, formal, "dead" preaching, and practiced a spontaneous, zealous personal religion. Separates, or Strict Congregationalists (as an association in Windham and New London counties styled themselves), with all their zeal and fervor, did not long survive as a distinct communion. Some of the churches quietly died out, while others returned to the mother church from which they had withdrawn. A few, retaining their organizational identity, came back into the Congregational fold as new churches of that denomination; some became Baptist (or later Methodist), and some continued the process of fractious dispute and contentious division into ever smaller and hardly recognizable groups. Other separations were more in the nature of a private protest by one or two individual malcontents out of which no organized church came. Yet with all its elusiveness and disorganization, the Separatist movement had an influence keenly felt.

The story of New Haven's North Church is typical of the manner in which a Separate church came into being.[58] Following Davenport's visit to that city, a group of forty-three persons withdrew in 1742 from Joseph Noyes' First Church, declaring their dissatisfaction with that pastor's dull, non-Calvinistic, and barren preaching. Only after appealing to the Act of Toleration (not yet stricken from the books) did these separatists succeed in getting permission from the General Assembly to form their own church. Property disagreements, however, between the old and new societies were not settled until 1758, while up to this time the New Lights continued under the requirements of the law to pay taxes for the support of Joseph Noyes.

In Norwich, where Benjamin Lord was pastor, there was much unrest among the extreme New Lights, despite the fact that Lord was sympathetic toward the revival.[59] The extremists insisted that none should be accepted as full church members who had not satisfactorily recounted their experience of grace. But in January, 1745, the majority of the church, with Lord's approval, voted: "Though it is esteemed a desireable thing that persons who come into full communion offer some publick relation of their experience; yet we do not judge or hold it a term of communion." The following month, thirteen persons, including the Baptist historian Isaac Backus, seceded from the church, protesting the neglect of church discipline, the coldness of preaching, the prohibition of lay exhortation and lay prayer—all this as well as the aforementioned laxity in the admission of church members. In October, Lord's church voted these reasons for separation "uncharitable and unwarrantable." Though subject to civil disabilities, these New Lights were always treated kindly by Lord who thus made possible the return of many to his church. Representatives of several separatist churches meeting at Norwich in 1753 decided to appeal to England if the General Assembly continued to ignore their petitions for tolerance. Solomon Paine and Ebenezer Frothingham were appointed the next year to go to England, but the mission was postponed when Paine died. In 1756, two new messengers having been appointed, the parliamentary committee in England heard their complaint, and concluded that if the king learned of this intolerance Connecticut might lose its charter. The committee thereupon sent by the two New Lights a letter of censure to the Connecticut government.[60] Modification of the oppressive measures gradually followed thereafter, but not until 1784 did the Assembly grant to all religious bodies recognized by law the same freedom in the management of their temporal affairs that the established churches enjoyed.[61] Up to that time the hand of government had been heavier on the Separates than upon the other extralegal groups.

Many other separations, not alone in Connecticut, obviously resulted from the Great Awakening. The effect of the schisms must be reckoned for the most part, however, in terms of their influence upon already existing denominations. As noted above, "Separtism" as a distinct communion was short-lived. Though the Separates often stood for principles worthy of continued emphasis, their "battle soon degenerated into a quarrel with the tax collector. . . ."[62] Usually led by a powerful individual, these aggrieved groups when deprived by death or defection of that leadership tended to disintegrate. The lack, moreover, of a trained or recognized ministry augured ill of Separatism's future. Finally, many of the older churches, as previously indicated, returned to a purer Congregationalism, thereby narrowing the gap between Old and New Lights and correspondingly diminishing the justification for separation.

Of the other denominations in New England upon which separatism in particular and the Awakening as a whole had marked effects, the Anglicans and the Baptists are the most notable. By 1740 the Church of England had become fairly comfortable in Connecticut. Having enjoyed a large measure of toleration since 1727, the Church in 1742 had seven clergymen in the colony and twice that number of edifices were "built and building."[63] There the revival unrest, and more particularly its extravagances, drove many anxious or offended persons into the less turbulent fold of Anglicanism. In 1744 a group of newly converted "churchmen" wrote the "Honorable Society"[64] in England as follows:

> We were all educated in this land, under the instruction of the Independent teachers, or (as they would be called) Presbyterians; and, consequently, we were prejudiced strongly against the Church of England from our cradles, until we had the advantage of books from your Reverend Missionaries and others, whereby we began to see with our own eyes that things were not as they had been represented to our view; and Mr. Whitefield passing through this land, condemning all but his adherents; and his followers and imitators—by their insufferable enthusiastic whims and extemporaneous jargon—brought in such a flood of confusion amongst us, that we became sensible of the unscriptural method we had always been accustomed to take in our worship of God, and of the weakness of the pretended constitution of the churches (so called) in this land; whereupon we fled to the Church of England for safety, and are daily more and more satisfied we are safe, provided the purity of our hearts and lives be conformable to her excellent doctrines.[65]

The missionary to Fairfield noted that "the effects of it [enthusiasm] at Stamford, Norwalk, Ridgefield, &c., where it has a large spread, has been the reconciling many sober, considerate people to the communion of our Church."[66]

While the Church of England endeavored to maintain itself as a haven for those who wished to flee the storm, its clergymen recognized that the Awakening was enormously powerful and threatening. The priest residing in North Groton admitted that "at the first rise of this enchanting delusion, I was under melancholy apprehensions that the infant Church of England, in this and the adjacent places, would be crushed. . . ." He was later convinced, however, that not even the gates of hell would prevail against the Church, and was content to request that more "good books" be sent to Connecticut "in this astonishing season in which the wildest enthusiasm and superstition prevail."[67] In March, 1743, Samuel Seabury of New London wrote the missionary society in England that "the Church . . . continueth steadfast in the midst of the wildest enthusiasms. . . ."[68] By June, however, he was less confident.

. . . truth obligeth me to say that the prospect of a large Church at Hebron is not so good as formerly, because the followers of Mr. Whitefield, Mr. Tennant, &c., do extremely abound there; the dissenting teacher at Hebron having gone the greatest lengths in pretensions to inspiration. . . . And I should the more rejoice in a resident minister there, because the same spirit of Methodism prevails mightily at New-London, increaseth my care and labours, and renders my absence on Sundays of dangerous consequence. The conformists, both at New-London and Hebron, indeed, are steadfast to the Church, though they are very much alarmed by the new doctrines and new propagation of religion. . . .[69]

The pressure of New Light zeal caused the Anglicans to order more "good books"—Arminian, of course—and carefully to instruct their adherents lest they be led astray. The Fairfield clergyman, untroubled by mixed metaphors, applied himself "closely to the duty of catechizing young and old who do not appear to have sufficiently digested the grounds of our most holy faith." An urgent need for additional ministers was keenly felt, together with a particularly pressing need for a bishop in this part of the world, or at the very least a commissary to reside in Connecticut as in the Boston area.

. . . the absence from our parishes, which such a distance requires, proves oftentimes great prejudice to our people, not only from the want of publick worship, but likewise in regard they are liable to be seduced by the indefatigable endeavours of enthusiastic teachers, who, since Mr. Whitefield's tour through this colony, have made an astonishing progress . . . we forbear to mention, the particular advantages to be enjoyed by the residence of a Commissary among us, especially at a time when enthusiasm, in its worst colors, is daily gaining ground.[70]

In Massachusetts, too, "the Church . . . stood steady in that Storm, which hath considerably shaken the Dissenters."[71] In Boston where the strength of episcopacy lay, the three Anglican Churches[72] were said to "live in Love and Peace; their Ministers preach against Enthusiasm and Bigottry every Day, not above three or four at most, of some thousands that are of the Episcopal Way, and these poor senseless Women, are taken in with the new Light."[73] The Anglican reaction to the Great Awakening is best seen in the letter of Timothy Cutler, rector of Christ's Church, to Zachary Grey, written September 24, 1743. After a damning caricature of Whitefield ("he forever lasht and anathematiz'd the Chh of England; and that was enough"), of Tennent ("a Monster! impudent & noisy"), and of Davenport ("a non-pareille.—The madder the Better"), Cutler declared that this wild revivalism "has turn'd to the growth of the Church in many Places, and it's Reputation universally; and it suffers no otherwise, than as Religion in general does, and that is sadly enough."[74]

The fact that Whitefield was still a priest of the Church of England, however joyfully this might be acknowledged by poor senseless women, was a bountiful source of confusion and irritation to his Anglican brethren in New England. With mournful disgust, Commissary Roger Price observed that "to the Quaker he becomes a Quaker; to the Anabaptist an Anabaptist; to the Presbeterian and Independent, a Presbeterian and Independent . . ."[75] Whitefield did nothing to allay suspicions, for he never even suggested that the dissenters were in error. On the contrary, he encouraged them "to persevere in their unreasonable separation from the Established Church of England, to contemn all lawful Ecclesiastical government and authority, and fondly taught [them] to expect no other proof of their acceptance with God than a fit of Madness and Enthusiasm. . . ." The Commissary's faith, though sorely tried, did not fail: ". . . the God of Peace and Order, who has already rescued us out of the paws of the Lyon and the Bear, from Popish and Fanatical fury, will also deliver us from the Rage of this Uncircumcised Philistine."[76]

At the Anglican mission in Scituate, the minister was ill at ease during all the excitement. In June, 1741, he informed the Bishop of London that the Wesleys were expected in New England in the fall, adding,

> Believe me, in a young (I may say as yet unsettled) church much depends on my deportment in this critical Juncture, which makes me thus pressingly intreat your Lordship's direction whether to receive them as brother clergymen into my church or Pulpit, or to reject them as those that are under the censure or displeasure of my Diocesan. . . .[77]

But the question was academic, for the Wesleys never appeared. The Society's missionary at Portsmouth, New Hampshire, Arthur Browne,[78] found it necessary to preach a weekly lecture to strengthen a congregation of fifty to sixty families, and to "guard them against the pernicious Doctrine of Enthusiasts. . . ."[79] The Great Awakening in large part flowed around the Church of England; yet the latter, sometimes fearful for its safety, more often concerned with maintaining and strengthening its position, did by its orderliness and calm prove attractive to many in the rough waters outside.

New England's Baptists were generally not characterized by orderliness and calm. Because of theological differences within their own communion, they were not uniformly affected by the Great Awakening. Prior to the revival, most of the Baptist churches were Arminian, and all Six-Principle Baptist churches[80] (such as the one gathered in Groton, Connecticut, in 1705, as well as many of the churches in Rhode Island) were of that theological bent. As such, most Baptists held aloof from the Awakening which was thoroughly Calvinistic in character.[81] Infant baptism was an even more conspicuous barrier than Calvinism in preventing an alliance with the revivalists. Isaac Backus wrote that

A measure of it [the Great Awakening] was granted to the Baptists in Boston, Leicester, Brimfield, Newport, Groton and Wallingford; but as the work was begun and carried on almost wholly by Pedo-baptists, from which denomination their fathers had suffered much, most of the Baptists were prejudiced against the work, and against the Calvinian doctrine by which it was promoted.[82]

The results of such a prejudice may be seen in the circumstances attending the Baptist church in Boston which, though originally Calvinistic, had under Jeremiah Condy (pastor from 1737 to 1764) become Arminian. This church strongly opposed the New Lights and in no way participated in or sympathized with the revival. In October, 1742, when on all sides church attendance in Boston was increasing and new services were being added, the Baptist church eliminated its traditional weekly lecture because of poor attendance! A faction favorable to the revival withdrew from Condy, protesting his Arminianism and lack of evangelistic zeal. In July, 1743, this group separated formally to establish what later became Warren Avenue Baptist Church.[83] During Condy's twenty-six-year ministry, which included the period of the Great Awakening, a total of only forty-three members was added to the church.

The greatest effect of the Awakening upon the Baptist fellowship was, however, not during the peak years of the revival, 1741-42, but in the subsequent period of decline, schism, and separation. The principal results were two: first, the ranks of the denomination were enormously swelled in the generation following the revival, often by entire churches switching from the status of Separates or Strict Congregationalists to that of Baptists; second, the major portion of the Baptist denomination took on a Calvinistic emphasis that altered its nature and subsequent history in America. Those few Baptist churches that were already Calvinist tended to expand more during the Awakening than non-Calvinist

Baptist churches. And the New Lights, invariably Calvinists, who styled themselves Baptists for one reason or another, augmented the growth of Calvinism within the denomination.[84] The Calvinistic character of the denomination was further enhanced by the now closer association with Baptists of the Middle Colonies. Calvinism had long been in the ascendancy among the Baptists of the Philadelphia Association, who immediately availed themselves of an opportunity to send their ministerial candidates to Princeton. James Manning, of Princeton's class of 1762 and Brown's first President, served also as pastor of the First Baptist Church in Providence where he demonstrated his Calvinism by firmly opposing the Six-Principle faction within the church.[85] While in 1740 there were less than half a dozen Calvinistic Baptist churches in all of New England, there were before the end of the century three hundred and twenty-five Baptist churches of which the overwhelming majority was Calvinist.[86]

Many of the new Baptist churches were comprised wholly or in part of disaffected Congregationalists, i.e., New Lights who moved directly into the Baptist communion, or those who had first become Separates. What was the affinity between the proponents of the Great Awakening and the Baptists? Both groups advocated a regenerate church membership, a gathering of visible saints. Both groups, moreover, reacted against governmental interference with the churches and against too strong an interchurch control. Agitation of this nature led to a more general interest in religious liberty which was characteristic of New Lights as well as of the Baptists.[87] These shared convictions were on occasion abetted by more practical considerations. In Connecticut, as has been observed, Baptists were under a lighter financial burden than unorthodox Congregationalists, an inequity which drove some Separates into the Baptist fold. In any case, it made return to the established communion difficult and humiliating.[88]

The disagreement concerning baptism, already briefly noted, remained a source of friction after the revival as it had been during the revival. Separates generally continued the practice of infant baptism, though Ezra Stiles described the worship of some "New Light Separatists" that included a baptism by immersion, presumably of an adult.[89] An attempt by Solomon Paine in 1753 to effect a compromise between Separates and Baptists on this issue was unsuccessful. Isaac Backus in his letter to Benjamin Lord stated that the Half-Way Covenant was the first thing that caused him to examine the whole question of infant baptism, which examination led him to conclude that it lacked "the stamp of divine institution upon it."[90] If the following letter is in fact from a New Light and not, as one suspects, from a propaganda-wise Baptist, it is a valuable revelation of the train of thinking which led some individual Separates to become Baptists.

Sir, I am one of the many in this Land, who in this Time of general Awakening and Enquiry, are unable to reconcile the Practice of Infant-Baptism with the Doctrine of the new Birth, that has of late been preached up with such great Power and remarkable Success. . . .

If the Baptism of Infants, don't avail to the Pardon of the Guilt of their original Sin, nor to the Renovation of their corrupt Nature, but such Infants remain under the condemning Sentence of the Law of God, and subject to the corrupt Desires of the Flesh and of the Mind, equally with others, that have not been baptis'd, and must be Converted, born again or regenerated, in order to their Salvation, and must make a public Declaration of it, in order to their Admission to Church Privileges and the Table of the Lord,—what Benefit or Advantage is it to them to be baptized, seeing they remain in the very same natural State of Sin and Guilt with other children, till they are afterwards effectually called, and are really born again?—And if it be no Advantage to them to be baptised, because, it alters not their Condition from what it is by Nature; how can it be thought a Divine institution, seeing God doth nothing in vain?—And if it be not a Divine Instituition, why is it practiced among us, seeing we profess to make the Scriptures the Rule of our Faith and Worship?[91]

A lesser obstacle to union of the groups was the practice in many Baptist churches of limiting the service of communion to members of their own fellowship. This practice, resented by the generally tolerant New Lights, was by no means universal among Baptists, the newly formed Calvinistic churches in particular tending to be more liberal in this respect.

These and other possible differences notwithstanding, New England, heretofore hostile to Baptist development, now became a fruitful area for the growth of that fellowship. One of the reasons for founding what was to become Brown University was "the great increase of the Baptist societies of late" in New England.[92] Before the Great Awakening there were in Massachusetts five Baptist churches; within the ensuing half-century, that number rose to one hundred and thirty-six. Though the growth in Connecticut was not so phenomenal, the number there rose from two in 1740 to sixty in 1796 and in Rhode Island, from eleven to forty. In neither Vermont nor New Hampshire were there any Baptist churches prior to the revival, but by 1800 over forty Baptist societies were in each state.[93] Henceforth, the Baptist denomination was for generations to retain its evangelistic, Calvinistic character, growing as America grew, in their common westward expansion.

Presbyterianism was affected chiefly, of course, by the Middle Colony Awakening. Yet the sympathetic alliance of New Lights with New Side Presbyterians, enhanced by the labors of Jonathan Parsons, Samuel Buell, David MacGregore, John Moorhead, Joseph Parks, Jonathan Dickinson, Ebenezer Pemberton, and Gilbert Tennent, subjected that communion also to the influence of the New England Awakening. In Milford, Connecticut, a group of New Lights separated from the regular society, expressing a desire to become affiliated with the New Brunswick (Tennent's) Presbytery. Hesitant about invading Connecticut territory, the latter group advised the Milford Separates to make another attempt at reconciliation. When such efforts failed, the presbytery decided to receive the church. Samuel Finley sent by the presbytery to Milford for that pupose was promptly arrested and ejected from the colony under its new law. The major influence of the New England revival party, however, was in the founding of the important Synod of New York in 1745 out of which Princeton and, to a great degree, subsequent American Presbyterianism grew.[34] Jonathan Dickinson's difficult decision to unite with the New Side faction of the Presbyterian church, finally made in 1745, may have been in part influenced by the support lent to the great colonial revival by Jonathan Edwards, as well as by Colman, Sewall, Prince, Webb, Cooper, Foxcroft, and Gee of Boston—all of whom had attested to Dickinson's A Display of God's special Grace.

The Indians, not exclusively members of any one denomination, were in many instances distinctly impressed by the revival. While the Congregationalist missionaries labored in special mission stations, Indians also attended and joined the parish churches. In Lyme, Connecticut, George Griswold reported that among the "Neantick Indians" a great revival followed Davenport's preaching. Nathanael Eells of Stonington and his neighbor, Joseph Parks of Westerly, had much success in their evangelistic labors among the Narragansett Indians. In Westerly alone, "The Number of Names who have yielded a professed Subjection to the Gospel of Christ among us are an Hundred and six, of which fifty-four are Indians."[95] Indians converted in Stonington became missionaries to other Indians in Rhode Island, and all gave up their "dances and drunken Frolicks."[96] Benjamin Colman, the great

Boston liberal, serving as a commissioner of the New England
Company in its work with the Indians, gladly noted the effect of
the Awakening upon them.

> ... the Clans or Tribes of *Indians*, the Reliques of the *Mokeage, Pequots,*
> and *Niantic's* in Connecticut Colony, who have obstinately continu'd in
> *Infidelity*, of their own accord, aply for Instruction to the Pastors about
> them, and receive it greedily, and with great Thankfulness, and Numbers
> of them seem savingly wrought upon. This is wondrous in our Eyes, and
> the Pastors about them are wonderfully spirited to serve them by the Grace
> of God, and see the Fruits of their Labours; The *Indian* Fund here, and
> private Helps will not be wanting to give Assistance.[97]

Colman was likewise instrumental in obtaining funds from England
with which to sustain the mission to the Housatonic Indians at
Stockbridge, Massachusetts. There from 1733 to 1749 John Sergeant
labored, reporting in 1743 significant evangelistic successes within
his heathen parish.[98] David Brainerd and Eleazer Wheelock were
particularly zealous in their respective labors among the Indians. To
Wheelock, Brainerd wrote, "When I consider the doings of the
Lord among these Indians, and then take a view of my journal, I
must say 'tis a faint representation I have given of them."[99] And
through Davenport's preaching to the Indians at New London had
come the conversion of Samson Occam (1723-1792), a Mohegan, who
became Wheelock's first Indian pupil and New England's first
ordained Indian missionary.

In July, 1742, the fiery Boston Presbyterian, John Moorhead, remarked, "I can't express the wonderful things which God is adoing,
and has already Manifested amongst Indians, Negros, Papists and
Protestants of all Denominations."[100] Though somewhat exaggerated,
Moorhead's enthusiastic observation indicated the truly ecumenical
character of the Awakening. Like its most powerful preacher, it crossed
denominational lines with little discrimination. Prorevivalists of Congregational, Baptist, Presbyterian, Reformed, and later Methodist
denominations found much ground for mutual appreciation and co-
operative undertakings. A modern Presbyterian, recently writing of
this unifying effect of the Great Awakening, reckons that "it gave to
nearly four-fifths of the Church a common understanding of the
Christian life and the Christian faith."[101] That common understanding
rested upon a practical piety which expressed itself most significantly
in an evangelical fervor. The missionary conquest of the west is no

small testimony to this piety's power. And from the interdenominational brothers-in-arms march came a functional catholicity which led to the creation of home and foreign mission boards, Bible societies, Christian associations, and the like. In the latter half of the eighteenth century, these sentiments of John Wesley had validity far beyond the limits of Methodism:

I will not quarrel with you about any mere opinion. Only see that your heart be right toward God; that you know and love the Lord Jesus Christ; that you love your neighbor and walk as your Master walked; and I desire no more. . . . Give me solid and substantial religion; give me a humble and gentle lover of God and man; a man full of mercy and good fruits, without partiality and without hypocrisy; a man laying himself out in the work of faith, the patience of hope, the labor love. Let my soul be with these Christians, whosoever they are, and whatsoever opinion they are of.[102]

Pietism does not deliberately or necessarily hack away at organizational unity; yet, the integrity of the institution is manifestly secondary to the integrity of the spirit. Churches were split, many and often; denominational synods and consociations were torn with bitter strife. But on the other hand, the common recovery of and attachment to evangelical piety made for a less rigid, even less conscious denominationalism. If the phoenix could rise from its ashes, ecumenicity could spring from "Dens of Disorder, Confustion, Noise and Clamour." A shared concern and a kindred spirit now drew together those Protestants who with a new sense of mission and a keen sense of responsibility turned to meet their own manifest destiny.

CHAPTER 8

THEOLOGICAL EFFECTS
of the GREAT AWAKENING

TO A SIGNIFICANT DEGREE, ANY ACCOUNT OF NEW England theology must be rendered in terms of movements first distinctly appearing in the generation following the Great Awakening. This generation, poised between an epochal revival and an epochal revolution, saw a more self-conscious theological development than had heretofore been visible in New England. "Calvinistical Schemes" were deliberately defended, while Arminianism was—on this side of the Atlantic, too—boldly espoused. Arianism, Unitarianism, and Universalism found advocates in eastern Massachusetts. Within the lifetime of many of the principals of the Awakening the central issues of an evangelical Christianity—general or particular atonement, a human or divine Christ, reason or revelation, reform or regeneration, free or earned grace—were subjected to severe testing.

In theology as within the churches and ministry, the immediate effect of the Awakening was divisive. But in theology, more than in any other area, that schism was rather an ever-widening divorce than a temporary alienation. In an election sermon delivered before the Connecticut legislature in 1758, Benjamin Throop of Norwich sadly observed the manner in which "the fear of God is amazingly cast off in this day."

While some are disputing the Personality of the Godhead, and denying the Lord that brought them; others are ridiculing the important Doctrine of Atonement, and casting contempt upon the efficacious Merits of a Glorious Redeemer; many are exploding the Doctrine of a free and Sovereign Grace, and exalting humane Nature under all its Depravity to a situation equal to all its Necessities; thereby perverting the Designs of the Gospel, and frustrating, as far as may be, the Means of our Salvation.[1]

Many of these points had long been controversial, but now it was possible to identify factions and fashionable to take sides. The great revival had destroyed the fetish of an undivided ministry.[2] Before 1740, church disputes could generally be settled by calling a council of churches. The practicality of this device was nearly obviated when now the decision of a council called by one faction of a church would be reversed by a later council called by the other faction. And so with heterodoxy. Heresy was more difficult to define and to extirpate. When, as in the case of John Bass of Ashford, a minister was deposed for Arminianism, it was because he was opposed by a majority sufficient to pack the council and to insure that no countercouncil would be called.[3]

Even catechetical instruction was now no longer feasible. Samuel Niles complained that the ministers were telling the people "(Practically at least, if not verbally) that the Catechism is corrupt, containing false Points of Doctrine." Parents as a result do not instruct their children and the minister "dare not teach the Children what he himself does not believe."[4] A committee defending Lemuel Briant of Braintree against charges of heresy acknowledged that "tho' Mr. Briant has too much neglected Catechising, yet he is now ready to teach our Children such Parts of the Catechism as he apprehends agreeable to the Scriptures."[55] The last clause is particularly significant. Enlightened liberals did not now feel under the necessity of waiting until the orthodox could keep pace with them. Open schism was the order of the day; theologians campaigned boldly, crystallized their ideology, and organized their forces.

The Awakening, moreover, by its extravagances in belief and behavior, pushed many of the normally orthodox into strongly anti-Calvinist positions. The countless accusations and defenses, the endless searching of the Scriptures, made men long for roomier, calmer meadows. Some, like William Hooper and Ebenezer Turell, overshot Congregational liberalism and landed in Anglicanism. Others, like Charles Chauncy, deliberately abandoned the theology which the revival espoused. Though certainly disposed by temperament toward a religion rather of the head than of the heart, Chauncy in 1741 displayed a healthy Calvinism.[6] In his published works he did not return to specifically theological matters until 1758 when he abandoned the doctrine of original sin. But in the years when ecclesiastical and doctrinal disorders were at their height, Chauncy's adamant opposition to the New Light party was accompanied by an opposition to the Calvinism in which that party lived. His *Seasonable Thoughts* was,

Wheelock reported with disdain, "never vendible, except among Arminians in the colony of Connecticut."[7]

The theological divisions which followed in the wake of the revival were more complex than the familiar Old Light—New Light dichotomy. Four parties may be distinguished. The extremists, least important of the four, were hyperzealous New Lights who were characterized either by theological novelty or theological vacuity. The traditional orthodoxy, that which existed before the Awakening and which tried desperately to maintain itself after, came to be known as "Old Calvinism." A third party, the Liberals, comprised a left wing within the older orthodoxy which spoke with new vigor and clarity. Finally, the Strict Calvinists or New Divinity men fully displayed and effectively extended the theological bias of the revival.

As with most periods of intense revival or missionary activity the years of New England's religious concern were filled with a hurried activity that usually precluded calm speculation. Eleazar Wheelock's words again suggest themselves: "I have a thousand things to say but the bearer is in hast. We are all in a Moving State thro' Divine Goodness."[8] The breathless quality of an inspired evangelism, too busy propagating a faith to inquire as to the nature of that faith, continued to characterize some elements of the New England clergy long after 1742. Whitefield, whose sole theological effort was a letter reproving John Wesley for his Arminianism,[9] was a perfect pattern for those who lacked the time or other essentials for making theology an essential part of their religion. How impressive was his example? It was certainly followed by many of the New Lights: Samuel Buell and Andrew Croswell for a time, together with James Davenport, John Moorhead, John Cleaveland, and Elisha Paine—to mention but a few. Laymen who suddenly felt an impulse or call saw no great incongruity in their proceeding, without benefit of theological education, to exhort sinners to repentance and faith. It was not difficult to reach the intellectual level of Whitefieldian sermonizing. A Boston newspaper in 1742 advertised for a runaway slave who could be identified because he is "very forward to mimick some of the strangers that have of late been preaching among us."[10]

Within this extreme faction, a minority of the New Light party, "human learning" was assigned a low value; it was noted that often a minister had zeal in inverse proportion to his knowledge. The precedent established in these years together with this prejudice against erudition made more facile and more probable the growth of an unlearned, untrained ministry. Congregationalists and the main body of the Presbyterian Church, however, refused to yield to these obscurantist pressures. When there was added to these pressures the influence of the frontier where no educated ministry was available, Baptists and Methodists utilized such leadership as there was, making possible their phenomenal expansion in America. To what extent the Awakening was responsible for a theological vacuum in given segments of American religion is problematic. That it demonstrated the feasibility of and made fashionable a fervent evangelism without intellectual discipline seems certain.[11] It was evident to all, moreover, that those who talked most of the value of reason adhered least to the dogmas of religion.

The extremists, when they did become theological, often produced doctrinal novelties. Enthusiasm and antinomianism, each with its several connotations, were extended by those whose "new light" was truly a will-o'-the-wisp. Beyond contributing to the rapid decline of the Awakening their perversions of dogma had little significance, though to some they occasionally served as convenient examples of the outcome of an unchecked Calvinism. One theological bypath of special interest led to a consideration of the imminent end of the world. It is surprising, not that millennial prophecies were a feature of this as of all periods of religious excitement, but that they occupied so minor a place in the popular preaching of the time. The court proceedings at the trial of James Davenport afford one of the few testimonies to their use. It was charged that Davenport affected and terrified his hearers by pretending to a revelation regarding the approaching end of the world.[12] Millennialism was popular not alone with the extremists, however. Edwards' concern with the future kingdom of Christ on earth is particularly evident in his *Humble Attempt*,[13] written in an effort to establish a "concert of prayer" for the revival of religion and return of Christ. Samuel Hopkins, according to Channing, was possessed by the subject: "The millennium was more than a belief to him. It had the freshness of visible things. He was at home in it. . . ."[14] Yet there is no evidence that any but extremists adopted millennialism as a lever to force conversion; it was hell, not Armageddon, which for most New Lights constituted the greater threat.

The "Old Calvinists," who continued to espouse a theology that gradually and painlessly adapted itself to cultural change, were made up of theological conservatives of both Old and New Light parties. These were the middle-of-the-road travelers. To many of this group the thunderous, turgid doctrinal battles that were waged around their heads seemed obstructive and unnecessary. They saw the wrangling between Strict Calvinists and liberals as the result of an overconcern for "metaphysical niceties," and advocated a "large measure of charity" on abstruse doctrinal matters. In 1760 Ezra Stiles viewed the conflict between Arminians and Calvinists as, in fact, only a verbal dispute. Interrogating so-called Arminians, he found they believed in the redemptive grace of Christ; inquiring of so-called Calvinists he learned that they did not deny the importance of good works. On the whole, "I cannot perceive any very essential real difference in their opinions respecting the fundamental principles of religion."[15]

In this discourse Stiles deliberately minimized all differences because he was trying to unify New England's tottering ecclesiastical structure. And with good reason. Old Calvinists, losing adherents both to liberalism and to a more consistent Calvinism, enjoyed ever fewer fellow travelers on their judicious middle path. They were not unlike the established clergy of England who at this time were fearful, Leslie Stephen observed, lest they "be thought to believe too much or too little." Men of great piety or ability abandoned the theology of compromise for the "New Divinity," while men of outstanding intellect or daring forsook the genial orthodoxy for a cautious testing of the Enlightenment's full force. Conscious of this depletion of their ranks, though somewhat mystified by it, even the Old Calvinists were on occasion aware that in current theological opinion there were some "very essential real differences." Braintree, whose ministers were as voluble as those of Boston, affords in the decade following the Awakening an instructive instance of the reaction of Old Calvinism to some real differences.

In 1749, Lemuel Briant of the First Church in Braintree, preached in Jonathan Mayhew's pulpit (West Church) in Boston, a sermon belligerently entitled, *The Absurdity and Blasphemy of depretiating Moral Virtue. . . ."* With Isaiah 64:6, the proof-text of the Calvinists, as his own text, Briant set out to demonstrate "that neither all, nor any part of our Righteousness when true and genuine, sincere and universal, can possibly consistent with Reason, Revelation, or indeed so much as common Sense, deserve this odious Character of filthy Rags."[16] To deprecate righteousness was to reflect dishonor on Christ, for "our Savior was the great Preacher of Righteousness: For this End was he born, and on this grand Design came he into the World, to propagate Truth and Vertue among Mankind." Though Christ was still "our Savior" the plan of salvation was no longer in evidence. The reduction of religion to morality by Briant lacked even the advantage of subtlety and finesse. Righteousness, he declared, is "that which the Son of God thought worth his coming down from Heaven to establish on Earth, that which is the Basis and in short the whole Superstructure of this his divine Religion." Divine grace, honored above all else by the Edwardean party and not at all forgotten by the Old Calvinists, was completely ignored by this Braintree liberal. "It is the Righteousness of the Saints that renders them amiable in God's Sight, that is the Condition of all his Favours to them, and the sole Rule he will proceed by in judging of them; and dispensing eternal Rewards to them." Upon this same righteousness "the general Good of all Mankind essentially depends."[17]

This sort of preaching, Briant acknowledged, is "not calculated for the general Taste of the present Age. . . . It may not, at present, be the Way to popular Applause. . . ."[18] He was right. Such a wholesale abandonment of orthodoxy would bestir Calvinists of any degree to a defense of the ancient faith. Upon the same text John Porter preached to the South Society in Braintree on *The Absurdity and Blasphemy of substituting the personal Righteousness of Men in the Room of the Surety-Righteousness of Christ.* . . . It is most proper and correct, Porter affirmed, to style the personal righteousness of the best of men as filthy rags in certain instances: viz., when that righteousness is viewed in comparison with the righteousness of God, or when it is viewed in "Point of Justification before God."[19] There can be no faith in Scripture nor semblance of orthodoxy that does not "include these two Things . . . (1) Renunciation of our own Righteousness as to Dependence—having no Confidence in the Flesh . . . (2) Appropriation of Christ's Righteousness to ourselves, and resting on it alone for Justification and Life."[20] Most Calvinists were quick to recognize that a moral reform was no substitute for a spiritual regeneration, and that true righteousness was the result, not the cause, of justification. In his seventy-eighth year, Samuel Niles of the Second Church, Braintree, also moved to counteract the tendencies of Briant's heresy. After waiting to see if Briant would make any respectable reply to Porter's sermon, Niles finally published in 1752 *A Vindication of Divers important Gospel-Doctrines* . . . Here he contended, not for novel doctrine or strange theology, but "for the Faith once delivered to the Saints; even that Faith, which the Churches of the Saints in New-England have been in the Possession and Profession of, now to the third Generation down from our renowned Ancestors. . . ."[21] Briant, on the other hand, denied and destroyed that faith, making "the whole Doctrine of Christ but a mere refined System of Morality."[22] In Braintree liberalism had proceeded with such haste and indiscretion that even Old Calvinists were aroused from a slumber of easy orthodoxy, rudely awakened by doctrinal differences both real and essential. To allow, as old orthodoxy had, the respectable unregenerate to come into the churches or even to partake of communion was one thing. It was quite another thing to admit these unregenerate into heaven.

Although this residual orthodoxy known as Old Calvinism spent some energy refuting the excesses of a strict Calvinism,[23] it was the liberal party which gave them greatest concern. The liberals had been tampering with natural reason even before the Awakening, but then it was less obtrusive and much less divisive. In the turbulence of 1741-1742, liberals found both incentive and justification for more emphatic declarations of their position. Ebenezer Gay of Hingham, described by John Adams as "perhaps equal to all, if not above all" the earliest New England Unitarians,[24] in 1745 signed a testimony against Whitefield.[25] Gay about this time was also busy tutoring Jonathan Mayhew who had graduated from Harvard the previous year. Mayhew while an undergraduate had visited York, Maine, in the midst of its spiritual convulsions. His criticism of the revival there was reserved, and there is some evidence that he was for a time swept along in its current. A short time later, however, he referred to the intellectual side of the Awakening with something less than appreciation:

. . . it is the manner of vain enthusiasts, when the absurdity of their doctrine is laid open, to fall a railing, telling their opposers that they are in a carnal state, blind, and unable to judge; but that themselves are spiritually illuminated. Thus they endeavor to palm the grossest absurdities on their neighbors, under a notion of their being divine and holy mysteries. . . . Whatever is reasonable, is with them carnal; and nothing is worthy of belief, but what is impossible and absurd in the eye of human reason.[26]

To those who like Samuel Niles complained of doctrinal disloyalty to the ancient and pious forefathers of New England, Mayhew had sharp words: ". . . nothing is more unworthy a reasonable creature, than to value principles by their age, as some men do their wines."[27] Or, ". . . no man in his senses will allow himself to be in error, because he cannot get as many hands held up in favor of his tenet, as another."[28]

Of the many forms which a natural or liberal theology might take, the prestige and prolixity of the revival party made the form of an intensified and accelerated reaction against Calvinism virtually inescapable. The "hardest" doctrines of Calvin were ridiculed and pronounced inhuman, unreasonable, and indefensible. The doctrine of original sin was treated in terms of thousands of innocent infants burning in hell. Predestination was viewed from the point of the reprobate, not of the regenerate, while the doctrine of free and irresistible grace was made to appear inimical to good works and all moral effort. If, furthermore, man's will was not free, then all men were simply automatons, victims of an impersonal and inexorable fate. To be sure, Christ's death provided an atonement, but that atonement was not *ex opere operato*. "That the merits of Christ's obedience and sufferings, may be so applied or imputed to sinners, as to be available to their justification and salvation, altho' they are destitute of all personal inherent goodness" is, asserted Mayhew, the "one grand, capital error." When this "grand mistake" is "cloathed in scripture language, it is expressed thus; that we are saved by grace. . . ."[29] Since the theological system of the early New Divinity men grew out of the doctrine of an unearned and all-powerful grace, the liberals were striking at the root.

Along with this attention to divine grace, there was a meticulous examination of the person of Christ, the instrument and manifestation of that grace. To what extent did the Christocentric preaching and writing of the revival provoke a liberal reaction against the Son? There were instances of New Light preaching that treated Christ with an intimacy that must have repulsed the more staid.[30] Yet the Arianism which Mayhew cautiously voiced in 1755 was rather a reflection of the growth of humanism abroad than a direct effect of the revival.[31] Like the fourth-century Arians, New England's unitarians sought to remove all mystery from religion, to eliminate that which defied the noble reason of man. And nothing was more mysterious or irrational than the dogmatic assertion of Jesus' equality with God. The Enlightenment in general, not the Great Awakening in particular, was responsible for New England's humanizing of Jesus.

This growing confidence in the powers and potentialities of human reason was not the possession alone of the liberal party. There, however, reason found its happiest home and some of its ablest exponents. Arminians and Arians began by quoting from the Bible to offset Calvinist texts, but before the argument was over there was sure to be some appeal, usually explicit, to Reason or mere Common Sense. Calvinists, particularly the less able among them, found it necessary to take refuge in revelation, depending "not upon human Tradition or Antiquity . . . But on the pure and unerring Word of God. . . ."[32] Whereas the Awakening provoked on the one hand a rapidly increased devotion to the dictates of reason, it resulted on the other hand in a dogged reaffirmation of the divine origin and infallible nature of the Bible. All three major parties, Old Calvinists, Liberals, and Strict Calvinists, imbibed enough of rationalism, however, to be aware of the fact that dogmatism and authority were not perfect persuaders. In their efforts to explain as well as to declare their doctrines, these parties developed theological schools, a new and important phenomenon in New England's religious history.

From this standpoint, i.e., of a theological school, the party of New or Strict Calvinists was the most significant; its relationship to the Great Awakening was, moreover, the most intimate. Indeed, this school of "The New England Theology"[33] is the monument of the Awakening. Old Calvinism prevailed before the revival, and a liberal faction would surely have risen within its fold whether or not the religious storm had swept New England. But that apart from the Awakening there would have ever been a powerful, vigorous Edwardean party is highly improbable. In order to appreciate the connection between that party and the revival, it is necessary to examine more closely the theology of the Awakening itself.

Edwards' series of sermons in 1734 on the doctrine of justification by faith was a major cause of the Northampton revival. In 1738 Edwards noted that the "Beginning of the late Work of God . . . was so circumstanced, that I could not but look upon it as a remarkable Testimony of God's Approbation of the Doctrine of Justification by Faith alone. . . ." Many were beginning to doubt "that Way of Acceptance with God" and Edwards was even "greatly reproached for defending this Doctrine in the Pulpit," when "God's Work wonderfully broke forth."[34] The validity of this teaching was thus confirmed. Thomas Foxcroft believed such was also the case during the later revival. In 1741, Jonathan Dickinson published a primer of Calvinism[35] in a preface to which Foxcroft observed:

. . . I'm persuaded, that few (or none) have to report any remarkable Fruits of their Ministry, in a prevailing Work of Conviction, and numerous effectual Conversions, where there has been either an open Opposition to the Doctrines of Grace, or a total Absence of them, or but a cold and unfrequent Glancing at them.—When there is an eminently successful Ministry, and when living practical Religion is restor'd to a flourishing State among a professing People in any Place, I believe it will very commonly . . . be found, there's a Proportionable Recovery of these Gospel-Principles [i.e., Calvinism] to their primitive Use and Esteem, Power and Influence.

I frankly confess it is a pleasing Reflection to me. . . . That this kind of Divinity, although run down by some as obsolete, jejune & insipid to the refin'd Taste of the present free and thinking Age, yet has of late in a happy Measure retriev'd its Reputation, & establish'd its Value and Improvement with Multitudes among us. It has highly delighted me, to observe, with what a singular Gust this old-fashion'd mystical Divinity (so called) has been entertain'd by our awaken'd Congregations. . . .[36]

In September, 1745, twenty New England ministers, apparently following a suggestion made the previous May, issued a testimony "Professing The ancient Faith"[37] that further reveals the close alliance between Calvinism and the Awakening. "We cannot but . . . observe," the group witnessed, "that the principal Means of the late Revival were the more than ordinary preaching of such Scripture and most important Doctrines as these . . ." and there follow one and one-half pages of what would then have been called "Solid Calvinism." Perfectly respectable and time-honored doctrines are often now ridiculed as New Light, "and they who Preach the same Truths of the Gospel and experimental Piety as those great Divines, Hooker, Cotton, Shepard, Goodwin, Owen, Flavel, the Mathers, Willard, Stoddard, are represented by some as New Light Enthusiastical or Antinomian Preachers. . . ."[38] The identification of the revival with Calvinism seemed complete. John Bass, removed from his pastoral office at Ashford because of his Arminianism, complained that "calvinistick Principles" were "at this Day a Clergyman's main Defence, the best he can hit upon to provide him Food and Raiment, and to fix him in the good Graces of the Populace. . . ."[39] For those to whom the revival was a time when "multitudes were seriously, soberly and solemnly out of their wits," the Awakening was a discrediting of this "Ancient Faith." For those to whom it was the occasion of "an extraordinary pouring out of the Spirit of God," the Great Awakening was the irrefragable argument which demonstrated the truth of Calvinist orthodoxy, and "retriev'd its Reputation."

In this manner, the religious upheaval brought about a revival of and renewed interest in Calvinism. The frequency with which Calvinism is said to revive may suggest that there is a type of religious experience, and of theology interpreting that experience, which arises independently of direct borrowing. Much of the similarity between

Augustine, Calvin, and Edwards is to be explained rather in terms of a common experience than of a common source. The personal piety of Edwards, considered with the many conversion experiences of the revival period, brought divine grace as an immediate indwelling reality to the consciousness of a great number. The theology of this school, thus as suited to the pulpit as to the professorial desk, enjoyed a wide and effectual dispersion. Joseph Bellamy's *True Religion delineated*[40] was the *Pilgrim's Progress* of New England.

It is of course incorrect to equate Edwardeanism with the Great Awakening, or to regard the former as the result of the latter. The revival had, however, very significant and marked effects upon Edwards and upon his theological school. In the first place, any doubts about the verity and efficacy of Calvinism which Edwards might have entertained were effaced by the Northampton and New England revivals. The later and more pervasive revival, moreover, in calling attention to Edwards' theological position, forced him to conclusions he otherwise might not have reached. This is obviously so in the case of the *Treatise Concerning Religious Affections* and the *Humble Inquiry*.[41] It is likewise true, but in a less direct way, of his later theological works. Though Edwards labored long upon a theological summa, the published portions of his system have a sequence that has order only in relation to the attacks which Calvinism, following the Awakening, sustained. His *Fredom of the Will*, published in 1754, was written in the recognition that

The decision of most of the points in controversy, between Calvinists and Arminians, depends on the determination of this grand article concerning the freedom of the Will, requisite to moral agency; and that by clearing and establishing the Calvinistic doctrine in this point, the chief arguments are obviated, by which Arminian doctrines in general are supported, and the contrary doctrines demonstratively confirmed.[42]

The treatise on *The Great Christian Doctrine of Original Sin*, prepared for publication just prior to his death in 1758, came out at a time when Samuel Webster, Peter Clark, Charles Chauncy, and Joseph Bellamy were considering the merits and demerits of that much-abused doctrine. Edwards' essay on *The Nature of True Virtue*, not published until 1765, was both the effect and cause of protracted controversy.[43]

In addition to its direct effect on Edwards, the Awakening had a determinative influence on the fate of his school by bringing to him his two earliest and most influential disciples, Joseph Bellamy (1719-

1790) and Samuel Hopkins (1721-1803). Bellamy and Hopkins found in the Awakening the verification of, if not the impetus for, their theology, even as they found in Edwards their mentor and standard of excellence. Ordained only a few years before the Great Awakening, Bellamy gave strong and able support to the movement. He was temporarily swept away from his parish by its force, preaching for some months in 1741 in both Connecticut and Massachusetts. Not wholly satisfied with the propriety of this method of evangelism, he returned to his church at Bethlehem which he pastored for fifty years. Bellamy, in whose home approximately sixty ministerial candidates were boarded, bedded, and instructed, extended to thousands through his teaching, his popular writing, and his even more popular preaching a faithful representation of Edwardean piety. Hopkins, while a senior at Yale, heard Edwards preach there his *Distinguishing Marks* in 1741 and thereupon decided that, after graduation from Yale, he would pursue his theological studies in Northampton. A powerful thinker, he propagated and modified Edwards' theology. Within a generation after the Awakening these three theologians had provided enough grist for the doctrinal mills to keep other theologians grinding for generations more.

Because it was Calvinistic, the New Divinity was concerned pre-eminently with the absolute sovereignty of God: God was almighty before He was loving and perfect before He was pliable. Because it was closely associated with the Great Awakening, the New Divinity School saw the operation of that sovereignty chiefly in the redemption of mankind. "God's Sovereignty in Man's Salvation,"[44] that is to say, the doctrine of a divine redeeming grace, was the heart of the Strict Calvinists' theology. That truth, above all else, must be honored and protected, at whatever cost to human pride, at whatever odds with human reason. In the religious experiences of the revival such theology found its stimulus. In 1742 Timothy Allen, leader of the short-lived Shepherd's Tent at New London, rhapsodized that he had been led to "the most wonderfull, wonderfull, views of Richest, Richest, freest Grace of God; oh the Grace! oh the Grace! My Soul sees Oceans, boundless Oceans of Grace. . . .[45] This is not theology; but it is a force for determining which direction theology shall take. This is the real clue to the revival's effect upon the New Divinity.

As the Liberals labored to reduce religion to morality, the New Calvinists made morality religious, and dependent upon divine grace. The Liberals thought upon the habits of man who made regular and free choices, and thereupon attributed to him a free will. The New Calvinists thought upon the nature of God, and thereupon found free will inconsonant with divine sovereignty. Common sense spiced with just a pinch of Arminianism enabled one to see that good men were nearer to God than evil men, that filthy rags could be exchanged for better attire. Revelation and history read through the lens of Calvinism and revival experiences disclosed that man was, apart from the work of the Holy Spirit in him, wholly depraved and rightfully damned. Thus the Awakening set in sharpest relief the Strict Calvinists opposing and opposed by those who would "substitute Man's moral Attainments in the Room of the Righteousness of God, by Faith in Jesus Christ."[46]

This clear confrontation accounts to a major degree for the persistent appeal of the Great Awakening. For nowhere else in the western world did the double reaction against the devotional decline and theological pedantry of the seventeenth century focus on a single movement. In New England, both pietism and the Enlightenment found their provocation in the revival's course and wake; that neither movement has yet fully dissipated its energies is a fact with which all subsequent American religious history must deal.

The Enlightenment, though logically blending into an amorphous cultural humanism, stubbornly clings to its genius, prodding and rankling the local church, the uneasy seminary, the established denomination. It impels men to seek daringly, yet often devotedly, after ultimate truth—all the while urging that they spurn the facile, comforting answers, the respected, hoary creeds. It aggravates the cosmic restlessness of all and irritates the naïve, pedestrian fundamentalism of some. New England's pietism, though logically evaporating into a lawless subjective mysticism, has with equal obstinacy refused to expire. It makes the ultimate truth worth seeking in the first instance, and constantly revises official orthodoxy—privately at least—in terms of new experience. Its zeal, on occasion without knowledge, inspires the church, establishes the seminary, and even now and then redeems the ecclesiastical machinery.

That New England's piety survived is due in part to its vigorous evangelism which found so gigantic a challenge in the expansion to the west. In part, it is due also to the dogged allegiance to an external, objective authority: the Scripture. But most peculiarly, it survived because the Edwardean theology was a powerful, capacious channel through which it could steadily flow. In western Christendom, the pietist movement did not generally produce a theological school.

Rather, in its reaction to arid scholasticism, it tended to minimize, even to ignore, particular systems of doctrine. Reawakened piety in New England, however, thanks to the genius of Jonathan Edwards, was followed by and incorporated in a theological school; it thereby stands unique; it thereby survived.

It seems hardly correct, then, to assert that Edwards was "a horrible example to his posterity" and "with his death his ideas lost their vitality."[47] True, multitudes no longer thronged ministers inquiring "What must I do to be saved?" nor sang of the "Richest, Richest, freest Grace of God." But it is no less true that Edwards' weighed reflection in his popular biography of Brainerd epitomized, for a large segment of later American Protestantism, the real nature of the religious life:

> . . . there is indeed such a thing as true experimental religion, arising from an immediate divine influence, supernaturally enlightening and convincing the mind, and powerfully impressing, quickening, sanctifying, and governing the heart; which religion is indeed an amiable thing, of happy tendency, and of no hurtful consequence to human society. . . .[48]

Personal piety, the life force of religion, was the legacy of the Great Awakening to those of its heirs who loved to ascribe absolute sovereignty, above all others, to God.

In the succeeding decades, however, this piety which had inspired so much theology found itself thriving on several shades of opinion and eventually on hardly any opinion at all. A pragmatic America and a frenetic frontier asked of the sermon only that it work. If effects were evident in terms of personal reform and multiplying churches, what more was required? Nothing. Thus, the discrediting of "human learning," characteristic of only a minority during the Awakening, later became typical of a majority of Protestantism. As Sidney Mead observes, "Since around 1800 Americans have in effect been given the hard choice between being intelligent according to the standards prevailing in their intellectual centers, and being religious according to the standards prevailing in their denominations."[49]

Happily, there remained a few for whom a warm heart was not quite enough. Notably in and around Edwards' own college, Yale, stalwarts standing on Edwardean ground grappled with strange tempers and manfully embraced hard facts. They assumed the task which the Edwardean school had set for itself: namely, to bring together faith and reason, experience and history, heart and head. In a word, to make men whole. This has always been the task of Christian theology and is unlikely ever to be otherwise. In this endeavor, the revival's own theological school was not completely successful, despite an ability to adapt and a readiness to conciliate. In the nineteenth century, the advent of critical biblical studies, Darwinism, and something approaching cultural unity made theological reconstruction more difficult and more urgent. In our own time, neo-orthodoxy probes diverging passes, each one supposedly leading to a pinnacle of synthesis. The fast-held faith that there is such a pinnacle, and that there are scalable approaches, urges the disciplined adventurer on. That the chasms below are littered with the remains of previous expeditions is really beside the point. Of course it is easier not to climb at all, to settle for Greek or Hebrew, science or poetry, mind or matter. But to accept one source of truth to the exclusion of all other sources is to court disaster on a fearfully grand scale. Besides, the climb is exhilarating—or so thought the Puritan.

NOTES

CHAPTER 1. PIETY AND THE PURITAN

1. Luke 9:50.
2. See L. J. Trinterud, "Origins of Puritanism," *Church History* XX:1, 37-57.
3. *The Keyes of the Kingdom of Heaven* (London, 1644), chap. 7.
4. *The Way of the Congregational Churches Cleared* (London, 1648), Pt. I, chap. 3.
5. John White, *The Planters Plea*, quoted in Perry Miller, *Orthodoxy in Massachusetts 1630-1650* (Cambridge, 1933), 141.
6. Only Massachusetts Bay and New Haven limited suffrage to church members. But in Plymouth and Connecticut as well the position of leadership enjoyed by Congregationalism, along with the need and desire for a careful, rigid control of behavior, led to a close co-operation between civil and religious authorities.
7. This rule of discipline which in its final form included the recently formulated Westminster Confession of Faith was presented to the Massachusetts General Court in 1649 and finally approved by it in 1651.
8. Quoted in Clifford Shipton, *Sibley's Harvard Graduates* (Boston, 1933-45) VII, 467, from Byles' Letter Book. See also Ola E. Winslow, *Meetinghouse Hill 1630-1783* (New York, 1952), chap. 10.
9. See W. A. Brown, "Covenant Theology," in Hastings' *ERE*; also Perry Miller, "The Marrow of Puritan Divinity," *Publications, The Col. Soc. of Mass.*, XXXII, 247-300; E. H. Emerson, "Calvin and Covenant Theology," *Church History*, XXV:2, 136-44.
10. See Perry Miller, *New England Mind* (New York, 1939), Bk. IV.
11. Williston Walker, *A History of the Congregational Churches in the United States* (New York, 1894), 104.
12. Thomas Hooker, *A Survey of the Summe of Church-Discipline* . . . (London, 1648), preface.
13. *Survey*, Pt. III, quoted in W. Walker, *The Creeds and Platforms of Congregationalism* (New York, 1893), 145, note 5.
14. Quoted *ibid.*, 252.
15. Later (1654) to become the second president of Harvard College.
16. Text in W. Walker, *Creeds*, 328. "Owning the Covenant" refers to the church covenant, not the covenant of grace. To "own" the latter would be the equivalent of a profession of faith, which was precisely what the members of this group lacked. "Publickly professing their assent" to the doctrines meant that they were disposed to agree with and believe the articles of faith so far as they could without possessing the gift of God's grace.
17. ". . . in these things, where moral fitness and spiritual qualifications are wanting, membership alone is not sufficient for full communion" Fourth Proposition, Synod of 1662, quoted in Walker, *Creeds*, 327.
18. *Ibid.*
19. So called from the name of its most influential, though not its first exponent,

Solomon Stoddard (1643-1729), powerful minister at Northampton, Massachusetts, and grandfather of Jonathan Edwards.

20. Reforming Synod of 1679, I, 1.
21. Text in Walker, *Creeds*, 486-89.
22. But see John White, *New England's Lamentations* (Boston, 1734), 33-36.
23. Text in Walker, *Creeds*, 426-432.
24. Perry Miller, "Declension in a Bible Commonwealth," *Proceedings of the American Antiquarian Society*, LI, 68 f.
25. *Ibid.*, 68; see also 84, 87, 92.
26. Joseph Haroutunian, *Piety Versus Moralism* (New York, 1932), xxiv.
27. Religion in colonial New England can be described for the most part in terms of these four religious bodies: Congregationalists (or Presbyterians), Anglicans, Quakers, and Baptists. The history of the Jews in Rhode Island is a fascinating chapter, as is the New England attitude toward Roman Catholicism. Yet these phases of New England's religious history, together with such minor movements as Gortonites, Seekers, and Sandemanians, are not the warp and woof of that history.
28. John Barnard, *Two Sermons* (Boston, 1714), quoted in Haroutunian, *op. cit.*, 3.
29. From John White's *Lamentations*, the full title of which is as follows: *New England's Lamentaitons* [*sic*], *Under these Three Heads, The Decay of the Power of Godliness; The Danger of Arminian Principles; The Declining State of our Church-Order, Government and Discipline. With the Means of these Declensions, and the Methods of our Recovery.*
30. *The Works of President Edwards in four volumes* (New York, 1843), III, 323. Hereafter *Works* refers to this edition.

CHAPTER 2. RIPPLES OF REVIVAL

1. B. Trumbull, *A Complete History of Connecticut Civil and Ecclesiastical* (New London, 1890), II, 104.
2. *Ibid.* The population of Windham at this time was only about two hundred families.
3. Edwards' *Works*, III, 232.
4. P. Miller, "Solomon Stoddard 1643-1729," *Harvard Theological Review*, XXXIV, 316.
5. Stoddard's *A Guide to Christ* and his *The Safety of Appearing* were both reprinted in Boston in 1742.
6. For life of Edwards (1703-1758), see S. E. Dwight, *The Life of President Edwards* (New York, 1829), or Ola E. Winslow, *Jonathan Edwards 1703-1758*, (New York, 1940); for his thought, see Frank Hugh Foster, *A Genetic History of New England Theology* (Chicago, 1907), and Perry Miller, *Jonathan Edwards* (New York, 1949).
7. *Works*, III, 232.
8. *Ibid.*, 234.
9. *Ibid.*, 235, *passim*.
10. *Ibid.*, 236.
11. See map, following p. 20.
12. For a full account of this epidemic, see Ernest Caulfield, *A True History of the Terrible Epidemic vulgarly called The Throat Distemper* (New Haven, 1939). For the epidemic in the Middle Colonies, see J. Dickinson, *Observations on that Terrible Disease . . .* (Boston, 1740).

13. Thomas Prince, *An Account of the Revival of Religion in Boston* (Boston, reprint 1823), 6.

14. How the *Narrative* came to be written is told most fully in the appendix to William Williams' *Duty and Interest of a People . . .* (Boston, 1736). The full title of that letter, as published in Boston in 1738, is as follows: *A Faithful Narrative of the Surprising Work of God in the Conversion of Many Hundred Souls in Northampton, and the Neighboring Towns and Villages of the County of Hampshire, in the Province of Massachusetts-Bay in New-England, In a Letter to the Reverend Dr. Colman of Boston. Written by the Rev*ᵈ*. Mr. Edwards, Minister of Northampton, Nov. 6, 1736. Published with a Large Preface by the Rev. Dr. Watts and Dr. Guyse of London: To Which a Shorter [Preface] is added by Some of the Reverend Ministers of Boston. Together with an Attestation from Some of the Reverend Ministers of Hampshire.* The Third Edition. Boston: N. E. Printed by S. Kneeland and T. Green, for D. Henchman, in Corn-Hill, 1738. It proved to be one of Edwards' most popular works, undergoing thirty editions, including Dutch and German.

15. In the Colman Papers at the Massachusetts Historical Society; the letter is dated May 19, 1737.

16. *Works*, III, 271.

17. Colman Papers, MHS.

18. ". . . this was the Doctrine on which this Work in its Beginning was founded, as it evidently was in the whole progress of it." Preface to *Discourses*.

19. T. Prince, *An Account*, 7.

20. *The Works of President Edwards in Ten Volumes* (New York, 1829), X, 48.

21. *Works*, III, 238.

22. Some direct influence may be inferred from the publication in Boston in 1735 of Gilbert Tennent's *A Solemn Warning to the Secure World . . .* and of John Tennent's *The Nature of Regeneration opened . . .* In 1739 the publication in Boston of the writings of Middle Colony revivalists was greatly accelerated.

23. E.g., Samuel Buell (pp. 102 f.), Samuel Finley (pp. 96 f.), David Brainerd (pp. 113 f.), Jonathan Dickinson (pp. 14 f.), and Gilbert Tennent (pp. 35 f.). All page references are to W. B. Sprague, *Annals of the American Pulpit* (New York, 1859), III.

24. See L. J. Trinterud, *The Forming of an American Tradition. A Re-examination of Colonial Presbyterianism* (Philadelphia, 1949); C. H. Maxson, *The Great Awakening in the Middle Colonies* (Chicago, 1920).

25. Ebenezer Pemberton, *Practical Discourses on Various Texts* (Boston, 1941).

CHAPTER 3. THE GRAND ITINERANTS

1. George Whitefield, *A Continuation of the Reverend Mr. Whitefield's Journal, From a few Days after his Return to Georgia To his arrival at Falmouth, on the 11th of March 1741. Containing An Account of the Work of God at Georgia, Rhode-Island, New-England, New-York, Pennsylvania and South-Carolina. The Seventh Journal* (London, 1741). Hereafter referred to as the *Seventh Journal*.

2. *Three Letters To The Reverend George Whitefield* (Philadelphia, n.d. [1739]). Colman wrote the first of these.

3. See the *Boston Weekly News-Letter* for the year 1740.

4. *Boston Weekly News-Letter*, Sept. 25, 1740.

5. *The Works of the Reverend George Whitefield, M.A. . . .* London, 1771-1772 (in seven volumes), I, 216. The letter is dated Sept. 28, 1740.

6. See map following p. 27.
7. *Seventh Journal.*
8. Whitefield's estimates of the number of his listeners are almost certainly exaggerated, yet not completely disproportionate. One Boston newspaper set the figure of those attending his farewell sermon at twenty-three thousand. See Joseph Tracy, *The Great Awakening. A History of the Revival of Religion in the time of Edwards and Whitefield* (Boston, 1845), 88.
9. T. Prince, *An Account*, 9.
10. *Seventh Journal.*
11. *Diary of the Rev. Daniel Wadsworth, seventh pastor of the First Church of Christ in Hartford*, (1737-1747), (Hartford, 1894).
12. From Franklin's *Memoirs* (I, 87), quoted in L. Tyerman, *The Life of the Rev. George Whitefield* (New York, 1877), I, 375-76.
13. Garden presided over the first Episcopal Court to be held in the Colonies. It met, July 15, 1740, for the purpose of suspending Whitefield from the privileges of his ministerial office for certain liturgical irregularities, particularly for his failure to follow the prescribed prayers in the Book of Common Prayer.
14. *Boston Evening-Post*, Nov. 10, 1740.
15. *Seventh Journal*, 54-55.
16. For the life of Charles Chauncy (1705-1787), see Sprague, *Annals*, VIII, 8-13; Shipton, *Harvard Graduates*, VI, 439-67; and *Dictionary of American Biography*, IV, 42, 43.
17. [Charles Chauncy] *A Letter from A Gentleman in Boston, to Mr. George Wishart, One of the Ministers of Edinburgh, Concerning the State of Religion in New-England* (Edinburgh, 1742). Though the letter is actually anonymous, it is generally and rightly thought to be Chauncy's.
18. Published in Boston, 1745.
19. Noted in Tyerman, *Life of Whitefield*, II, 124-25.
20. *Boston Weekly News-Letter*, April 22, 1742.
21. *Works*, I, 296-97.
22. *The Testimony of the President, Professors, Tutors and Hebrew Instructor of Harvard College in Cambridge, Against the Reverend Mr. George Whitefield, And his Conduct* (Boston, 1744). *The Declaration of the Rector and Tutors of Yale-College in New-Haven, against the Reverend Mr. George Whitefield, his principles and designs. In a letter to him* (Boston, 1745).
23. On the life of Gilbert Tennent (1703-1764), see Sprague, *Annals*, III, 35-41; A. Alexander, *Biographical Sketches of the Founder and Principal Alumni of the Log College* . . . (Princeton, 1845); R. Webster, *A History of the Presbyterian Church in America* (Philadelphia, 1857), 387-97; and the sketch in *Dictionary of American Biography*, XVIII, 366-69.
24. *Seventh Journal*, 62-63.
25. *Works*, I, 220-21.
26. C. H. Maxson, *The Great Awakening in the Middle Colonies*, 28.
27. *Boston Weekly Post-Boy*, Jan. 12, 1741.
28. Quoted in Tyerman, *Life of Whitefield*, II, 125. The letter is dated Dec. 28, 1740; original in Boston Public Library, Chamberlain A3, 5.
29. T. Prince, *An Account*, 12.
30. Chauncy, *Letter to Wishart*, 10 f.
31. *The Examiner, Examined* . . . (Philadelphia, 1745), 3.
32. Because the *News-Letter* did not bother to give Tennent's daily itinerary, and because Tennent kept no journal, it is not possible to follow his journeying in detail. In a letter written to Whitefield April 25, 1741, he refers, however, to many of the places he visited. Among those mentioned are Ipswich, Hamlet,

Marblehead, Plymouth, Providence, Newport, New London, Lime, Guilford, and New Haven. See John Gillies, *Historical Collections* (Glasgow, 1754), II, 132-33.

33. T. Prince, *An Account*, 19.

34. The letter is printed in Gillies, *Hist. Collections*, II, 132 f.

35. All quotations in this paragraph are from Gilbert Tennent, *The Danger of an Unconverted Ministry, Considered in a Sermon on Mark vi.34 . . . From the Second Edition printed at Philadelphia* (Boston, 1742).

36. For life of John Hancock (1703-1744) of Braintree, see Sprague, *Annals*, I, 240-41.

37. [John Hancock,] *The Examiner, or Gilbert against Tennent. Containing a Confutation of the Reverend Mr. Gilbert Tennent and his Adherents: Extracted chiefly from his Own Writings, and formed upon his Own Plan of comparing the Moravian Principles, with the Standard of Orthodoxy, in distinct Columns. Together with some Strictures on the Preface to the Rev. Mr. Tennent's Five Sermons and Appendix lately published, and subscribed by Six Reverend Ministers of Boston. The whole being an Essay towards answering three important Queries, viz. 1. What is Truth in the present Religious Commotions in the Land? 2. What is the shortest Method finding the whole Truth? 3. Whether such as are given to Change, ought not in Conscience to make their publick Retractions, according to St. Austin? [sic] The whole Essay is submitted to the Judgment of Common Sense. By Philalethes . . .* (Boston, 1743).

38. See Evans, *American Bibliography*, #5298.

39. For biographical sketch of Davenport (1710-1757), see Sprague, *Annals*, III, 80-92; Webster, *Presbyterian Church*, 531-45; and F. B. Dexter, *Biographical Sketches of the Graduates of Yale College* (New York, 1885), I, 447-50.

40. Samuel Blair (1712-1751) was one of the important "New Sides" of the New Brunswick Presbytery. A friend of Tennent's and pastor at Londonderry (Pennsylvania), he had little direct influence on the revival in New England.

41. Eleazar Wheelock was apparently instrumental in Davenport's coming to Connecticut. See the letter to his wife, dated May 5, 1740, from Southold, Long Island, in Dartmouth College Library.

42. The letter is in the *Boston Weekly Post-Boy*, printed August 20, 1741.

43. "Diary of Joshua Hempstead of New London, Connecticut, 1711-1758," *Collections of the New London County Historical Society* (New London, 1901), I, entry for Feb. 27, 1742.

44. Biographical sketch of Pomeroy (1704-1784) in Sprague, *Annals*, I, 394-97; Dexter, *Graduates of Yale*, I, 485-88.

45. This order of the Assembly is reprinted in the *Boston Weekly News-Letter*, July 10, 1742.

46. *Boston Evening-Post*, July 5, 1742.

47. T. Prince, *An Account*, 32.

48. The document was signed by Benjamin Colman, Joseph Sewall, Thomas Prince, John Webb, William Cooper, Thomas Foxcroft, Samuel Checkley, William Wellsteed, Joshua Gee, Mather Byles, Ellis Gray, Andrew Eliot, Hull Abbot, and Thomas Prentice.

49. Andrew Croswell, *Reply to the Declaration of a Number of the associated Ministers in Boston and Charlestown, with Regard to the Rev. Mr. James Davenport and his Conduct . . .* (Boston, 1742).

50. Jonathan Dickinson (1688-1747) was the influential Presbyterian minister at Elizabethtown, New Jersey. Second only to Edwards as a leading American Calvinist of his day, he, like Edwards, was president of the College of New Jersey (Princeton) and, also like Edwards, died soon after taking that office;

Sprague, *Annals*, III, 14-18; H. C. Cameron, *Jonathan Dickinson and the College of New Jersey* (Princeton, 1880).

51. Tennent's remarks on Davenport actually constitute a postscript to his letter to Dickinson, and were published (in the *Boston Weekly News-Letter*, July 22, 1742) perhaps without his permission.

52. Quoted from *Boston Weekly News-Letter*, Aug. 26, 1742.

53. The incident here referred to is the famous "burning of the books" episode. For an eyewitness and tongue-in-cheek account, see the *Boston Weekly Post-Boy*, March 28, 1743; or a different report in the *Boston Evening-Post*, April 11, 1743.

54. Both of Lebanon, Williams (1700-1776) pastored the First Church there, while Wheelock (1711-1779), later first president of Dartmouth, presided over the Second or North Society. Sprague, *Annals*, I, 321-26, 397-403.

55. *Two Letters From the Reverend Mr. Williams & Wheelock of Lebanon, To the Rev. Mr. Davenport, Which were The principal Means of his late Conviction and Retraction. With A Letter from Mr. Davenport, desiring their Publication, for the Good of others. And His Explanation of some Passages in his late Confession* (Boston, 1744).

56. The "Confessions" are enclosed in a letter from Solomon Williams to Thomas Prince, and printed in Boston in 1744. Reprinted in Sprague, *Annals*, III, 86-88; and in Tracy, *History of the Revival*, 249-52.

CHAPTER 4. THE FLOOD, 1741-1742

1. John C. Miller, "Religion, Finance and Democracy in Massachuetts," *New England Quarterly*, VI, 29-58.

2. Perry Miller, *Jonathan Edwards*, 175.

3. Eugene E. White, "Decline of the Great Awakening in New England: 1741 to 1746," *New England Quarterly*, XXIV:1, 35-52.

4. Richard D. Mosier, *The American Temper* (Berkeley and Los Angeles, 1952), 76 f. See also Clinton Rossiter, *Seedtime of The Republic* (New York, 1953), 57.

5. Mosier, *The American Temper*, 77.

6. See chap. 2.

7. For life of Buell (1716-1798) see Dexter, *Graduates of Yale*, I, 664-69; Sprague, *Annals*, III, 102-13; and S. Beull, *A Faithful Narrative* . . . (Sag-Harbor, 1803). While a student at Yale, Buell kept a diary which, unfortunately, was destroyed by fire in 1911.

8. The letter, dated April 20, 1742, is in the Dartmouth College Library (DCL).

9. W. Patten, *Reminiscences of the late Rev. Samuel Hopkins* . . . (Boston, 1843), 26.

10. Quoted in Sprague, *Annals*, III, 103.

11. A. M., *The State of Religion in New-England* . . . (Glasgow, 1742), 16.

12. On life of Wheelock, see J. D. McCallum, *Eleazar Wheelock Founder of Dartmouth College* (Hanover, 1939); Sprague, *Annals*, I, 397-403; Dexter, *Graduates of Yale*, I, 493-97; and E. H. Gillett, "President Wheelock and the Great Revival," *Amer. Presb. Review*, I (n.s.), 1869, 520-35. The letters in DCL, written and received by Wheelock in the revival period, reveal the depth to which he was involved in the movement and furnish valuable data on many aspects of it.

13. Unlike Whitefield's *Journal*, however, Wheelock's was not published until long after his death, and then only partially. See *American Quarterly Register*, X:1, 12 f.

14. *Ibid.* The letter is dated June 9, 1741.
15. *American Quarterly Register*, X, 1, 12 f.
16. *Ibid.*, 11-12.
17. On life of Josiah Cotton (1703-1780), see Shipton, *Harvard Graduates*, VII, 50-56. Cotton was installed with much pomp in 1728 as a part of Massachusetts' missionary work, his salary subsidized by Old South Church, Boston.
18. *Amer. Quar. Register, op. cit.*
19. See the fascinating sketch of Daniel Rogers (1707-1785) in Shipton, *Harvard Graduates*, VII, 554-60.
20. Letter to Daniel Rogers, Jan. 18, 1741/42, in DCL.
21. Letter to Stephen Williams, February 3, 1741/42, in DCL.
22. Dexter, *Graduates of Yale*, I, 485-88; Sprague, *Annals*, I, 394-97; and Webster, *Presbyterian Church*, 592-99.
23. Shipton, *Harvard Graduates*, VII, 244-47.
24. Webster, *Presbyterian Church*, 583-85.
25. Shipton, *Harvard Graduates*, VI, 556-60.
26. *Ibid.*, V, 396-403.
27. Benjamin Trumbull, *A Complete History of Connecticut Civil and Ecclesiastical* . . . II, 138 f.
28. *Boston Weekly News-Letter*, Nov. 13, 1741.
29. Letter to Wheelock, Feb. 27, 1742/43, in DCL.
30. T. Pickering, *The Rev. Mr. Pickering's Letters To the Rev. N. Rogers and Mr. D. Rogers* . . . (Boston, 1742).
31. Shurtleff reported in the *Christian History*, I, 382-94.
32. The characterization is Trumbull's, *Hist. of Conn.*, II, 112. Only to a Calvinist could persons be both secure and loose at the same moment. Eleazar Wheelock, who heard the sermon, described it for his friend, Benjamin Trumbull.
33. *Works*, IV, 313-21. This notorious sermon has had twenty-three editions. One of the passages on which its fame rests is here reproduced.
    "The God that holds you over the pit of hell, much as one holds a spider or some loathsome insect, over the fire, abhors you, and is dreadfully provoked; his wrath towards you burns like fire; he looks upon you as worthy of nothing else, but to be cast into the fire; he is of purer eyes than to bear to have you in his sight; you are ten thousand times so abominable in his eyes, as the most hateful and venomous serpent is in ours. You have offended him infinitely more than ever a stubborn rebel did his prince; and yet it is nothing but his hand that holds you from falling into the fire every moment: it is ascribed to nothing else, that you did not go to hell the last night; that you was suffered to awake again in this world, after you closed your eyes to sleep; and there is no other reason to be given, why you have not dropped into hell since you arose in the morning, but that God's hand has held you up: there is no other reason of God, provoking his pure eyes by your sinful wicked manner of attending his solemn worship: yea, there is nothing else that is to be given as a reason why you do not this very moment drop down into hell." (317, 318.)
    The original manuscript of this sermon shows that Edwards had not at the time of preaching written the sermon out in full. The tradition that Edwards quietly read the sermon to the congregation is then not very credible. See Dexter, "The Manuscripts of Jonathan Edwards," in *Proceedings of MHS*, XV. Nor is it probable that he stared at the bell rope (P. Miller, *Jonathan Edwards*, 145). See Edwards' remarks on how to preach about eternal damnation, which remarks were written just two months after the Enfield sermon, *Works*, I, 538.
34. Published in Boston the same year with a preface by William Cooper and

letters from Benjamin Colman describing the revival in and around Boston. For a discussion of the contents, see chap. 6.

35. The "Errours" to which Edwards refers were of Davenport's doing; Davenport had just a few days before this letter was written perpetrated the bonfire episode in New London . . . Proceedings of the MHS, XV.

36. Sidney Mead, Nathanael Taylor (Chicago, 1942), 128.

37. Christian History, I, 367-81.

38. Ibid., 372.

39. Benjamin Colman (1673-1747) enjoyed the favor and, in the colonies, uncommon honor of a contemporary biographer. His son-in-law and student, Ebenezer Turell (1702-1778) left a valuable and useful account in The Life and Character of the Reverend Benjamin Colman, D.D. . . . (Boston, 1749). Of Colman's participation in the Great Awakening, Turell is, however, singularly uncommunicative. See Sprague, Annals, I, 223-29; Shipton, Harvard Graduates, IV, 120-37; C. H. Chapman, Life and Influence of Benjamin Colman, Boston University School of Theology Th.D. dissertation, abstract published, 1948.

40. Turell, Benjamin Colman, 168-70.

41. Benjamin Colman, Souls flying to Jesus Christ pleasant and admirable to behold. A Sermon Preach'd at the Opening an Evening-Lecture, in Brattle-Street, Boston . . . To a very crowded Audience . . . (Boston, 1740), 5, 22.

42. Ibid., 26.

43. Proceedings of the MHS, LIII, 197 f.

44. Benjamin Colman, The Great GOD has magnified his WORD to the Children of Men . . . (Boston, 1742), 32.

45. Proceedings of the MHS, LIII, 203.

46. Christian History, I, 412-16; II, 80-91.

47. Ibid., II, 13-21 (pp. 15-16 wanting).

48. Christian History, I, 397-98.

49. American Quarterly Register, X, 1, 12.

50. Quoted in G. L. Walker, Some Aspects of the Religious Life of New England (Boston, 1897), 89-91.

51. S. L. Blake, The Separates or Strict Congregationalists of New England (Boston, 1902), 143 f.

52. Colman, Souls flying to Jesus Christ . . . (Boston, 1740), 5.

53. See C. Chauncy, Letter to Wishart . . . (Edinburgh, 1742), 7.

54. Letter to Wheelock, April 20, 1742, in DCL.

55. The opposition of Chauncy to the revival is treated in chap. 6.

56. Three other Boston ministers, William Welstead and Ellis Gray of New Brick Church, and William Hooper of West Church, followed a sort of wavering neutrality. See the latter's Apostles Neither Imposters nor Enthusiasts . . . (Boston, 1742). Hooper entered the Anglican fold unexpectedly in 1746. Anglican and Baptist attitudes toward the revival are considered in chap. 7.

57. On life of Samuel Mather (1706-1785), see Sprague, Annals, I, 371-74; Shipton, Harvard Graduates, VII, 216-38.

58. Quoted in Sprague, Annals, I, 371.

59. With Mather went ninety-three members of Second Church to form a separate congregation (Bennett Street Church). They continued to meet separately until Mather's death, when most of the members returned to Second.

60. Mather Byles (1707-1788) was the wit among Boston's clergy; his inability to resist a pun, even more than his fancy for writing poetry, caused him to be regarded with much suspicion and occasionally with disgust. Most of the Byles anecdotes are preserved in William Tudor, Life of James Otis (Boston, 1823),

and some are reprinted in Sprague, *Annals*, I, 376-82, and in Shipton, *Harvard Graduates*, VII, 464-93.

61. On the life of Cooper (1694-1743), see Sprague, *Annals*, I, 288-91; Shipton, *Harvard Graduates*, V, 624-34; and the funeral sermon preached by Colman, *Jesus Weeping over his dead Friend* . . . (Boston, 1744), 26 f.

62. William Cooper, *The Doctrine of Predestination unto Life* . . . (Boston, 1740), particularly 130 f.

63. William Cooper, *One shall be taken and another left* . . . *A Season wherein there was a remarkable Display of the sovereign Grace of God in the work of Conversion* . . . (Boston, 1741), 14.

64. *Ibid.*, 16, 20.

65. A sketch of Thomas Foxcroft (1696-1769) is in Sprague, *Annals*, I, 308-10. The funeral sermon was preached by his surviving colleague, Charles Chauncy, with whom, despite profound theological differences, amicable relations had been maintained.

66. Thomas Foxcroft, *Some seasonable Thoughts on Evangelic Preaching* . . . (Boston, 1740), 43.

67. For remarks on the life of Joseph Sewall (1688-1769), see Sprague, *Annals*, I, 278-80; and Shipton, *Harvard Graduates*, V, 376-93.

68. Joseph Sewall, *The Holy Spirit Convincing the World of Sin, of Righteousness, and of Judgment* . . . (Boston, 1741), 19.

69. Joseph Sewall, *God's People must Enquire of Him to bestow the Blessings promised in his Word* . . . (Boston, 1742), 29.

70. T. Prince, *An Account of the Revival of Religion in Boston, in the Years 1740-1-2-3* (Boston, reprint 1823). For Prince's life (1687-1758), see Sprague, *Annals*, I, 304-7; and Shipton, *Harvard Graduates*, V, 341-68.

71. For a discussion of this magazine, see L. N. Richardson, *A History of Early American Magazines* (New York, 1931), 58 f. It probably came into being as a result of a suggestion by Jonathan Edwards; *Works*, III, 425.

72. *Christian History*, I, 160.

73. Regarding John Webb (1687-1750), see Shipton, *Harvard Graduates*, V, 463-71.

74. John Webb, *Christ's Suit to the Sinner, while he stands and knocks at the Door. A Sermon Preach'd in a Time of Great Awakening* . . . (Boston, 1741).

75. Andrew Eliot (1719-1778) felt as late as 1745 that though Whitefield was probably the accidental cause of many of the errors, nevertheless, to call him a "rank enthusiast" was to carry "the matter too far." Sprague, *Annals*, I, 417.

76. See chap. 5, p. 65.

77. See Shipton, *Harvard Graduates*, VI, 74-78; and sermon by Checkley (1696-1769), *Little Children brought to Christ* . . . (Boston, 1741).

78. See chap. 3, p. 27.

79. The nine "new lights" were Gee, Foxcroft, Colman, Cooper, Sewall, Prince, Webb, Eliot, and Checkley. The three "old lights" were Byles, Mather, and Chauncy (the neutrals are mentioned above, note 56).

80. Facts on Moorhead's life (d. 1773) are meager. Coming from Ireland, this Scotsman was in 1730 invited to pastor the "Church of Presbyterian strangers" in Boston. Moorhead accepted the position, continuing in it until his death. Fiery and unlearned, he was an extreme supporter of the revival, but published nothing in this period—a rare virtue. See Sprague, *Annals*, III, 44-46; A. M., *State of Religion in New England* (Glasgow, 1742), 11; and *Proceedings of MHS*, LIII, 211-13.

81. See chap. 7, p. 116 f.

82. Cooper's preface to Edwards' *Distinguishing Marks*.

83. Examples of such reprints are J. Alleine (1633-1688), *An Alarm to Unconverted Sinners* (Boston, 1741 and again in 1743); Samuel Corbin, *Advice to Sinners Under Conviction* (Boston, 1741), and his *An Awakening Call from the eternal God to the Unconverted* (Boston, 1742); Thomas Shepard (1605-1649), *The Sincere Convert* and his *The Sound Believer* (Boston, 1742); and Solomon Stoddard (1643-1729), *A Guide to Christ. Or, the Way of Directing Souls That are Under the Work of Conversion* (Boston, 1742).

84. [Jonathan Dickinson,] *A Display of God's special Grace in A Dialogue Between A minister & a Gentleman of his Congregation About The Work of God, in the Conviction of Sinners, so remarkably of late begun and going on in these American Parts* . . . (Boston, 1742).

CHAPTER 5. THE EBB, 1742-1743

1. Watts and Guyse, preface to Edwards, *A Faithful Narrative* . . . (London, 1738).
2. William Cooper, *One Shall be taken* . . . (Boston, 1741), 19, 20.
3. Samuel Niles, *Tristitiae Ecclesiarum* . . . (Boston, 1745), 4.
4. Isaac Stiles, *A Prospect of the City of Jerusalem* . . . (New London, 1742), 46.
5. [John Hancock,] *The Examiner, or Gilbert Against Tennent*, 2.
6. Letter from Timothy Allen to Eleazar Wheelock, Feb. 27, 1742/3, in Dartmouth College Library.
7. Benjamin Colman, *The Great GOD has magnified his WORD* . . . (Boston, 1742), 32.
8. Letter from Tennent to Whitefield in Gillies, *Historical Collections*, II, 132 f.
9. *The Testimony of the Pastors of the Churches In The Province of the Massachusetts-Bay in New-England, at their Annual Convention in Boston, May 25, 1743. Against several Errors in Doctrine, and Disorders in Practice, Which have of late obtained in various Parts of the Land; as drawn up by a Committee chosen by the said Pastors, read and accepted Paragraph by Paragraph, and voted to be sign'd by the Moderator in their Name, and Printed* (Boston, 1743), 13 pp. Signed by Nathanael Eells, Moderator.
10. Joshua Gee charged that only about one-fifth of the ministers of Massachusetts approved it.
11. Joshua Gee, *A Letter To the Reverend Mr. Nathanael Eells, Moderator of the late Convention of Pastors in Boston* . . . (Boston, 1743, second edition), 13. It is from this letter and a reply to it by Benjamin Prescott of Salem that the "backstage" planning at the convention is known.
12. A. M., *The State of Religion in New-England* . . . ; John Caldwell, *An impartial Trial of the Spirit operating in this Part of the World* . . . (Boston, 1742).
13. Gee, *Letter to Eells*, 6.
14. *Ibid.*, 10-11. Later, Gee stated that this thirty-eight represented about one-fifth of Massachusetts' ministers, and that Nathanael Eells—the only one to sign the Testimony—did so unwillingly.
15. Benjamin Prescott, *A Letter To the Reverend Mr. Joshua Gee, In Answer to His of June 3, 1743* . . . (Boston, 1743), 10, 11. See also John Hancock, *An Expostulatory and Pacifick Letter* . . . (Boston, 1743).
16. Quoted from *Christian History*, I, 155-56.
17. The committee members were Joseph Sewall, Samuel Wigglesworth, Thomas Prince, Joseph Adams, William Cooper, Nathanael Rogers, Nathanael Leonard, and William Hobby.
18. Numbers 20 through 24.
19. Published in Boston in 1743.

20. *The Testimony and Advice* . . . , 15.
21. F. B. Dexter (ed.), *Extracts from the Itineraries and other Miscellanies of Ezra Stiles* . . . (New Haven, 1916), 414.
22. *The Testimony and Advice of a Number of Laymen respecting Religion, and the Teachers of it. Address'd to the Pastors of New-England* (Boston [1743]). The tract is signed by "J. F., Moderator."
23. Edwards, quoted in Perry Miller, *Jonathan Edwards*, 179.
24. J. Parsons, *A Needful Caution in a Critical Day* . . . (New London, 1742), quoted in Tracy, *History of the Revival*, 147.
25. For biographical references, see above, chap 3, note 50. Dickinson's theological ability is perhaps best revealed in a work issued contemporaneously with the Great Awakening in New England: *The True Scripture-Doctrine Concerning Some Important Points of Christian Faith* . . . (Boston, 1741).
26. [Jonathan Dickinson,] *A Display of God's special Grace in A familiar Dialogue Between A Minister & a Gentleman of his Congregation* . . . , 38-39, 62-70.
27. *Mr. Croswell's Reply to a Book Lately Publish'd, entitled, A Display of God's Special Grace* . . . (Boston [1742]), 4.
28. [Jonathan Dickinson,] *A Defense of the Dialogue Intitled, A Display* . . . (Boston, 1743).
29. See N. Appleton's *God, and not Ministers to have the Glory of all Success given to the preached Gospel* . . . , Boston, 1741; and especially his *The clearest and surest Marks of our being so led by the Spirit of God, as to demonstrate that we are Children of God* . . . (Boston, 1743). (Cf. Edwards' *Distinguishing Marks*.) Also see Turell's *Directions to his people with relation to the present times* . . . (Boston, 1742).
30. See *Boston Weekly News-Letter*, Dec. 23, 1741.
31. A. M., *The state of Religion in New-England*, 3, 4.
32. *An Impartial Examination of Mr. Davenport's Retractions* . . . (Boston, 1744), 3, 5.
33. Most often mentioned are Whitefield, Davenport, Buell, Tennent, Wheelock, and Croswell. See *Evening-Post*, Dec. 12, 1743, "A Letter to one in the Country"; and the issue of Jan. 17, 1743.
34. Samuel Niles, *Tristitiae Ecclesiarum, OR, A brief and sorrowful Account of the Present State of the Churches in New-England* . . . (Boston, 1745).
35. Timothy Walker, *The Way to Try all Pretended Apostles* . . . (Boston, 1743). See also *News-Letter*, Nov. 18 and 25, 1742.
36. Published in Boston in 1743. In his preface [i.e., in the "N. B."], Hancock let it be known that it was Tennent's divisive sermon which he sought to counteract and refute.
37. T. Walker, *Pretended Apostles*, 19.
38. *News-Letter*, April 22, 1742.
39. *Ibid.*, Oct. 28, 1742; Dec. 2, 1742.
40. *Ibid.*, Nov. 18, 1742; Nov. 25, 1742.
41. See p. 65.
42. A. M., *State of Religion in New-England* . . . , 8, 9.
43. *News-Letter*, April 15, 1742.
44. Extract of a letter from A. Croswell to T. Prince, dated May 17, 1743, in the *Boston Evening-Post*, May 30, 1743.
45. *The Reverend Mr. James Davenport's Confessions & Retractions* (Boston, 1744).
46. Yet the similarity between the exhorter of this period and America's frontier preacher of a later period should not be overlooked.

47. Jonathan Ashley, *The Great Duty of Charity* . . . (Boston, 1742). Cooper's objections appear in the *Boston Gazette* the week preceding Jan. 18, 1742.
48. "J. F.," *Remarks on the Rev. Mr. Cooper's Objections to the Rev. Mr. Ashley's Sermon* (Boston, 1742).
49. See particularly two sermons preached at Medfield in November, 1748: Samuel Dunbar, *Brotherly Love, The Duty and Mark of Christians;* and, Jonathan Townsend, *A Caveat Against Strife, Especially among Christian Brethren,* both published in Boston, 1749.
50. *News-Letter,* Dec. 10, 1741.
51. Isaac Stiles, *A Prospect of the City of Jerusalem* . . . (New London, 1742), 46.
52. Quoted in Trumbull, *History of Connecticut,* II, 127-30.
53. The letter, dated Sept. 1743, is in Dartmouth College Library.
54. See Webster, *Presbyterian Church,* 488-91.
55. *News-Letter,* Dec. 16, 1742.
56. Because the group had only recently separated from Whittelsey's church in Wallingford, the name "Baptist" was more convenient than descriptive.
57. Philemon Robbins, *A Plain Narrative of The Proceedings of the Reverend Association and Consociation of New-Haven County, Against the Reverend Mr. Robbins of Brandford, Since the Year 1741. And the Doing of His Church and People* . . . , Boston, 1747. For rebuttal and correction, see *A Defense of the Doings of the Reverend Consociation and Association of New-Haven County, Respecting Mr. Philemon Robbins of Branford: Or, An Answer to Mr. Robbins's plain Narrative* . . . (New Haven, 1748).
58. John Cotton, *Seasonable Warning* . . . (Boston, 1746).
59. Theophilus Pickering, *A Bad Omen* . . . (Boston, 1747).
60. *Boston Gazette,* Dec. 16, 1746.
61. *A Result of the Council of Churches at Grafton, October 2d. 1744,* n.d., n.p.
62. *The Result of a Council of Ten Churches; Conven'd at Exeter* . . . (Boston, 1744).
63. J. Parson, *Wisdom Justified of her Children* . . . (Boston, 1742), preface, v.
64. *Ibid.,* 43.
65. *Mr. Parson's corrected* . . . (Boston, 1742), 13.
66. Two notable exceptions to this are Chauncy's delineation in his *Seasonable Thoughts* and a single paragraph from the Annual Convention testimony issued at Boston in May, 1743.
67. Chauncy, for example, writes that among the revival doctrines there is a vilifying of good works and a decrying of sanctification as an evidence of justification. *Seasonable Thoughts,* Pt. I.
68. The word "enthusiasm" was of course also used then, as now, to describe a great zeal and fervor, a "Religious Phrenzy" as Chauncy says. Used in that sense, however, the word had more to do with ecclesiastical disorders than with doctrinal errors.
69. On the title page of his *More last Words to these Churches* . . . (Boston, 1746).
70. See chap. 6, p. 87 f.
71. William Hooper, *The Apostles Neither Imposters nor Enthusiasts* . . . , Boston, 1742.
72. Published in Boston, 1743. Doolittle (1695-1749) had a keen, incisive mind; see Dexter, *Graduates of Yale,* I, 151-54.
73. See chap. 8.
74. Published in Philadelphia, n.d.
75. Published in Boston, 1746.
76. Foxcroft, *A seasonable Memento for New Year's Day* . . . (Boston, 1747).

CHAPTER 6. CASCADES: CHAUNCY AND EDWARDS

1. Otto Neugebauer, *The Exact Sciences in Antiquity* (Princeton, 1952), preface.
2. *Works*, III, ix (introduction to *A Treatise Concerning Religions Affections*).
3. Chauncy, *The out-pouring of the Holy Ghost* (Boston, 1741), 43.
4. Chauncy, *Seasonable Thoughts . . .* (Boston, 1743), 34.
5. Perry Miller, *Jonathan Edwards*, 305, xiii. Vincent Tomas questions the modernity of Edwards in *New England Quarterly*, xxv:1, 60-84.
6. Published in Boston, 1741, with a preface by William Cooper and some letters from Benjamin Colman describing the revival in Boston. *Works* I, 519-62.
7. This sermon was reprinted in Philadelphia by Benjamin Franklin and was endorsed in London by Isaac Watts and later by John Wesley. It found welcome reception among the revival party in Scotland, one of whose number wrote to T. Prince (Sept. 13, 1742) that "those who are friendly to this Work among us have a high Sense of the Worth of Mr. Edwards of Northampton; and reckon themselves exceedingly obliged to him for that incomparable Sermon on the *Marks of a Work of the Spirit of God*: wherein he reasons with greatest Judgment and Solidity, and a Mind perfectly free of all enthusiastic or Party Humours. . . ." *Christian History*, I, 77-79. Note influence of this sermon in N. Appleton, *The Clearest and Surest Marks . . .* (Boston 1743); J. Seccombe, *Some Occasional Thoughts . . .* (Boston, 1742); the sermonic feud of J. Caldwell and D. MacGregore in Londonderry, New Hampshire; and Jonathan Parsons' report of the revival in Lyme in *Christian History*, II, 118-62.
8. *Works*, I, 446.
9. *Ibid.*, I, 550.
10. Published in Boston, 1741.
11. Charles Chauncy, *The New Creature Describ'd, and consider'd as the sure Characteristick of a Man's being in Christ: Together with some Seasonable Advice to those who are New-Creatures* (Boston, 1741), 20.
12. *Ibid.*, 17.
13. *Ibid.*, 26.
14. Chauncy, *The New Creature . . .* , 35 f. Cf. Edwards, *Works*, I, 556 f.
15. In *The out-pouring of the Holy Ghost . . .* (Boston, 1742), Chauncy speaks with reservation about the Awakening in only one-half page, 43.
16. Chauncy, *The Gifts of the Spirit to Ministers consider'd in their Diversity: with the wise Ends of their various Distribution, and the good Purposes it is adapted to serve . . .* (Boston, 1742), 34-35.
17. Chauncy, *Enthusiasm described and caution'd against . . . With a Letter to the Reverend Mr. James Davenport* (Boston, 1742), 15.
18. *Ibid.*, 26.
19. Long after the Awakening, Chauncy wrote to Ezra Stiles, "I wrote and printed in that day more than two volumes in octavo. A vast number of pieces were published also as written by others; but there was scarce a piece against the times but was sent to me, and I had labour some measures of preparing it for the press, and always of correcting the press. I had also hundreds of letters to write, in answer to letters received from all parts of the country." Letter in *Collections of Mass. Hist. Soc.*, 1s. X, 162.
20. Published in Edinburgh in 1742. Reprinted in *Clarendon Historical Society Reprints*, March, 1883.
21. *Ibid.*, 21. Yet even this late (August, 1742), Chauncy concedes, "I am of opinion also, that the Appearances among us . . . have been the Means of awakening the Attention of many; and a good Number, I hope, have settled into a truly Christian Temper . . ." 21.

22. *The Wonderful Narrative: OR, A Faithful Account of the French Prophets, their Agitations, Extasies, and Inspirations: To which are added, Several other remarkable Instances of Persons under the Influence of the like Spirit, in various Parts of the World, particularly in New-England* . . . , Boston, 1742. For a recent, readable account of these "Prophets," see R. Knox, *Enthusiasm* (Oxford, 1950), chap. XV.

23. It should be remembered that "Methodist" was in the 1740's a term of reproach only, not yet the title of a separate ecclesiastical organization.

24. For this and other bibliographical problems connected with Chauncy's literary activity at this time, see Edwin S. Gaustad, "Charles Chauncy and the Great Awakening: A Survey and Bibliography," Bibliographical Society of America, *Papers*, XLV, Second Quarter, 125-35.

25. Published in Boston in 1743, with a preface of twenty pages which was intended to answer William Cooper's preface to Edwards' *Distinguishing Marks*.

26. Bibliographical Soc. of Amer., *Papers*, XLV, Second Quarter, 131.

27. *New England Historical and Genealogical Register*, X, 332. The letter is dated March 16, 1742/3.

28. *Works*, III, 275 (preface).

29. *Ibid.*, 288.

30. *Ibid.*, 313-16.

31. *Ibid.*, 326-29.

32. *Ibid.*, 355. There follows an excellent, compact essay on spiritual pride.

33. *Ibid.*, 391.

34. *Ibid.*, 414.

35. *News-Letter*, March 17, 1743.

36. *News-Letter*, March 25, 31, 1743.

37. *News-Letter*, Sept. 15, 1743.

38. *Seasonable Thoughts*, vii. Chauncy follows and quotes liberally from T. Welde's *A Short Story of the Rise, reign, and ruine of the Antinomians, Familists & Libertines, that infected the Churches of New England* . . . (London, 1644), reprinted by the Prince Society, Boston, 1894.

39. *Seasonable Thoughts*, xxix.

40. *Ibid*, 2, 3.

41. Chauncy, *The New Creature described* . . . , 25, 26.

42. *Seasonable Thoughts*, 77.

43. *Ibid.*, 136-37.

44. *Works*, III, 336.

45. *Letter to Wishart*, 22.

46. *Seasonable Thoughts*, 144.

47. *Ibid.*, 178.

48. *Ibid.*, 217. Cf. *Letter to Wishart*, 23.

49. *Seasonable Thoughts*, 307 f.

50. *Ibid.*, 332. There is more here in a similarly sarcastic vein.

51. *Ibid.*, 408 f.

52. *Seasonable Thoughts*, 422.

53. Published in Boston in 1746, *Religious Affections* was with the possible exception of his *Life of Brainerd* the most popular of Edwards' works; it went through thirty editions (T. H. Johnson, *The Printed Writings of Jonathan Edwards*, Princeton, 1940). *Works*, III, 1-228.

54. *Works*, III, 2, 5, 7.

55. *Ibid.*, 15, 17.

56. Miller, *Jonathan Edwards*, 176.

57. *Works*, III, 70 f.

58. See *Works*, IV, 438-50. This sermon, published in 1732, is a clear, informative statement of the presuppositions underlying the extended exposition in this portion of *Religious Affections*. Compare C. Chauncy's, *The Method of the Spirit, in the Work of Illumination*, published in a volume of twelve of his sermons, Boston, 1765.
59. See P. Miller, "Jonathan Edwards on A Sense of the Heart," *Harvard Theological Review*, XLI, 122-45.
60. *Works*, III, 442.
61. *Ibid.*, 10, 11.
62. II Cor. 5:17, KJV.
63. Miller, *Jonathan Edwards*, 193.

CHAPTER 7. INSTITUTIONAL EFFECTS OF THE GREAT AWAKENING

1. See R. J. Purcell, *Connecticut in Transition 1775-1818* (Washington, 1918).
2. H. R. Niebuhr, *The Kingdom of God in America* (Chicago, 1937), 126.
3. See chap. 5.
4. The return of Whitefield to New England in 1745 was the occasion for this evaluation of the revival's effects.
5. William Shurtleff, *A Letter To Those of his Brethren In the Ministry Who refuse to admit The Rev. Mr. Whitefield Into their Pulpits* . . . (Boston, 1745).
6. [Isaac Stiles,] *The Declaration of the Association of the County of New-Haven in Connecticut* . . . (Boston, 1745), 6.
7. E. Stiles, *A Discourse on the Christian Union* . . . (Boston, 1760), 50.
8. See Edwards' *Works*, III, 296 f.; and William Cooper, preface to *Distinguishing Marks*, I, 522 f.
9. H. M. Dexter (*Congregationalism . . . As Seen in Its Literature*, [New York, 1880] 502) reckons the number of converts in New England as between forty and fifty thousand; Trumbull, as between thirty and forty thousand, *Hist. of Conn.*, II, 218. These estimates require drastic revision downward.
10. *Christian History*, II, 14, 20.
11. *Ibid.*, II, 105-14.
12. M. H. Mitchell, *The Great Awakening and other Revivals in Connecticut* (New Haven, 1934), 12. For the number of baptisms in Northampton in years 1735-1741, see E. Stiles, *Itineraries* . . . , 201.
13. Thomas Prince, *An Account*, 18.
14. In a letter to Whitefield, dated April 25, 1751, in *Proceedings of the MHS*, LIII, 197.
15. Thomas Prince, *An Account*, 19.
16. William Cooper, in preface to *Distinguishing Marks*.
17. *Christian History*, II, 146.
18. *Letter to Wishart*, 7.
19. See the *News-Letter*, Oct. 29, 1741.
20. Published in Boston, 1749; *Works*, I, 83-192. The *Humble Inquiry* caused a flurry of reaction; see bibliography in W. Walker, *Creeds*, 243.
21. *Works*, I, 85 (preface), 89.
22. Cambridge Platform, chap. 3, in Walker, *Creeds*, 205.
23. *Ibid.*, 206-29.
24. This dispute between defenders and opponents of the Half-Way Covenant is described in excellent fashion by J. Haroutunian, "Sinners and Saints in Full Communion" (chap. 5), in *Piety Versus Moralism*.
25. Stiles, *Itineraries*, 472.
26. See chap. 8, p. 134.

27. As reported in the *News-Letter*, Nov. 12, 1742. The law is given in C. J. Hoadly, *Public Records of Conn.* (Hartford, 1874-1876), VIII, 500 f.
28. Timothy Allen, letter to Wheelock, Feb. 27, 1743, in DCL.
29. See *News-Letter*, Nov. 12, 1742, and *Evening-Post*, Aug. 2 and Sept. 13, 1742.
30. See L. B. Richardson, *History of Dartmouth College* (Hanover, 1932).
31. See L. J. Trinterud, *The Forming of an American Tradition. A Re-examination of Colonial Presbyterianism* (Philadelphia, 1949), 84-85; T. J. Wertenbaker, *Princeton 1746-1896*, (Princeton, 1946).
32. *Official Register of Princeton University*, XLII, I, 90.
33. See R. A. Guild, *Early History of Brown University.* . . . (Providence, 1897).
34. C. J. Hoadly, *Public Records of Conn.*, VIII, 522.
35. The intolerant acts of 1742-43 were never formally repealed but in the revision of laws in 1750 were quietly omitted.
36. Solomon Paine, *A Short View of the Difference Between the Church of Christ, and the established Churches in the Colony of Connectuicut* . . . (Newport, 1752) quoted in S. L. Blake, *The Separates or Strict Congregationalists of New-England* (Boston, 1902), 58.
37. Quoted in S. L. Blake, *Separates*, 58.
38. ". . . the opposers remained . . . students of the free and catholic spirit." P. Miller, *Jonathan Edwards*, 168; see also 174.
39. Reuben Fletcher, *The Lamentable State of New-England* . . . (Boston, 1772).
40. See E. Stiles, *A Discourse on the Christian Union*.
41. John Devotion, in Stiles, *Itineraries*, 474.
42. Quoted in Trumbull, *History of Conn.*, II, 429.
43. Leonard Bacon, "Historical Discourse," *Contributions to the Eccl. Hist. of Conn.* (New Haven, 1861), 55 f.
44. Trumbull, *Hist. of Conn.*, II, 432.
45. John Devotion, in Stiles, *Itineraries*, 472.
46. Mar. 9, 1765, *ibid.*, 586.
47. Walker, *Creeds*, 524 f.
48. Stiles, *Itineraries*, 583.
49. The Consociation called by the Connecticut legislature in 1741 to meet at Guilford "was the last synod of Congregational Churches called under the auspices of an American commonwealth." A. P. Stokes, *Church and State in the United States* (New York, 1950), I, 241.
50. Quoted in Walker, *Congregational Churches*, 307.
51. Though Bacon is speaking primarily of Connecticut, his remarks, delivered in 1859, applied to the whole of New England; *Contributions to the Eccl. Hist. of Conn.*, 64-65.
52. *Discourse on Christian Union*, 94.
53. *News-Letter*, Sept. 16, 1747.
54. S. Dunbar, *Brotherly Love* . . . (Boston, 1749), 19.
55. See article, "A Dissertation on the State of Religion in North America," in *The American Magazine and Historical Chronicle* (Boston, Sept., 1743).
56. E. Stiles, *Discourse on Christian Union*, 51. By "revival period" he probably means at least ten to fifteen years.
57. William Shurtleff, *A Letter to Those of his Brethren In the Ministry* . . . (Boston, 1745).
58. S. W. S. Dutton, *The History of the North Church in New Haven* . . . (New Haven, 1842).
59. F. M. Caulkins, *History of Norwich, Connecticut* . . . (n.p., 1866), chap. 23.
60. I. Backus, *A History of New-England, With particular Reference to the*

Denomination of Christians called Baptists . . . (Boston, 1777-1796), II, 204 f. Hereafter referred to as *Church History*.

61. M. L. Greene, *The Development of Religious Liberty in Connecticut* (Boston, 1905), 338.
62. S. L. Blake, *Separates*, 124.
63. Letter reprinted in F. L. Hawks and W. S. Perry, *Documentary History of the Protestant Episcopal Church* . . . *in Connecticut* (New York, 1893), I, 181-82.
64. The Society for the Propagation of the Gospel in Foreign Parts.
65. Quoted in E. E. Beardsley, *The History of the Episcopal Church in Connecticut* . . . (Boston, 1883), 132-33.
66. Hawks and Perry, *Documentary History*, I, 180.
67. *Ibid.*, I, 178.
68. *Ibid.* Letter dated Mar. 25, 1743.
69. *Ibid.* Letter dated June 5, 1743.
70. *Ibid.*, I, 181-82.
71. The words are those of the Commissary, Roger Price (see Sprague, *Annals*, V, 69-75); quoted in H. W. Foote, *Annals of King's Chapel* (Boston, 1896), I, 509.
72. King's Chapel, the first Anglican church of Boston, was built in 1688, Christ's Church in 1723, and Trinity Church in 1734.
73. A. M., *The State of Religion in New-England* . . . 16.
74. Boston Public Library, Chamberlain MSS, A3, 1-5. Some excerpts from it have already been given in chap. 3.
75. H. W. Foote, *King's Chapel*, I, 511.
76. *Ibid.*, I, 514.
77. H. W. Foote, *King's Chapel*, I, 508.
78. Sprague, *Annals*, V, 76-82.
79. H. W. Foote, *King's Chapel*, I, 509. But in December of 1741, Thomas Prince reported that he had seen a letter which stated that Browne "who has often preach'd against The Work with distinguish'd Violence, has now declar'd he is convinc'd it is a wondrous Work of God." The words are Prince's, in a letter to Whitefield. *Proceedings of the MHS*, LIII, 204, 5.
80. So called from the six principles set forth in Heb. 6:1, 2.
81. A. H. Newman, *A History of the Baptist Churches* . . . (New York, 1894), 243. See also p. 117 where a report of 1729 mentions only three Calvinistic Baptist churches in New England at this time: at Newport, Swansea, and Boston.
82. I. Backus, *Church History*, II, 134.
83. Nathan Wood, *The History of the First Baptist Church of Boston* (Philadelphia, 1899), 236-41. See also I. Backus, *Church History*, II, 149.
84. Arminian Baptist churches were by no means smothered out of existence; indeed it was because of their reaction against the mounting allegiance to Calvinism that the "free will" Baptist movement arose.
85. R. A. Guild, *Brown University*, 213-17.
86. See statistics in Backus, *Church History*, III, 93 f. The rapidly expanding, revival-holding Baptist faith on the frontier was of Calvinistic character.
87. One of the most revealing features of the New Lights' concern for religious liberty is the tolerance explicit in the charters of Princeton, Brown, and Dartmouth.
88. It is significant that no New Side Presbyterian Churches in the Middle Colonies became Baptist. Though there were doubtless several reasons for this, an obvious one is that the formation of the more flexible and liberal

New York Synod made possible an expression of New Light sympathies and interests within Presbyterianism. See L. J. Trinterud, *Colonial Presbyterianism*, 122.

89. E. Stiles' *Literary Diary*, edited by F. B. Dexter (New York, 1901), I, 234. See also S. L. Blake, *Separates*, 146.
90. Quoted by Backus, *A Letter to the Reverend Mr. Benjamin Lord . . .* (Providence, 1764), 35.
91. The letter is printed in the *Boston Weekly-Post-Boy* of Feb. 21, 1743.
92. R. A. Guild, *Brown University*, 11.
93. Backus, *Church History*, III, 93 f.
94. Trinterud, *Colonial Presbyterianism*, 118, 122 f.
95. *Christian History*, II, 113 f., 23 f.
96. *Ibid.*, I, 201-10.
97. Letter dated May 27, 1742, in *Proceedings of the MHS*, LIII, 213.
98. *Christian History*, I, 151-54. In 1751, Jonathan Edwards removed from Northampton to this mission station at Stockbridge, remaining there until 1758 when he was called as president to the College of New Jersey.
99. Quoted in Sprague, *Annals*, III, 115.
100. *Proceedings of the MHS*, LIII, 212.
101. L. J. Trinterud, *Colonial Presbyterianism*, 197; also 307, 308.
102. Quoted in F. E. Mayer, *The Religious Bodies of America* (St. Louis, 1954), 296 f.

CHAPTER 8. THEOLOGICAL EFFECTS OF THE GREAT AWAKENING

1. Quoted in G. L. Walker, *Some Aspects of the Religious Life*, 112.
2. That this fetish was a real power prior to the revival is evident in the undeclared war between Stoddard and Increase Mather; see P. Miller, "Solomon Stoddard 1643-1729," *Harvard Theological Review*, XXXIV, 301.
3. John Bass, *A True Narrative . . .* (Boston, 1751).
4. S. Niles, *A Vindication . . .* (Boston, 1752), 3.
5. *The Report of a Committee of the First Church in Braintree . . .* (Boston, 1753), 5.
6. See chap. 6.
7. J. D. McCallum, *Eleazar Wheelock*, 24.
8. Letter, Feb. 3, 1742, in DCL.
9. G. Whitefield, *A Letter to the Rev. Mr. John Wesley, in Answer to his Sermon, entitled "Free Grace" . . .* (London, 1741).
10. *Boston Weekly News-Letter*, April 15, 1742.
11. See Sidney E. Mead, "Denominationalism . . ." *Church History* XXIII: 4, 310. The entire article is most illuminating.
12. *Boston Weekly News-Letter*, July 1, 1742.
13. Edwards, *Works*, III, 492-508.
14. Channing, *Works* (Boston, 1888), 427 f.
15. E. Stiles, *Christian Union*, pt. I, 2.
16. L. Briant, *The Absurdity and Blasphemy . . .* (Boston, 1749), 11.
17. *Ibid.*, 17-21.
18. *Ibid.*, 30.
19. John Porter, *The Absurdity and Blasphemy . . .*, 7.
20. *Ibid.*, 19.
21. S. Niles, *A Vindication*, 3.
22. *Ibid.* (preface), 13.

23. See, e.g., the writings of William Hart, Moses Hemmenway, Solomon Williams, and Israel Holly.
24. See W. B. Sprague, *Annals*, VIII, 6.
25. *The Sentiments and Resolutions . . . of Ministers, convened at Weymouth . . .* (Boston, 1745).
26. Quoted in Alden Bradford, *Memoir of . . . Jonathan Mayhew* (Boston, 1838), 50.
27. *Ibid.*, 63.
28. *Ibid.*, 48.
29. J. Mayhew, *Sermons . . .* (Boston, 1755), 107.
30. For an extreme example of such intimacy, see the erotic Christ-mysticism of Gilbert Tennent in his letter to Whitefield: *Three Letters To The Reverend Mr. George Whitefield* (Philadelphia, n.d. [1739]), 8-12.
31. Extracts from Emlyn's *Humble Inquiry into the Scripture Account of Jesus Christ* were printed in Boston in 1756. For an excellent discussion of the history and literature of Unitarianism in this period, see E. H. Gillett, *Historical Magazine*, XIX, 221-324.
32. S. Niles, *A Vindication* (preface), 1.
33. F. H. Foster, *A Genetic History of the New England Theology* (Chicago, 1907).
34. J. Edwards, *Discourses on Various Subjects* (Boston, 1738), preface.
35. J. Dickinson, *The True Scripture-Doctrine Concerning Some Important Points of Christian Faith, Particularly Eternal Election, Original Sin, Grace in Conversion, Justification by Faith, And the Saints Perseverance . . .* (Boston, 1741).
36. *Ibid.* (preface), vi. That feelings ran high in this period is evidenced by the fact that Foxcroft was rebuked for not being sufficiently enthusiastic about Calvinism! Foxcroft had acknowledged the possibility of salvation for those "who do not Calvinize in every point." In the intense days of the revival, such magnanimity had to be justified. See *Boston Weekly Post-Boy*, April 12 and 26, 1742.
37. *The Testimony of a Number of New-England Ministers Met at Boston Sept. 25. 1745 . . .* (Boston, 1745).
38. *Ibid.*, 7-9.
39. Quoted in S. Niles, *A Vindication*, 95.
40. Published in Boston in 1750 with a preface by Edwards. See H. B. Stowe's chapter on "My Grandmother's Blue Book" in *Oldtown Folks* (New York, 1869).
41. See above, 97 f. and page 105 f.
42. Edwards, *Works*, II, 176.
43. See J. Haroutunian, *Piety Versus Moralism*, chap. 3, and bibliography thereof.
44. S. Niles, *A Vindication*, 25.
45. In a letter to Wheelock, Feb. 27, 1743.
46. S. Niles, *A Vindication*, 119. A clear instance of these diverging theologies is the dispute at this time regarding original sin; see H. Shelton Smith, *Changing Conceptions of Original Sin* (New York, 1955).
47. H. W. Schneider, *The Puritan Mind* (New York, 1930), 155.
48. Edwards, *Works* (ten-volume edition, New York, 1829), X, 430.
49. *Church History*, XXIII:4, 314.

BIBLIOGRAPHY

The primary sources are listed here as a step toward a complete bibliography of the Great Awakening in New England.

The American Magazine and Historical Chronicle. Boston, 1743-1746.

Appleton, Nathanael. *God, and not Ministers to have the Glory of all Success given to the preached Gospel* . . . Boston, 1741.

———. *The clearest and surest Marks of our being so led by the Spirit of God, as to demonstrate that we are the Children of God* . . . Boston, 1743.

Ashley, Jonathan. *The Great Duty of Charity* . . . Boston, 1742.

———. *The Great Concern of Christ for the Salvation of Sinners, and the Duty of his Ministers earnestly to perswade Man into his Kingdom* . . . Boston, 1743.

Backus, Isaac. *Backus Papers*, 1750-1806, in Brown University Library.

———. *A Letter To the Reverend Mr. Benjamin Lord, of Norwich* . . . Providence, 1764.

———. *A History of New-England, With particular Reference to the Denomination of Christians called Baptists* . . . (3 vols.). Boston, 1777-1796.

Barnard, John. *A Zeal for Good Works Excited and Directed* . . . Boston, 1742.

Barnard, Thomas. *Tyranny and Slavery in Matters of Religion, caution'd against; and True Humility recommended to Ministers and People*. Boston, 1743.

Beckwith, George. *Christ the alone Pattern of True Christian Obedience*. N. London, 1742.

Bellamy, Joseph. *The Works of the Rev. Joseph Bellamy, D. D.* . . . (3 vols.). New York, 1811-1812.

———. *True Religion delineated; Or, Experimental Religion, As distinguished from Formality on the one Hand, and Enthusiasm on the other, set in a Scriptural and Rational Light* . . . *With a Preface by the Rev. Mr. Edwards* . . . Boston, 1750.

[———]. *A Letter To the Reverend Author of The Winter-Evening Conversation on Original Sin, From one of his candid Neighbours* . . . Boston, 1758.

The Boston Evening-Post. Boston: Printed by T. Fleet, at the Heart and Crown in Cornhill, 1735-1775.

The Boston Gazette, or, Weekly Journal. Boston: Printed by S. Kneeland & T. Green, 1719-1798.

The Boston Weekly News-Letter. Boston: Printed by J. Draper, at his Printing-House in Newbury-Street where Advertisements are taken in, 1704-1776.

The Boston Weekly Post-Boy. Boston: Printed for E. Huske, Post-Master. 1734-1775.

Bradstreet, Benjamin. *Godly Sorrow described, and the Blessing annexed consider'd. In a Discourse Deliver'd* . . . *At a Time of Great Awakenings. When many were under deep Concern for their Souls, and many full of Joy* . . . Boston, 1742.

A Brief Narrative of some of the Brethren Of the Second Church in Bradford . . . Boston, 1746.

Buell, Samuel. *A Faithful Narrative of the Remarkable Revival of Religion, in the Congregation of Easthampton, on Long-Island, In the year of our Lord, 1764;*

with some reflections . . . To which are added, Sketches of the author's life . . .
Sag-Harbor, 1803.

Caldwell, John. *An impartial Trial of the Spirit operating in this Part of the World* . . . Boston, 1742.

Campbell, John. *A Treatise of Conversion, Faith and Justification, &c.* . . . Boston, 1743.

A Caveat Against Unreasonable and unscriptural Separations . . . Boston, 1748.

Chauncy, Charles. *The New Creature Describ'd, and consider'd as the sure Characteristick of a Man's being in Christ* . . . Boston, 1741.

———. *An Unbridled Tongue a sure Evidence, that our Religion is Hypocritical and Vain* . . . Boston, 1741.

———. *The Gifts of the Spirit to Ministers consider'd in their Diversity* . . . Boston, 1742.

———. *The out-pouring of the Holy Ghost* . . . Boston, 1742.

[———]. *A Letter from a Gentleman in Boston, To Mr. George Wishart, One of the Ministers of Edinburgh, Concerning the State of Religion in New-England.* Edinburgh, 1742.

———. *Enthusiasm described and caution'd against* . . . *With a Letter to the Reverend Mr. James Davenport.* Boston, 1742.

———. *Seasonable Thoughts on the State of Religion in New England, A Treatise in five Parts* . . . Boston, 1743.

———. *Ministers cautioned against Occasions of Contempt* . . . Boston, 1744.

———. *Ministers exhorted and encouraged to take heed to themselves, and to their Doctrine* . . . Boston, 1744.

———. *A Letter to the Reverend Mr. George Whitefield, Vindicating certain Passages he has excepted against* . . . Boston, 1745.

[———]. *The Opinion of one that has perused the Summer Morning's Conversation* . . . *In a Letter to a friend.* Boston, 1758.

———. "Sketch of eminent men in New England," *Collections of the Massachusetts Historical Society,* X.

———. *Twelve Sermons.* Boston, 1765.

———. *Five Dissertations on the Scripture Account of the Fall; and its Consequences.* London, 1785.

Checkley, Samuel. *Little Children brought to Jesus Christ* . . . Boston, 1741.

[Clap, Thomas]. *The Declaration of the Rector and Tutors of Yale-College in New-Haven, against the Reverend Mr. George Whitefield, his principles and designs. In a letter to him.* Boston, 1745.

Clark, Peter. *The Scripture-Doctrine of Original Sin, stated and defended. In A Summer-Morning's Conversation, between a Minister and a Neighbour* . . . Boston, 1758.

[———]. *Remarks On A late Pamphlet, Intitled, "The Opinion of One that has perused the Summer-Morning's Conversation . . ." Detecting and correcting the Mistakes of that Writer* . . . Boston, 1758.

———. *A Defence Of the Principles of The "Summer-Morning's Conversation— Concerning the Doctrine of Original Sin." Against The Exceptions of the Author of the "Winter Evening's Conversation vindicated."* . . . Boston, 1760.

Cleaveland, John. *The Cleaveland Papers,* in Essex Institute.

Colman, Benjamin. *Colman Papers,* II, in Massachusetts Historical Society.

———. *Souls flying to Jesus Christ pleasant and admirable to behold* . . . Boston, 1740.

———. *The Lord Shall Rejoice in his Works* . . . Boston, 1741.

———. *The Great GOD has magnified his WORD to the Children of Men* . . . Boston, 1742.

————, et al. *The Declaration of a Number of associated Pastors of Boston and Charles-Town relating to the Rev. Mr. James Davenport*. Boston, 1742.

————. *The Glory of God in the Firmament of his Power* . . . Boston, 1743.

————. *Jesus weeping over his dead Friend, and with his Friends in their Mourning* . . . Boston, 1744.

Cooke, Samuel. *Divine Sovereignty in the Salvation of Sinners* . . . Boston, 1741.

Cooper, William. *The Doctrine of Predestination unto Life, Explained and Vindicated* . . . Boston, 1740.

————. *One shall be taken, and another left* . . . Boston, 1741.

————. *The Sin and Danger of quenching the Spirit* . . . Boston, 1741.

Corbin, Samuel. *An Awakening Call from the Eternal God, to the Unconverted*. Boston (reprint), 1742.

Cotton, John. *Seasonable Warning to these Churches. A Narrative of the Transactions at Middleborough* . . . Boston, 1746.

Croswell, A. *An Answer to The Rev. Mr. Garden's Three First Letters To The Rev. Mr. Whitefield. With An Appendix* . . . Boston, 1741.

————. *A Letter to the Rev. Mr. Turell, In Answer to his Direction to his People* . . . Boston, 1742.

————. *Mr. Croswell's Reply to a Book Lately Publish'd, entitled, A Display of God's Special Grace*. Boston, 1742.

————. *Reply to the Declaration of a Number of the associated Ministers in Boston and Charlestown, with Regard to the Rev. Mr. James Davenport and his Conduct* . . . Boston, 1742.

————. *A Narrative of the Founding and Settling The New-gathered Congregational Church in Boston* . . . Boston, 1749.

Davenport, James. *The Reverend Mr. James Davenport's Confessions & Retractions*. Boston, 1744.

A Defence Of the Doings of The Reverend Consocation and Association of New-Haven County, Respecting Mr. Philemon Robbins of Branford . . . Printed for the Consocation & Association of N. Haven County, 1748.

Dexter, F. B. (ed.). *The Literary Diary of Ezra Stiles, D. D., LL.D.* (3 vols.). New York, 1901.

————. *Extracts from the Itineraries and other Miscellanies of Ezra Stiles, D. D., LL. D. 1755-1794 with a selection from his correspondence*. New Haven, 1916.

Dexter, Samuel. *Diary of Rev. Samuel Dexter 1721-1752*, in Dedham Historical Society.

Dickinson, Jonathan. *The True Scripture-Doctrine Concerning Some Important Points of Christian Faith* . . . With a Preface by Mr. Foxcroft. Boston, 1741.

[————]. *A Display of God's special Grace in A familiar Dialogue Between A minister & a Gentleman of his Congregation About The Work of God, in the Conviction and Conversion of Sinners, so remarkably of late begun and going on in these American Parts* . . . To which is prefixed an Attestation, by several Ministers of Boston. Boston, 1742.

————. *The Nature and Necessity of Regeneration* . . . New York, 1743.

[————]. *A Defence of the Dialogue Intitled, A Display of God's special Grace* . . . Boston, 1743.

————. *Familiar Letters To a Gentleman, Upon a Variety of seasonable and important Subjects in Religion*. Boston, 1745.

Doolittle, Benjamin. *An Enquiry Into Enthusiasm, Being an Account what it is, the Original, Progress, and Effects of it* . . . Boston, 1743.

Dunbar, Samuel. *Brotherly Love, The Duty and Mark of Christians* . . . Boston, 1749.

Edwards, Jonathan. *The Works of President Edwards in four volumes*. New York, 1843. (cited as *Works*)

———. *The Works of President Edwards in Ten Volumes*. New York, 1829.

———. *A Faithful Narrative of the Surprising Work of God in the Conversion of Many Hundred Souls in Northampton, and the Neighboring Towns and Villages of the County of Hampshire, in the Province of the Massachusetts-Bay in New-England*. Boston (third edition), 1738.

———. *Discourses on Various Important Subjects, Nearly concerning the great Affair of the Soul's Eternal Salvation . . . Delivered at Northampton, chiefly at the Time of the late wonderful pouring out of the Spirit of God there . . .* Boston, 1738.

———. *The Distinguishing Marks of a Work of the Spirit of God, Applied to that uncommon Operation that has lately appeared on the Minds of many of the People in New-England: With A Particular Consideration of the extra-ordinary Circumstances with which this Work is attended . . . With a Preface by the Rev. Mr. Cooper of Boston, and Letters from the Rev. Dr. Colman, giving some Account of the present Work of God in those Parts*. Boston, 1741.

———. *Some Thoughts Concerning the Present Revival of Religion in New England*. (Boston, 1743.) *Works*, III.

———. *The great Concern of A Watchman For Souls . . .* Boston, 1743.

———. *An Expostulatory Letter From the Rev. Mr. Edwards of Northampton, To The Rev. Mr. Clap, Rector of Yale College in New-Haven . . .* Boston, 1745.

———. *Copies of Two Letters Cited by The Rev. Mr. Clap, Rector of the College at New-Haven . . . With some Reflections on the Affair those Letters relate to, and Rector Clap's Management therein . . .* Boston, 1745.

———. *A Treatise concerning Religious Affections*. (Boston, 1746.) *Works*, III.

———. *An humble Inquiry into the Rules of the Word of God, concerning the Qualifications requisite to a complete Standing and full Communion in the visible Church*. (Boston, 1749.) *Works*, I.

———. *An Account of the Life of the Late Reverend Mr. David Brainerd . .* Boston, 1749.

———. *A careful and strict Enquiry into the modern prevailing Notions of that Freedom of Will, which is supposed to be essential to moral Agency, Virtue and Vice, Reward and Punishment, Praise and Blame*. (Boston, 1754.) *Works*, II.

———. *The great Christian Doctrine of Original Sin defended*. (Boston, 1758.) *Works*, II.

———. *A Dissertation concerning the End for which God created the World*. (Boston, 1765.) *Works*, II.

———. *A Dissertation concerning the Nature of true Virtue*. (Boston, 1765.) *Works*, II.

———. *Sermons, Works*, IV.

Eells, Nathanael. *Religion is the Life of God's People . . .* Boston, 1743.

Eliot, Andrew. *The Faithful Steward*. Boston, 1742.

Emerson, J. *Exhortation to his People with Respect to Variety of Ministers . . .* Boston, 1742.

Finley, Samuel. *Christ Triumphing and Satan Raging . . .* Philadelphia, 1741.

Flavel, John. *A Word to the Well-Wishers of the good Work of God in this Land; in a seasonable Extract from that holy Man of God, Mr. John Flavel*. Boston, 1742.

Fletcher, Reuben. *The Lamentable State of New-England; Being An Account of the Beginning, or Original of the Separates in New-England, And their Progress, with their Errors and Faults . . .* Boston, 1772.

Flynt, Henry. *Diary of Henry Flynt 1724-1747*, in Harvard Library.

Foxcroft, Thomas. *Some seasonable Thoughts on Evangelic Preaching; its Nature, Usefulness, and Obligation . . . Occasion'd By the late Visit, and uncommon Labours, in daily and powerful Preaching, of the Rev. Mr. Whitefield . . .* Boston, 1740.

———. *An Apology in Behalf of the Rev^d Mr. Whitefield . . .* Boston, 1745.

———. *A seasonable Memento for New Year's Day . . .* Boston, 1747.

Freeman, Samuel (ed.). *Extracts from the Journals kept by the Rev. Thomas Smith, Late Pastor of the First Church of Christ in Falmouth . . .* Portland, 1821.

Frothingham, Ebenezer. *A key To unlock the Door, that leads in, to take a Fair View of the Religious Constitution, Established by Law, in the Colony of Connecticut . . .* n.p., 1767.

Gay, Ebenezer. *The Alienation of Affections from Ministers consider'd, and improv'd . . .* Boston, 1747.

Gee, Joshua. *A Letter To the Reverend Mr. Nathanael Eells, Moderator of the late Convention of Pastors in Boston; Containing Some Remarks on their Printed Testimony Against several Errors and Disorders in the Land . . .* Boston (second edition), 1743.

Gillies, John. *Historical Collections Relating to Remarkable Periods of The Success of The Gospel and Eminent Instruments Employed in Promoting It,* II. Glasgow, 1743.

The Glasgow-Weekly-History Relating to the Late Progress of the Gospel At Home and Abroad; Being A Collection of Letters, partly reprinted from the London-Weekly-History, and partly printed first here at Glasgow. For the Year 1742. Glasgow, 1743.

Gray, Ellis. *The Fidelity of Ministers to Themselves, and to the Flock of God, consider'd and enforc'd.* Boston, 1742.

Hall, David. *Diary of David Hall 1740-1789,* in Massachusetts Historical Society.

H[all], E[lihu]. *The present way of the Country in Maintaining the Gospel Ministry by a publick Rate or Tax is Lawful, Equitable & Agreeable to the Gospel . . .* New London, 1749.

Hancock, John. *A Discourse upon the Good Work . . .* Boston, 1743.

[———]. *The Examiner, or Gilbert against Tennent. Containing a Confutation of the Reverend Mr. Gilbert Tennent and his Adherents: Extracted chiefly from his Own Writings . . .* Boston, 1743.

———. *An Expostulatory and Pacifick Letter, By Way of Reply to the Rev^d Mr. Gee's Letter of Remarks . . .* Boston, 1743.

———. *The Danger of an Unqualified Ministry . . .* Boston, 1743.

Hart, William. *A Discourse Concerning the Nature of Regeneration, and the Way Wherein it is wrought.* New London, 1742.

Haven, Elias. *A Sermon wherein is shown that youthful Pleasures must be accounted for in the Day of Judgment . . .* Boston, 1742.

Hempstead, Joshua. *Diary of Joshua Hempstead of New London, Connecticut (1711-1758),* (Collections of the New London County Historical Society), I. New London, 1901.

Henchman, Nathanael. *Reasons offered by Mr. Nathanael Henchman, Pastor of the first Church of Christ in Lynn, For declining to admit Mr. Whitefield into his Pulpit.* Boston, 1745.

Holyoke, Edward. *The Duty of Ministers of the Gospel to guard against the Pharisaism and Sadducism, of the present Day . . .* Boston, 1741.

Hooper, William. *Jesus Christ the only Way to the Father . . .* Boston, 1742.

Hopkins, Samuel. *The System of Doctrines, contained in Divine Revelation, Explained and Defended . . .* (2 vol.). Boston, 1793.

An Impartial Examination of Mr. Davenport's Retractions. n.d., n.p., [Boston, 1744].

Jewet, Jedidiah. *The Necessity of good Works, as the Fruit and Evidence of Faith* . . . Boston, 1742.

K., L. *A Letter to the Reverend Mr. George Whitefield, Publickly calling upon him to vidicate his conduct or confess his faults.* (Signed L. K.) Boston, 1744.

The Late Religious Commotions in New-England considered. An Answer to the Reverend Mr. Jonathan Edwards's Sermon, Entitled, The distinguishing Marks of a Work of the Spirit of God . . . *Together with A Preface Containing an Examination of the Rev. Mr. William Cooper's Preface to Mr. Edwards's Sermon* . . . Boston, 1743.

A Letter from A Gentleman in Scotland, to His friend in New-England. Containing An Account of Mr. Whitefield's Reception and Conduct in Scotland . . . Boston, 1743.

A Letter to the Reverend Mr. Foxcroft, Being an Examination of his Apology for the Rev. Mr. Whitefield . . . Boston, 1745.

Lord, Benjamin. *Believers in Christ, only, the true Children of God, and Born of Him alone* . . . Boston, 1742.

Loring, Israel. *Ministers insufficient of themselves rightly to discharge the Duties of their sacred Calling* . . . Boston, 1742.

M., A. *The State of Religion in New-England, Since the Reverend Mr. George Whitefield's Arrival there. In A Letter from a Gentleman in New-England to his Friend in Glasgow* . . . Glasgow, 1742.

MacGregore, David. *Professors warn'd of their Danger* . . . Boston, 1742.

———. *The Spirits of the present Day Tried* . . . *With a Preface by some Ministers of Boston. The Second Edition* . . . Boston, 1742.

[March, Edmund]. *Fair Play! Or, A needful Word, To temper the Tract, Entitled, A Summer Morning's Conversation, &c.* . . . Portsmouth, 1758.

Niles, Samuel. *Tristitiae Ecclesiarum OR, A brief and sorrowful Account of the Present State of the Churches in New-England* . . . Boston, 1745.

———. *The true Scripture-Doctrine of Original Sin stated and defended* . . . Boston, 1757.

Paine, Solomon. *A Short View of the Difference Between the Church of Christ, and the established Churches in the Colony of Connecticut* . . . Newport, 1752.

Parsons, Jonathan. *Wisdom justified of her Children* . . . Boston, 1742.

———. *A Needful Caution in a Critical Day* . . . New London, 1742.

Peabody, Oliver. *The Foundations, Effects and Distinguishing Properties of a Good and Bad Hope of Salvation* . . . Boston, 1742.

Pemberton, E[benezer]. *Practical Discourses on Various Texts.* Boston, 1741.

———. *The Knowledge of Christ Recommended* . . . New London, 1741.

———. *The Duty of Committing Our Souls to Christ* . . . Boston, 1743.

Pickering, Theophilus. *The Rev. Mr. Pickering's Letters to the Rev. N. Rogers and Mr. D. Rogers of Ipswich: With their Answer to Mr. Pickering's First Letter. As also His Letter To the Rev. Mr. Davenport of Long-Island* . . . Boston, 1742.

———. *A Bad Omen To the Churches of New-England: In the Instance of Mr. John Cleaveland's Ordination so termed, over a Separation in Chebacco-Parish in Ipswich* . . . Boston, 1747.

Prescott, Benjamin. *A Letter To the Reverend Mr. Joshua Gee, In Answer to His of June 3. 1743. Address'd to the Reverend Mr. Nathanael Eells, Moderator of the late Convention of Pastors in Boston* . . . Boston, 1743.

Prince, Thomas. *An Account of the Revival of Religion in Boston, in the Years 1740-1-2-3.* Boston (reprint), 1823.

———. *The Salvation of God* . . . Boston, 1746.

Prince, Thomas, Jr. (ed.). *The Christian History, containing Accounts of the*

Revival and Propagation of Religion in Great-Britain & America. For the Year 1743. Boston, 1744. (cited as volume I)

————. *The Christian History, containing Accounts of the Revival and Propagation of Religion in Great-Britain, America &c. For the Year 1744.* Boston, 1745. (cited as volume II)

Rand, William. *The ministers of Christ are to enrich those they minister unto . . .* Boston, 1741.

————. *Ministers should have a sincere and ardent Love to the Souls of their People . . .* Boston, 1742.

The Result of A Council of the Consociated Churches of the County of Windham . . . Boston, 1747.

The Result of a Council of Ten Churches; conven'd at Exeter, Jan. 31. 1743 . . . Boston, 1744.

Robbins, Philemon. *A Plain Narrative Of The Proceedings Of the Reverend Association and Consociation of New-Haven County . . .* Boston, 1747.

Seabury, Samuel. *A Sermon Preach'd at New-London, Sunday The 21st of February, Anno Domini, 1741,2.* N. London, 1742.

Seccombe, Joseph. *Some Occasional Thoughts on the Influence of the Spirit. With Seasonable Cautions against Mistakes and Abuses . . .* Boston, 1742.

A Second Letter to the Rev. Mr. George Whitefield, Urging upon him the Duty of Repentance. By Canonicus. Boston, 1745.

Separate Church Papers, I, 1733-1772, in Connecticut Historical Society.

Sergeant, John. *The Causes and Dangers of Delusions in the Affairs of Religion, Consider'd and caution'd against, With particular Reference to the Temper of the present Times . . .* Boston, 1743.

Sewall, Joseph. *All Flesh is as Grass; but the Word of the Lord endureth for ever . . .* Boston, 1741.

————. *The Holy Spirit Convincing the World of Sin, of Righteousness, and of Judgment . . .* Boston, 1741.

————. *God's People must Enquire of Him to bestow the Blessings promised in his Word . . .* Boston, 1742.

Shepard, Thomas. *The Sincere Convert.* Boston (reprint), 1742.

————. *The Sound Believer.* Boston (reprint), 1742.

Shurtleff, William. *The Obligation upon all Christians to desire and endeavour the Salvation of others . . .* Boston, 1741.

————. *A Letter To Those of his Brethren In the Ministry Who refuse to admit The Rev. Whitefield Into their Pulpits . . .* Boston, 1745.

Smith, Josiah. *The Character, Preaching &c. Of the Reverend Mr. George Whitefield . . . With a Preface by the Reverend Dr. Colman and Mr. Cooper of Boston, New-England . . .* Boston, 1740.

Some Remarks on a late pamphlet intitled, The State of Religion in N. England . . . Boston, 1743.

Stiles, Ezra. *A Discourse on the Christian Union . . .* Boston, 1760.

————. (See Dexter, F. B., above).

Stiles, Isaac. *A Prospect of the City of Jerusalem, in it's [sic] Spiritual Building, Beauty and Glory . . .* New London, 1742.

————. *A Looking-glass for Changlings. A Seasonable Caveat against Meddling with them that are given to Change . . .* New London, 1743.

[————]. *The Declaration of the Association of the County of New-Haven in Connecticut, Conven'd at New-Haven, Feb. 19. 1744,–5. Concerning the Reverend Mr. George Whitefield, His Conduct, and the State of Religion at this Day.* Boston, 1745.

Stoddard, Solomon. *A Guide to Christ. Or, the Way of Directing Souls That are Under the Word of Conversion* . . . Boston (reprint), 1742.

Tennent, Gilbert. *The Danger of an Unconverted Ministry* . . . *From the Second Edition printed at Philadelphia.* Boston, 1742.

——. *The Necessity of holding fast the Truth* . . . *With an Appendix, Relating to Errors lately vented by some Moravians in those Parts* . . . Boston, 1743.

——. *Some Account of the Principles of the Moravians* . . . *Recommended by the Reverend Dr. Colman, and other Ministers of Boston* [Prince, Webb, Cooper, Foxcroft and Gee] . . . London, 1743.

——. *The Examiner, Examined or Gilbert Tennent, Harmonious. In Answer to a Pamphlet entitled The Examiner, or Gilbert against Tennent, etc.* Philadelphia, 1743.

——. *Twenty Three Sermons Upon the Chief End of Man. The Divine Authority of the Sacred Scriptures, the Being and Attributes of God, and the Doctrine of the Trinity* . . . Philadelphia, 1744.

——. *The necessity of studying to be quiet, and doing our own Business. A Sermon at Philadelphia, September 30th.* 1744. Philadelphia, n. d.

The Testimony and Advice of a Number of Laymen respecting Religion, and the Teachers of it. Address'd to the Pastors of New-England. Boston, 1743.

The Testimony and Advice of an Assembly of Pastors of Churches in New-England, At a Meeting in Boston July 7. 1743. *Occasion'd By the late happy Revival of Religion in many Parts of the Land. To which are added, Attestations contain'd in Letters from a Number of their Brethren who were providentially hinder'd from giving their Presence.* Boston [1743].

The Testimony of a Number of New-England Ministers Met at Boston Sept. 25. 1745. *Professing The ancient Faith of these Churches* . . . Boston, 1745.

The Testimony of the Pastors of the Churches In the Province of the Massachusetts-Bay in New-England, at their Annual Convention in Boston . . . *Against several Errors in Doctrine, and Disorders in Practice* . . . Boston, 1743.

The Testimony of the President, Professors, Tutors and Hebrew Instructor of Harvard College in Cambridge, Against the Reverend Mr. George Whitefield, And his Conduct. Boston, 1744.

Three Letters To The Reverend Mr. George Whitefield [By Benjamin Colman, Gilbert Tennent and William Tennent]. Philadelphia, n. d. [1739].

Townsend, Jonathan. *A Caveat Against Strife, Especially among Christian Brethren* . . . Boston, 1749.

Turell, Ebenezer. *Directions To his People with Relation to the present Times* . . . Boston (second edition), 1742.

——. *The Life and Character of the Reverend Benjamin Colman, D. D. Late pastor of a church in New-England. Who Deceased August 29th 1747.* Boston, 1749.

Wadsworth, Daniel. *Diary of the Rev. Daniel Wadsworth seventh Pastor of the First Church of Christ in Hartford.* (1737-1747). Hartford, 1894.

Walker, Timothy. *The Way to try all Pretended Apostles* . . . Boston, 1743.

Walter, Nathanael. *The Thoughts of the Heart The Best Evidence of a Man's Spiritual State* . . . Boston, 1741.

——. *An heavenly and God-like Zeal the grand Characteristick of a true Christian* . . . Boston, 1742.

Webb, John. *Christ's Suit to the Sinner, while he stands and knocks at the Door. A Sermon Preach'd in a Time of Great Awakening, at the Tuesday-Evening Lecture in Brattle-Street, Boston, October 13.* 1741 . . . Boston, 1741.

[Webster, Samuel]. *The Winter Evening Conversation Vindicated; Against the Remarks of the Rev. Mr. Peter Clark of Danvers* . . . Boston, n. d. [1758].

[Weller, Samuel]. *The Trial of Mr. Whitefield's Spirit. In some Remarks upon his Fourth Journal* . . . Boston, 1741.

Wheelock, Eleazar. *Wheelock Collection,* in Dartmouth College Library. (Includes many valuable letters by Wheelock and important letters to him by such revivalists as Samuel Buell, James Davenport, Benjamin Pomeroy, Daniel Rogers, and Timothy Allen.)

Whitefield, George. *The Works of the Reverend George Whitefield, M. A.* . . . (seven volumes). London 1771-1772. Principally letters and sermons.

————. *A Continuation of the Reverend Mr. Whitefield's Journal, From a few Days after his Return to Georgia To his Arrival at Falmouth, on the 11th of March 1741. Containing An Account of the Work of God at Georgia, Rhode-Island, New-England, New-York, Pennsylvania and South-Carolina. The Seventh Journal.* London, 1741. (Cited as *Seventh Journal*)

————. *A Letter to the Reverend Dr. Chauncy, On Account of some Passages relating to the Rev. Mr. Whitefield, in his Book intitled Seasonable Thoughts on the State of Religion in New-England.* Boston, 1745.

Wigglesworth, Edward. *A seasonable Caveat against believing every Spirit: with some Directions for trying the Spirits, whether they are of God* . . . Boston, 1745.

————. *A Letter To the Reverend Mr. George Whitefield by Way Reply To his Answer to the College Testimony against him and his Conduct* . . . Boston, 1745.

Williams, Solomon. *The Comfort and Blessedness of Being at Home in God, Or Dwelling with Him* . . . New London, 1742.

————. *The More Excellent Way. Or, the ordinary renewing and sanctifying graces of the Holy Spirit, more excellent than all extraordinary gifts* . . . New London, 1742.

————. *The surprizing Variety of the Acts of Divine Providence in the Government of the World* . . . N. London, 1742.

————, and Wheelock, Eleazar. *Two Letters From the Reverend Mr. Williams & Wheelock of Lebanon, To The Rev. Mr. Davenport, Which were The principal Means of his late Conviction and Retraction. With A Letter from Mr. Davenport, desiring his Publication, for the Good of others. And His Explanation of some Passages in his late Confession.* Boston, 1744.

————. *The Sad Tendency of Divisions and Contentions in Churches To bring on their Ruin and Desolation* . . . Newport, n. d. [1750?].

Williams, William. *The Duty and Interest of a People among whom Religion has been planted, To Continue Stedfast and Sincere in the Profession and Practice of it* . . . *Preach'd at a Time of General Awakenings* . . . *To which is added, Part of a large Letter from the Rev. Mr. Jonathan Edwards of Northampton. Giving an Account of the late wonderful Work of God in those Parts* . . . Boston, 1736.

Williams, William (of Weston). *A Discourse on Saving Faith. Designed as some Assistance, to serious Christians concerned to know the Difference, between it and that common Faith, which many have, who will not be acknowledged by Christ. Preached at Newton, June 14th 1741* . . . Boston, 1741.

The Wonderful Narrative: OR, A faithful Account of the French Prophets, their Agitations, Extasies, and Inspirations: To which are added, Several other remarkable Instances of Persons under the Influence of the like Spirit, in various Parts of the World, particularly in New-England. In a Letter to a Friend. Boston, 1742.

Z., A. *Mr. Parsons Corrected. Or An Addition of some Things to his late Sermon and Preface, tending to set them in a true and just Light* . . . (signed A. Z.). Boston, 1743.

INDEX

QUADRANGLE PAPERBACKS

History

Frederick Lewis Allen. *The Lords of Creation*. QP35
William Sheridan Allen. *The Nazi Seizure of Power*. QP302
Lewis Atherton. *Main Street on the Middle Border*. QP36
Thomas A. Bailey. *Woodrow Wilson and the Lost Peace*. QP1
Thomas A. Bailey. *Woodrow Wilson and the Great Betrayal*. QP2
Charles A. Beard. *The Idea of National Interest*. QP27
Carl L. Becker. *Everyman His Own Historian*. QP33
Ray A. Billington. *The Protestant Crusade*. QP12
Kenneth E. Boulding. *The Organizational Revolution*. QP43
John Chamberlain. *Farewell to Reform*. QP19
Alice Hamilton Cromie. *A Tour Guide to the Civil War*.
Robert D. Cross. *The Emergence of Liberal Catholicism in America*. QP44
Chester McArthur Destler. *American Radicalism, 1865-1901*. QP30
Robert A. Divine. *The Illusion of Neutrality*. QP45
Elisha P. Douglass. *Rebels and Democrats*. QP26
Herman Finer. *Road to Reaction*. QP5
Felix Frankfurter. *The Commerce Clause*. QP16
Lloyd C. Gardner. *A Different Frontier*. QP32
Edwin Scott Gaustad. *The Great Awakening in New England*. QP46
Ray Ginger. *Altgeld's America*. QP21
William B. Hesseltine. *Lincoln's Plan of Reconstruction*. QP41
Raul Hilberg. *The Destruction of the European Jews*. QP301
Frederic C. Howe. *The Confessions of a Reformer*. QP39
Louis Joughin and Edmund M. Morgan. *The Legacy of Sacco and Vanzetti*. QP7
Edward Chase Kirkland. *Dream and Thought in the Business Community, 1860-1900*. QP11
Edward Chase Kirkland. *Industry Comes of Age*. QP42
Adrienne Koch. *The Philosophy of Thomas Jefferson*. QP17
Gabriel Kolko. *The Triumph of Conservatism*. QP40
Walter LaFeber. *John Quincy Adams and American Continental Empire*. QP23
David E. Lilienthal. *TVA: Democracy on the March*. QP28
Arthur S. Link. *Wilson the Diplomatist*. QP18
Huey P. Long. *Every Man a King*. QP8
Gene M. Lyons. *America: Purpose and Power*. QP24
Jackson Turner Main. *The Antifederalists*. QP14
Ernest R. May. *The World War and American Isolation, 1914-1917*. QP29
Henry F. May. *The End of American Innocence*. QP9
George E. Mowry. *The California Progressives*. QP6
Frank L. Owsley. *Plain Folk of the Old South*. QP22
David Graham Phillips. *The Treason of the Senate*. QP20
Julius W. Pratt. *Expansionists of 1898*. QP15
John P. Roche. *The Quest for the Dream*. QP47
David A. Shannon. *The Socialist Party of America*. QP38
Richard W. Van Alstyne. *The Rising American Empire*. QP25
Willard M. Wallace. *Appeal to Arms*. QP10
Norman Ware. *The Industrial Worker, 1840-1860*. QP13
Albert K. Weinberg. *Manifest Destiny*. QP3
Bernard A. Weisberger. *They Gathered at the River*. QP37
Bell I. Wiley. *The Plain People of the Confederacy*. QP4
William Appleman Williams. *The Contours of American History*. QP34
William Appleman Williams. *The Great Evasion*. QP48
Esmond Wright. *Causes and Consequences of the American Revolution*. QP31

Philosophy

James M. Edie. *An Invitation to Phenomenology*. QP103
James M. Edie. *Phenomenology in America*. QP105
Manfred S. Frings. *Heidegger and the Quest for Truth*. QP107
Moltke S. Gram. *Kant: Disputed Questions*. QP104
George L. Kline. *European Philosophy Today*. QP102
Lionel Rubinoff. *Faith and Reason*. QP106
Pierre Thévenaz. *What Is Phenomenology?* QP101

Social Science

George and Eunice Grier. *Equality and Beyond*. QP204
William Loren Katz. *Teachers' Guide to American Negro History*. QP210
Charles O. Lerche, Jr. *Last Chance in Europe*. QP207
David Mitrany. *A Working Peace System*. QP205
Martin Oppenheimer and George Lakey. *A Manual for Direct Action*. QP202
Fred Powledge. *To Change a Child*. QP209
Lee Rainwater. *And the Poor Get Children*. QP208
Clarence Senior. *The Puerto Ricans*. QP201
Sidney Trubowitz. *A Handbook for Teachers in a Ghetto School*. QP211

H 1101

LIBRARY
FLORISSANT VALLEY COMMUNITY COLLEGE
ST. LOUIS, MO.

INVENTORY 74

JAN 12 1978

FALL 77

INVENTORY 1983